Telecourse Student Guide

to accompany

Psychology
The Human Experience

Ken Hutchins

Coast Community College District

William M. Vega, Chancellor, Coast Community College District
Ding-Jo H. Currie, President, Coastline Community College
Dan C. Jones, Administrative Dean, Instructional Systems Development
Laurie R. Melby, Director of Production
Lynn M. Dahnke, Marketing Director
Judy Garvey, Publications Supervisor
Wendy Sacket, Senior Publications Assistant
Thien Vu, Publications Assistant

The Telecourse *Psychology: The Human Experience* is produced by the Coast
Community College District in cooperation with Worth Publishers; NILRC: A Consortium
of Midwest Community Colleges, Colleges, and Universities; HETA: Higher Education
Telecommunications Association of Oklahoma; DALLAS TeleLearning; and KOCE-TV,
Channel 50.

ISBN: 0-7167-5524-6

Printing: 5 4 3 2 1
Year: 04 03 02 01

Worth Publishers
41 Madison Avenue
New York, NY 10010
www.worthpublishers.com

The stunning artwork that appears on the cover of this guide and on the cover and chapter-
opening pages of *Psychology*, third edition, was created by award-winning artist and
lithographer, Phoebe Beasley.

Contents

Introduction

To the Student

Welcome to *Psychology: The Human Experience*. This course has been designed to cover the concepts, vocabulary, and subjects that are typical of an on-campus, college-level introductory psychology course.

Psychology is a broad and exciting field, but it is also very challenging. This course will introduce many new words, concepts, and theories. You will learn that psychology is, above all else, a science. Psychology is the science of behavior and mental processes. There is a major difference between psychology and most other academic courses. While psychology is both an academic discipline and a field of scientific inquiry, it is also personal. Psychology is about *you*.

Consider the subject matter of psychology. You probably already know that psychology deals with things like learning, motivation, thinking, memory, and emotions. Yet psychology is so much more than this. How you see the world, how your brain communicates, why you and I behave as we do, all this—and much more—is the subject of the adventure you are about to begin.

"Who are you?" Can you describe your personality, your interests, your innate abilities? Why are some people happy and others depressed? Why is it that some people become addicted to cigarettes, others are unable to attract friends, and others are subject to periods of anxiety or fits of anger? Psychology is the science that strives to answer these very personal questions, questions about who we are and why we behave as we do.

While it is the goal of this course to introduce you to the fundamentals of introductory psychology, this course has been designed so that it is of personal value to you. Throughout this course we will emphasize how psychology and the psychological principles you will be learning can be used to improve the quality of your everyday life.

As with any college-level course, this course has a textbook, a student guide, assignments, and tests. In lieu of classroom lectures, however, you will be watching half-hour video programs. The designers, academic advisors, and producers of this telecourse have produced an engaging and comprehensive course that will entertain you as you learn about the fascinating field of psychology.

Telecourse Components

Student Guide

The telecourse student guide is an integral part of this course. Think of this guide as your "road map." This guide gives you a starting point for each lesson, as well as directions and exercises that will help you successfully navigate your way through each lesson. Reading this guide will provide you with all the information that you normally would receive in the classroom if you were taking this course on campus. Each lesson in this telecourse student guide includes the following components:

- **Course Compass:** A tool designed to help you stay focused on the various aspects and branches of psychology covered in this telecourse. The compass is provided in each of the 26 lessons. In each lesson, the applicable branch and subject are highlighted. This compass will help you understand the big picture of the course: where you are, where you have been, and where you are headed.

- **Questions to Consider:** These questions give you topics to think about as you read, watch, and study each subject.

- **Lesson Assignments:** Detailed instructions on activities to be completed before, during, and after viewing the video program.

- **Lesson Preview:** An overview of the lesson that informs you of the importance of the subject you are about to study and gives you a brief snapshot of the upcoming video lesson.

- **Learning Objectives:** A list of what you'll know and be able to do after you complete each lesson. Upon completing each lesson, you should be able to satisfy each of the learning objectives. (Hint: Instructors often develop test questions directly from learning objectives.)

- **Key Terms and Concepts:** Much of education is learning the meaning of new words, terms, and concepts. It is important to be able to define each of the key terms and concepts for each lesson.

- **Study Activities:** These Study Activities or self-tests (multiple-choice questions, short-answer questions, matching exercises, and completion exercises) help you master the most important information in each lesson.

- **Answer Key:** Answers to the test items are conveniently located at the end of each lesson so that you can get immediate feedback. After completing a study activity or self-test, be sure to check the Answer Key to make sure you correctly understand the material.

- **Study Matrix:** This matrix has been designed to act as a study tool to help strengthen your knowledge of each learning objective or concept. Pages in the textbook and sections in the telecourse student guide where you can find more information on the objectives are listed next to each learning objective. Use this tool to master learning objectives you feel are your weak points.

Textbook

The recommended textbook for this course is *Psychology*, third edition, by Don Hockenbury and Sandra E. Hockenbury (Worth Publishers, 2003). As you read the textbook, you will come to know the authors, Don and Sandra E. Hockenbury, not only as teachers but also as caring people. In much the same way as the telecourse lessons, the textbook is complete with real-life stories—some funny, some dramatic, others quite personal. This textbook allows you to learn about psychology by observing and hearing about the lives of real, ordinary people. You will repeatedly discover how psychology can enrich the lives of everyone who takes the time to look deeply into the science of human behavior.

Video Programs

Each of the video lessons features a real-life situation—a story line that will help you recognize and appreciate how psychology affects the lives of ordinary people. The award-winning producers and directors at Coast Learning Systems have brought together top professionals from every field of psychology to help explain different aspects of psychology.

How to Take a Telecourse

If this is your first experience with a college telecourse, welcome. Telecourses are designed for busy people whose schedules do not permit them to take a traditional on-campus college course.

This guide is designed to help you study effectively and learn the material presented in both the textbook and the video lessons. To complete a telecourse successfully, you will need to schedule sufficient time to watch each lesson, read the textbook, and study the materials outlined in this guide. In conjunction with your instructor, this guide will provide you with:

- directions on how to take this course.

- study recommendations.

- preview questions for each lesson.

- a brief synopsis of each lesson.

- a set of learning objectives for each lesson.

- a list of key terms and concepts for each lesson.

- several different types of study activities and self-tests for each lesson.

The telecourse student guide is a complement to the textbook and the video lessons. It is not a substitute. You will not be able to complete this course successfully unless you purchase and read the textbook, watch the video program—and study. By following the instructions in this guide, you should be able to easily master the learning objectives for each lesson.

To complete this course successfully, you will need to:

- contact your instructor to find about any course requirements, time lines, meetings, and scheduled exams.

- purchase a copy of the course textbook.

- read and study the textbook.

- view each program in its entirety.

- understand the key terms and concepts presented in this guide.

- be able to satisfy the learning objectives for each lesson.

- complete the Study Activities.

- complete any additional assignments your instructor may require.

Even though you do not have a scheduled class to attend each week, please keep in mind that this is a college-level course. You will not be able to "look at some of the videos" or "just scan the text" and pass this course. It is important that you schedule sufficient time to watch, read, study, and reflect. While taking a telecourse provides you the convenience of not having to meet at a prearranged time, do not make the mistake of not scheduling enough time to complete the work and study. All learning demands a good measure of self-discipline. Unless you put in the effort, take the time to study, and think about what you are learning, you will not learn.

Try your best to keep up with your work. It is very difficult to catch up if you allow yourself to get a few weeks behind schedule. We strongly recommend that you set aside specific times each week for viewing, reading, and studying. You will do better and will be more likely to succeed if you make a study schedule and stick to your schedule. When you watch the programs, try to do so without any interruptions. Each program is approximately thirty minutes long. If you are interrupted during your viewing time, you may miss an important point. If possible, take some time immediately after watching the video program to reflect on what you have just viewed. This is an excellent time to discuss the video lesson with a friend or family member. Remember that your active involvement promotes your success.

It is our goal to give you a good, basic understanding of the field of psychology. This course will provide you with all the basic information required for a college-level introductory class in psychology.

Minds are like parachutes; they only function when open.

—Thomas R. Dewar

And, don't forget to always check with your instructor. He or she will explain the specific course requirements for your assigned class. We sincerely hope you enjoy your introduction to the field of psychology, the science of behavior and mental processes.

Study Recommendations

Everyone has his or her own unique learning style. Some people learn best by reading alone the first thing each morning, others by discussing ideas with a group of friends, still others by listening to experts and taking notes. While there is no "best" way to learn, psychologists and educators have identified several things you can do that will help you study and learn more effectively.

One of the advantages of telecourse learning is that you have many choices in how you learn and study. You can tailor this course to fit your "best" way to learn. Below are several study tips. These are proven methods that will help you learn and retain what you are studying. Please take the time to read through this list. You will discover that by using one or more of these techniques you can significantly improve your ability to learn and remember new information.

Open your mind: One of the major obstacles to learning new information is that new information often differs from what we already "know." For example, if you believe that obesity is caused by depression, it will be difficult for you to learn about new information that reveals that there is no cause-and-effect relationship between obesity and depression. To learn, you need to have an open mind. We are not suggesting you simply believe everything you are told. We want you to think critically about what you are told. However, be cautious and guard against letting old beliefs or opinions stop you from learning anything new.

Reduce interference: One of the major reasons for forgetting information is that new information interferes with other information. When you are studying more than one subject at a time, you are increasing the likelihood of interference occurring. If possible, try to study one thing at a time. If you must take multiple subjects, try to take courses with very different subjects, such as art and psychology or math and history. For example, it would not be a good idea to take Child Development and Introduction to Psychology during the same semester. Of course, visiting with friends, watching television, listening to the radio, or any distraction while you are studying will also interfere with your ability to learn new information. When you engage in these types of activities during or just after studying, you risk letting the information you have just learned interfere with other information. Give yourself time to absorb new information.

Don't cram: You probably already know that staying up all night cramming for an exam the following morning is not a good way to study. The opposite of cramming is, in fact, one of the best ways to study. Spacing out your studying into smaller and more frequent study periods will improve retention. Instead of studying for six hours in one evening, you will learn more and retain more if you study one hour per night for six nights.

Reduce stress: In addition to being bad for your health, stress is bad for learning. Stress and anxiety interfere with learning. You will learn more and enjoy it more if you are relaxed when you study. One of the most effective ways of relaxing that does not interfere with learning is exercise. A good brisk walk or run before you settle in to study is a good prescription for success. Ideally, you would study some, take a break, then get some exercise while you think about what you have just learned. And later, when you are relaxed, return and study some more.

Be a Smart Student: Most top students have one thing in common. They all have excellent study habits. Students who excel have learned, or were fortunate enough to have someone teach them, how to study effectively. There is no magic formula for successful studying. However, there are a few universal guidelines.

Do make a commitment to yourself to learn.

Don't let other people interrupt you when you are studying.

Do make a study schedule and stick to it.

Don't study when you are doing something else, like watching television.

Do create a specific place to study.

Don't study if you are tired, upset, or overly stressed.

Do exercise and relax before you study.

Don't study for extended periods of time without taking a break.

Do give yourself ample time to study.

Don't complain that you have to go study.

Do take a positive approach to learning.

Make the most of your assignments: You will master this material more effectively if you make a commitment to completing all your assignments. The lessons will make more sense to you, and you will learn more, if you follow these instructions:

- Set aside a specific time to view, read, and study each lesson.

- Before you view each video lesson, read the Questions to Consider, Lesson Preview, and Learning Objectives outlined in this guide.

- Read the assigned textbook pages for the lesson you are studying.

- View the video lesson.

- Review the Key Terms and Concepts. Check your understanding of all unfamiliar terms in the glossary notes in the textbook.

- Complete the Study Activities for each lesson.

Think about what you have learned: You are much more likely to remember new information if you use it. Remember that learning is not a passive activity. Learning is active. As soon as you learn something, try to repeat it to someone or discuss it with a friend. If you will think about what you just learned, you will be much more likely to retain that information. The reason we remember certain information has to do mostly with (1) how important that information is to us, and (2) whether or not we actively use the information. For example, if you suffer from headaches and the textbook or video is discussing various headache remedies, this information will be valuable to you. Because of your personal interest in this subject, you will have little difficulty remembering this information. What do you do, however, when you need to learn some information that is not personally valuable or interesting to you? The best way to remember this type of information is to reinforce it—and the best reinforcer is actively using the information.

Get feedback on what you are studying: Study alone, learn with others. You need feedback to help reinforce learning. Also, feedback helps make sure you correctly understand the information. The study activities and self-tests in this guide are specifically designed to give you feedback and reinforce what you are learning. The more time and practice you devote to learning, the better you will be at remembering that information. When you take a self-test, make sure you immediately check your answers with the answer key. Don't wait and check your answers later. If you miss a question, review that section of the textbook to reinforce the correct understanding of the material.

A good gauge of how well you understand some information is your ability to explain that information to another person. If you are unable to explain some term or concept to a friend, you probably will need to review and study that term or concept further.

Contact your instructor: If you are having an especially difficult time with learning some information, contact your instructor. Your instructor is there to help you. Often a personal explanation will do wonders in helping you clear up a misunderstanding. Your instructor wants to hear from you and wants you to succeed. Don't hesitate to call, write, e-mail, or visit your instructor.

Some students do better with study groups; others do better studying alone. If study groups are helpful to you, let your instructor know of your preference. However, be aware that study groups are not a substitute for studying alone. Study groups often turn into friendly chats and not much actually gets learned. So, remember that study groups are not a substitute for individual effort.

Learn it well: Retention is the key to long-term knowledge. One of the best methods to increase your retention is to overlearn material. It is a common mistake to think that just because you can answer a question or give a brief definition of a term or concept, you really know and will remember that term or concept. Think back about how many things you have already "learned." How much do you really remember? Much of what we learn is quickly forgotten. If you want to really learn some information, learn it in a way that you will not forget it—overlearn it.

Overlearning is simple. After you have learned a fact or new word, spend an additional ten or fifteen minutes actively reviewing that fact or word. You will be amazed how much this will increase your long-term retention.

Enjoy learning: You do not need to suffer to learn. In fact, the opposite is true. You will learn more if you enjoy learning. If you have the attitude that "I hate to study" or "schoolwork is boring," you are doing yourself a real disservice.

You will to progress better and learn more if you adopt a positive attitude about learning and studying. Since you are choosing to learn, you will be well served by also choosing to enjoy the adventure.

We are sure you will enjoy *Psychology: The Human Experience.*

Acknowledgments

Several of the individuals responsible for the creation of this telecourse are listed on the copyright page of this book. In addition to those people, appreciation is expressed for the contributions of the following people:

Members of the Telecourse Advisory Committee

The following gifted scholars and teachers on the National Academic Advisory Team helped focus the approach and content of the video programs, faculty manual, and telecourse student guide to ensure accuracy, academic validity, accessibility, significance, and instructional integrity.

Frank Bagrash, Ph.D., California State University, Fullerton
Ted Barnes, M.S., Coastline Community College
Elizabeth Bjork, Ph.D., University of California, Los Angeles
Stephen Burgess, Ph.D., Southwestern Oklahoma State University
Michael Catchpole, Ph.D., North Island College, British Columbia
Marte Fallshore, Ph.D., Central Washington University
Deborah Finkel, Ph.D., Indiana University Southwest
Erin Fisher, Ed.D., Rock Valley College
Ken Hutchins, M.A., Orange Coast College
Joann Jelly, Ed.D., Barstow College
Robert Jensen, Ph.D., California State University, Sacramento
Karsten Look, Ph.D., Columbus State Community College
Robert Lugar, Ed.D., Dallas County Community College District
Jeffery Mio, Ph.D., California State Polytechnic University, Pomona
Alan Monat, Ph.D., California State University, Hayward
Joel Morgovsky, M.A., Brookdale Community College
Christine Padesky, Ph.D., Center for Cognitive Therapy
Steve Saunders, Ph.D., Marquette University

Lead Academic Advisors

Stephen Burgess, Ph.D., Southwestern Oklahoma State University
Michael Catchpole, Ph.D., North Island College, British Columbia
Ken Hutchins, M.A., Orange Coast College, author of Telecourse Student Guide
Jeffery Mio, Ph.D., California State Polytechnic University, Pomona
Ohr Olivkovich, Ed.D., Milestone Learning, Inc.

Television Production Team

Vanessa Chambers, Jason Daley, Aaron Estrada, Steve Hawk, Alex Lopez, Steve Marino, Keith Martin, Salma Martinez, Dorothy McCollom, Harry Ratner, Greg Rogers, Mike Rust, Wendy Moulton-Tate, Susan Wilcox, and the many other talented people who helped make the programs.

Use the Course Compass to orient yourself in the road that you are taking to explore branches and aspects of psychology. The branch and aspects that are covered in this lesson are highlighted in the compass.

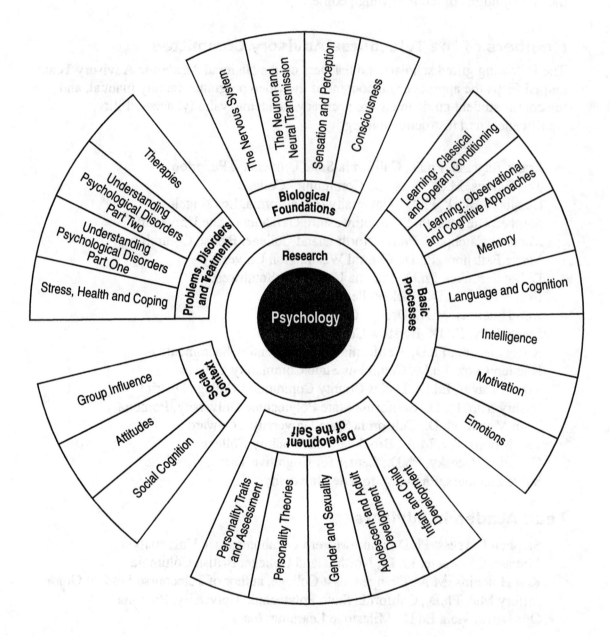

Please note: This compass does not represent the full range of topics comprising the field of psychology; it represents a map for this course only. Each of the five branches represented above has many aspects and subjects that are covered in the 26 lessons of this telecourse. You should remember that these branches and subjects all interrelate.

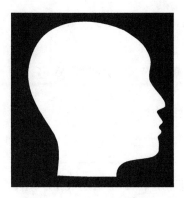

Why Study Psychology?

Questions to Consider

What exactly is psychology?

Why do people study psychology?

When did psychology begin? Who founded it?

What do psychologists do?

What are the major perspectives in psychology?

In what ways can the study of psychology personally benefit me?

Lesson Assignments

Before viewing the video program

Read the Questions to Consider, Lesson Preview, and Learning Objectives for this lesson. Use this information to guide your reading, viewing, and thinking.

Read Chapter 1, "Introduction and Research Methods," pages 1–16, in the textbook.

View the video program, "Why Study Psychology?"

After viewing the video program

Review the vocabulary listed in the Key Terms and Concepts section. (Page references are keyed to the Hockenbury textbook, *Psychology*. Remember: there is a complete Glossary at the end of the textbook.)

Review the reading assignments for this lesson.

Complete the exercises found in the Study Activities section and check your answers with the Answer Key at the end of this lesson.

Use the Study Matrix found at the end of this lesson to review and assess your knowledge of each Learning Objective.

Lesson Preview

This lesson will introduce you to the exciting field of psychology. You will learn why people study psychology. This video follows an expedition team as they struggle during a mountain climb. Against the backdrop of breathtaking scenery, you will hear ordinary people tell you about the importance of studying human behavior. You will discover that, even in this unique and life-threatening situation, human behavior remains at the core of everything we do.

You will hear from psychologists, educators, and researchers as they explain the breadth of the field of psychology. You will also hear ordinary people explain why they think it is important to study psychology. This video concludes with a discussion by psychologist Peter Salovey of Yale University.

As you will learn in this video series, the work of psychologists is very diverse. Psychologists can be found wherever people are found—from helping police solve crimes to developing educational material; from studying brain activity to helping teachers understand childhood behavior; and from helping families cope with aging parents to advising employers on how to increase employee productivity. If human behavior is involved, look closely and you will find a psychologist studying, researching, and working hard to better understand why people behave as they do. While the work of psychologists varies greatly, all psychologists share the common goal of trying to improve our understanding of the complex world of human behavior.

As you will also discover in this video series, each of the lessons is a story of real people and real events. We are using true-to-life stories to help you see the very practical role psychology plays in everyday life.

Psychology is, at its core, about you and other people. Studying psychology can make a difference in your life by helping you understand yourself—what motivates you, why you behave as you do, what kind of person you are. Psychology will help you understand what you need to do to live a full, productive, and happy life.

Psychology can also help you better understand other people. You will learn how other people learn and grow. Psychology can help you understand all manners of human behavior, from why we sleep and the causes of obesity to why some people get addicted to drugs or why some people have poor memories. Psychology is about the people you meet every day, in every walk of life.

Psychology is not a cold science—a collection of hard facts and firm conclusions. Rather, psychology is the science of real people. Psychology is the way each of us can use the power of science to help us live better, solve problems, understand the world, and enrich our own lives and the lives of those people we meet in the adventure we call life.

Welcome to *Psychology: The Human Experience*.

Learning Objectives

When you have completed this lesson, you should be able to:

1. Define psychology.

2. Discuss how philosophy and physiology influenced the development of the field of psychology.

3. Identify the contributions to psychology made by Wilhelm Wundt, Sigmund Freud, Ivan Pavlov, B. F. Skinner, and Carl Rogers.

4. Describe some of the various types of work done by psychologists.

5. Distinguish between psychodynamic, behavioral, and humanistic perspectives in psychology.

6. Explain the biological and cognitive perspectives in psychology.

7. Distinguish between organizational/industrial psychology and clinical psychology.

8. Describe what is meant by cross-cultural psychology, including the concepts of individualistic cultures and collectivistic cultures.

9. Explain the evolutionary perspective in psychology.

Key Terms and Concepts

Page references are keyed to the Hockenbury textbook, *Psychology*.

Psychology: The scientific study of behavior and mental processes. (page 3)

Psychoanalysis: Personality theory and form of psychotherapy that emphasizes the role of unconscious factors in personality and behavior. (page 7)

Behaviorism: School of psychology and theoretical viewpoint that emphasizes the study of observable behaviors, especially as they pertain to the process of learning. (page 8)

Humanistic psychology: School of psychology and theoretical viewpoint that emphasizes each person's unique potential for psychological growth and self-direction. (page 8)

Wilhelm Wundt: A German physiologist who is generally credited as being the founder of psychology. Founded the first psychology research laboratory in 1879. (page 4)

Sigmund Freud: An Austrian physician who developed the personality theory based on uncovering the hidden, or unconscious, causes of behavior. Largely credited as making psychology a household word. Recognized as one of the most influential thinkers of the twentieth century. (page 7)

Ivan Pavlov: A Russian physiologist whose pioneering work led to the creation of behaviorism. (page 8)

B. F. Skinner: An American psychologist who is famous for his study of observable behaviors and experiments using reinforcement and punishment to shape behavior. (page 8)

Carl Rogers: An American psychologist who is credited with the development of humanistic psychology and the emphasis on each person's individual potential. (page 9)

Clinical psychology: A specialty area of psychology that studies the causes, treatment, and prevention of different types of psychological disorders. (page 15)

Experimental psychology: A term traditionally used to describe research focused on basic topics, such as sensory processes or principles of learning. However, psychologists in every field conduct research and perform experiments. (page 15)

Industrial/organizational psychology: A specialty area of psychology that is concerned with the relationship between people and work. Includes such topics as worker productivity, job satisfaction, and personnel testing and selection. (page 15)

Social psychology: Explores how people are affected by their social environments, including how people think about and influence others. (page 15)

Biological psychology: A specialty area of psychology that focuses on the relationship between behavior and the body's physical systems. (page 10)

Educational psychology: A specialty area of psychology that studies how people learn. Develops instructional methods and materials. (page 15)

Evolutionary psychology: The application of principles of evolution, including natural selection, to explain psychological processes and phenomena. (pages 12–13)

Cross-cultural psychology: Branch of psychology that studies the effects of culture on behavior and mental processes. (pages 11–12)

Study Activities

These self-test questions are designed as a study exercise to aid you in understanding the most important terms and concepts in this lesson. To ensure that you have an accurate understanding of the key terms and concepts in this lesson, please check your answers with the Answer Key provided at the end of this lesson.

Multiple-Choice Questions

1. Sigmund Freud was the father of

    a. the science of psychology.

    b. the psychodynamic theory of personality.

    c. behaviorism.

    d. humanism.

2. The specialty area of psychology that focuses on the relationship between behavior and the body's physical systems is called

    a. evolutionary psychology.

    b. experimental psychology.

    c. biological psychology.

    d. clinical psychology.

3. The Russian physiologist whose pioneering work led to the creation of behaviorism was

    a. Wilhelm Wundt.

    b. Ivan Pavlov.

    c. E. B. Titchener.

    d. René Descartes.

4. Psychology is defined as the

    a. study of human and animal behavior.

    b. study of human behavior and mental processes.

    c. science of human and animal behavior.

    d. science of behavior and mental processes.

5. Humanistic psychology is a school of psychology and theoretical viewpoint that emphasizes

    a. each person's unique potential.

    b. how people learn.

    c. the importance of childhood conflicts and unconscious motivation.

    d. the need for each person to avoid personal suffering.

6. The school of psychology that emphasizes the study of observable behaviors, especially as they pertain to the process of learning, is called

   a. psychoanalysis.

   b. experimental psychology.

   c. behaviorism.

   d. educational psychology.

7. Industrial/organizational psychology is a specialty area of psychology that is concerned with the relationships between people and their work and includes topics such as

   a. worker productivity and job satisfaction.

   b. group influences.

   c. each person's unique potential for psychological growth.

   d. conducting research and developing instructional methods.

8. Studying the differences among cultures and the influences of culture on behavior are the fundamental goals of

   a. collectivistic cultures.

   b. individualistic cultures.

   c. cross-cultural psychology.

   d. social psychologists.

9. The specialty area of psychology that studies how people learn is called

   a. clinical psychology.

   b. educational psychology.

   c. experimental psychology.

   d. applied psychology.

10. The person who is generally credited as being the founder of psychology is

    a. an Austrian physician named Sigmund Freud.

    b. an American educator and researcher named B. F. Skinner.

    c. the Greek philosopher Aristotle.

    d. a German physiologist named Wilhelm Wundt.

11. In the video, textbook author Sandy Hockenbury explained that, while difficult to define, stress essentially is a negative emotional state that results when you perceive

    a. a major change in your life.

    b. something dangerous.

    c. a threatening event as more than you can handle.

    d. yourself getting anxious.

12. In this video, you learned that psychology is a science that

    a. focuses only on mental illness.

    b. is very diverse.

    c. wants to change how people behave.

    d. is practiced only at university and health clinics.

13. In this video, psychologist Steven James discussed his belief that the reason most people study psychology is

    a. that we all need to learn more about science.

    b. to better understand ourselves.

    c. to learn how to manipulate other people.

    d. that it will reduce stress and make us happy.

14. In this video, Dr. Judy Rosener explained that the two things you never forget when you meet someone are

    a. their age and occupation.

    b. their names and sex.

    c. their overall appearance and age.

    d. the color of their skin and their sex.

Short-Answer Questions

15. Define psychology.

_____

_____

_____

16. Discuss how philosophy and physiology influenced the development of the field of psychology.

_____

_____

_____

17. Identify the contributions to psychology made by Wilhelm Wundt, Sigmund Freud, Ivan Pavlov, B. F. Skinner, and Carl Rogers.

_____

_____

_____

18. Describe some of the various types of work done by psychologists.

_____

_____

_____

19. Distinguish between psychodynamic, behavioral, and humanistic perspectives in psychology.

_____

_____

_____

20. Explain the biological and cognitive perspectives in psychology.

_____

_____

_____

21. Distinguish between organizational/industrial psychology and clinical psychology.

_____

_____

_____

22. Describe what is meant by cross-cultural psychology, including the concepts of individualistic cultures and collectivistic cultures.

_____

_____

_____

23. Explain the evolutionary perspective in psychology.

_____

_____

_____

Matching Exercises

Match the following terms and concepts with the correct definition.

Carl Rogers   Ivan Pavlov   experimental psychology

psychoanalysis   behaviorism   clinical psychology

psychology   Sigmund Freud   evolutionary psychology

24. _____ Founded the school of psychology that emphasizes free will, self-determination, and the importance of choice in human behavior.

25. _____ Has grown out of a renewed interest in the work of English naturalist Charles Darwin and the concept of natural selection.

26. _____ The scientific study of behavior and mental processes.

27. _____ The primary goal of this school of psychology was to discover the fundamental principles of learning.

28. _____ A term traditionally used to describe research that focused on such basic topics as sensory processes, principles of learning, emotion, and motivation.

29. _____ Believed that human behavior was motivated by unconscious conflicts that were almost always sexual or aggressive in nature.

30. _____ Demonstrated that dogs could learn to associate a neutral stimulus, such as the sound of a bell, with an automatic response, such as reflexively salivating to food.

31. _____ A specialty area of psychology that studies the causes, treatment, and prevention of different types of psychological disorders.

32. _____ A distinct form of psychotherapy that continues to influence many psychologists and mental health professionals.

Completion Exercises

Fill in each blank with the most appropriate term or terms from the list of answers provided.

B. F. Skinner   industrial/organizational psychology

biological   motivation

biological psychology   science

cross-cultural psychology   self-efficacy

educational psychologists   social psychologists

group influence   Wilhelm Wundt

humanistic psychology

33. Rather than emphasizing unconscious experience, _____ emphasizes the conscious experiences of patients, including each person's unique potential for psychological growth and self-direction.

34. Studying the differences among the values, attitudes, and behaviors shared by a group of people and their influences on behavior is the fundamental goal of _____.

35. Group influence, interpersonal attraction, helping behavior, and prejudice beliefs are typical of the topics that _____ would research.

36. _____ focuses on the relationship between behavior and the body's physical systems, including the brain, the rest of the nervous system, the endocrine system, the immune system, and genetics.

37. Consumer reactions, work productivity, and the interaction between people and equipment are typical of the work performed by people with an interest in _____.

38. In 1879, _____ realized his goal of establishing psychology as a separate science when he opened the first psychology research laboratory.

39. The famous American psychologist _____ believed that psychology should restrict itself to studying outwardly observable behaviors that could be measured and verified.

40. _____ help develop the instructional methods and materials used to train people in both educational and work settings.

41. In this video, the study of psychology was defined as being the _____ of human behavior.

42. In the video, you learned that _____ can strongly affect the way an individual behaves.

43. In the video, Yale University psychologist Peter Salovey stated that the future of psychology will involve studying and learning more about the interplay between what is _____ and what is behavioral.

44. In the video, Stanford University psychologist Albert Bandura discussed the concept of _____ as the foundation of human motivation and action.

45. In the video, you learned that _____ is a key element in the study of human behavior.

Answer Key

Multiple-Choice Questions

1. b	4. d	7. a	10. d	13. b
2. c	5. a	8. c	11. c	14. d
3. b	6. c	9. b	12. b	

Short-Answer Questions

Your answers should include the following:

15. Psychology is defined as the science of behavior and mental processes. (page 3)

16. Throughout history, many great philosophers have been concerned with the same issues that psychologists now study. For example, Aristotle wrote extensively about such topics as sleep, dreaming, and memory. Physiology, the biological study of living organisms, contributed greatly to the emergence of psychology as a distinct science. Scientific discoveries, such as how human senses function, made in the 1800's by physiologists became foundation for the scientific research of human behavior. (pages 3–4)

17. Wilhelm Wundt established the first research laboratory exclusively for psychology; he is credited as the founder of psychology as an experimental science. Sigmund Freud developed psychoanalysis, a personality theory and the form of psychotherapy; he is recognized as one of the most influential thinkers of the twentieth century. Ivan Pavlov first discovered classical conditioning, which became the foundation of behaviorism. B. F. Skinner popularized behaviorism by experimentally demonstrating various learning principles. Carl Rogers is credited as being the principal founder of the school of psychology called humanism. (pages 4–5, 7–9)

18. Psychologists' work is very diverse. The most common type of work done by psychologists is in the study and treatment of psychological disorders. Studying the relationship between behavior and biological forces, conducting research experiments, and developing educational material and tests are also common of the work performed by psychologists. (pages 14–16)

19. The psychodynamic perspective is based on the key ideas of Sigmund Freud, who emphasized the importance of unconscious influences and early life experiences to explain human behavior. The behavioral perspective focus is on observable behavior and the fundamental laws of learning. The humanistic perspective focuses on the motivation of people to grow psychologically, and the importance of self-direction and personal choice. (pages 10–11)

20. The biological perspective emphasizes studying the physical bases of human and animal behavior, including the nervous system, the endocrine system, the immune system, and genetics. The cognitive perspective focuses on the

important role of mental processes in how people process information, develop language, solve problems, and think. (pages 10–11)

21. Organizational/industrial psychology is a specialty field of psychology that is concerned with the relationship between people and work. It includes such topics as worker productivity, job satisfaction, and personnel testing and selection. Clinical psychology is a different specialty area of psychology that studies the causes, treatment, and prevention of different types of psychological disorders. (page 15)

22. Cross-cultural psychology is the branch of psychology that studies the effects of culture on behavior and mental processes. Individualistic cultures are cultures that emphasize the needs and goals of the individual over the needs and goals of the group. Collectivistic cultures emphasize the needs and goals of the group over the goals of the individual. (pages 11–13)

23. The evolutionary perspective refers to the application of the principles of evolution to explain psychological processes and phenomena. (pages 12–13)

Matching Exercises

24. Carl Rogers

25. evolutionary psychology

26. psychology

27. behaviorism

28. experimental psychology

29. Sigmund Freud

30. Ivan Pavlov

31. clinical psychology

32. psychoanalysis

Completion Exercises

33. humanistic psychology

34. cross-cultural psychology

35. social psychologists

36. biological psychology

37. industrial/organizational psychology

38. Wilhelm Wundt

39. B. F. Skinner

40. educational psychologists

41. science

42. group influence

43. biological

44. self-efficacy

45. motivation

Study Matrix

Lesson 1

Why Study Psychology?

Please Note: Use this matrix to guide your study and achieve the learning objectives of this lesson. It will also help you to view the video, which defines and demonstrates important concepts and objectives as they relate to everyday life and actual case studies.

Learning Objective	Textbook	Telecourse Student Guide
Define psychology.	p. 3	Key Terms and Concepts; Study Activities 4, 12, 13, 15, 26, 41.
Discuss how philosophy and physiology influenced the development of the field of psychology.	pp. 3–4	Key Terms and Concepts; Study Activity 16.
Identify the contributions to psychology made by Wilhelm Wundt, Sigmund Freud, Ivan Pavlov, B. F. Skinner, and Carl Rogers.	pp. 4–9	Key Terms and Concepts; Study Activities 1, 3, 10, 17, 24, 29, 30, 38, 39.
Describe some of the various types of work done by psychologists.	pp. 14–16	Key Terms and Concepts; Study Activities 7, 9, 18, 28, 31, 35, 37, 40.
Distinguish between psychodynamic, behavioral, and humanistic perspectives in psychology.	pp. 10–11	Key Terms and Concepts; Study Activities 5, 6, 19, 27, 32, 33, 45.
Explain the biological and cognitive perspectives in psychology.	pp. 10–11	Key Terms and Concepts; Study Activities 2, 11, 14, 20, 21, 36, 43, 44.
Distinguish between organizational/industrial psychology and clinical psychology.	p. 15	Key Terms and Concepts; Study Activity 21.
Describe what is meant by cross-cultural psychology, including the term individualistic cultures and collectivistic cultures.	pp. 11–13	Key Terms and Concepts; Study Activities 8, 22, 34.
Explain the evolutionary perspective in psychology.	pp. 12–14	Key Terms and Concepts; Study Activities 23, 25.

Use the Course Compass to orient yourself in the road that you are taking to explore branches and aspects of psychology. The branch and aspects that are covered in this lesson are highlighted in the compass.

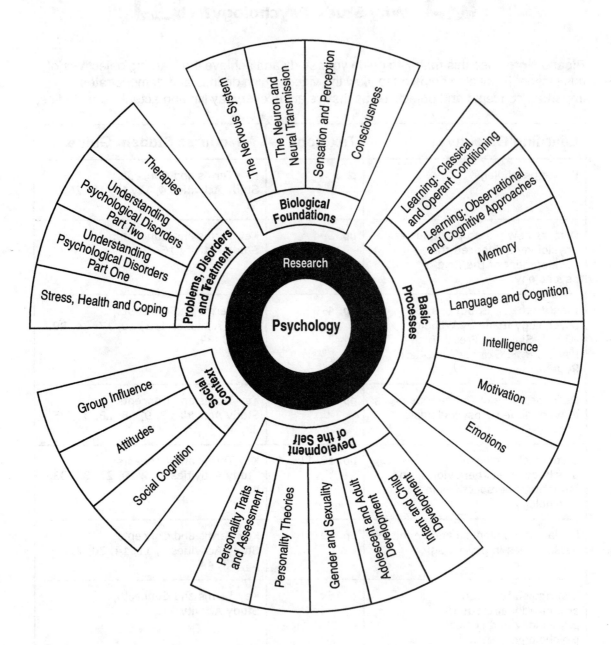

Please note: This compass does not represent the full range of topics comprising the field of psychology; it represents a map for this course only. Each of the five branches represented above has many aspects and subjects that are covered in the 26 lessons of this telecourse. You should remember that these branches and subjects all interrelate.

Research Methods in Psychology

Questions to Consider

Why do psychologists conduct psychological research?

What is the scientific method?

How is a psychological experiment performed?

What are the two basic categories of research methods?

How accurate is psychological research?

How does science prove cause and effect?

Lesson Assignments

Before viewing the video program

Read the Questions to Consider, Lesson Preview, and Learning Objectives for this lesson. Use this information to guide your reading, viewing, and thinking.

Read Chapter 1, "Introduction and Research Methods," pages 16–38, in the textbook.

View the video program, "Research Methods in Psychology"

After viewing the video program

Review the vocabulary listed in the Key Terms and Concepts section. (Page references are keyed to the Hockenbury textbook, *Psychology*. Remember: there is a complete Glossary at the end of the textbook.)

Review the reading assignments for this lesson.

Complete the exercises found in the Study Activities section and check your answers with the Answer Key at the end of this lesson.

Use the Study Matrix found at the end of this lesson to review and assess your knowledge of each Learning Objective.

Lesson Preview

Often people simply believe what they are told. "Everyone knows that if you get drunk you can sober up more quickly if you take a shower and drink some coffee. It is common sense." It is also not true. If a drunken person takes a shower and drinks coffee, he or she will be wet, wide awake, … and still drunk. The scientific fact is that neither cold water nor caffeine alters the rate at which the human body metabolizes alcohol.

From losing money to bogus "cures" for cancer, believing everything you hear or read can, and often does, cause people all types of problems. To combat false claims, psychologists have become scientists.

In this lesson, you will learn that psychology is a science. And, like all other sciences, psychology uses strict rules and methods to gather and evaluate information.

In this video, you will be introduced to the scientific method and the various research methods psychologists use when conducting experiments. To help you understand how psychologists use research, this video explores the research of psychologist Craig Anderson and Karen Dill as they explore whether there is any connection between video games and tragedies such as the shooting that occurred at Columbine High School in April, 1999.

In this video, you will learn why psychologists use the scientific method and very rigid guidelines whenever conducting research experiments. You will also learn about the two basic categories of research: the descriptive method and the experimental method. Dr. Elaine Vaughn will examine the pros and cons of the different types of research, including many of the errors commonly made when reviewing the results of psychological research.

By better understanding how and why psychologists conduct different methods of research, and by understanding the limitations of these various methods, you will be better equipped to distinguish between scientific fact and speculation or personal opinion.

Learning Objectives

When you have completed this lesson, you should be able to:

1. List the four goals of psychology.

2. List the steps that comprise the scientific method.

3. Define the concepts of hypothesis, empirical evidence, and critical thinking.

4. Define what is meant by the concept of descriptive methods of research.

5. Compare and contrast the three categories of descriptive research.

6. Define what is meant by the concept of correlational method of research.

7. Explain the difference between correlation and cause and effect.

8. Define what is meant by the concept of experimental method of research.

9. Explain the difference between an independent variable and a dependent variable as used in the experimental method.

10. Explain the difference between an experimenter group and a control group as used in the experimental method.

11. Describe how statistics are used in research.

Key Terms and Concepts

Page references are keyed to the Hockenbury textbook, *Psychology*.

Scientific method: A set of assumptions, attitudes, and procedures that guide research. (page 16)

Hypothesis: A tentative statement about the relationship between two or more variables. (page 19)

Empirical evidence: Evidence that is based on objective observation or measurement. (page 19)

Critical thinking: A rational thinking process used to evaluate evidence and minimize the influence of preconceptions and biases. (page 16)

Statistics: A mathematics method used by researchers to summarize data and draw conclusions based on data. (page 19)

Statistically significant: A mathematics conclusion that something is very likely to be the result of some event and not a factor of chance. (page 19)

Descriptive research methods: A category of scientific procedures that are used to observe and describe behavior. (page 23)

Naturalistic observation: A descriptive method of research used when the experiment is conducted in a natural setting. (page 23)

Survey research method: A descriptive method of research that uses questionnaires or interviews to collect data. (pages 23–24)

Case study: A descriptive method of research where one individual is intensely studied. (page 23)

Random selection: A common strategy to ensure that every member of a group has an equal chance of being selected. (page 25)

Correlational studies: A research method that investigates how strongly two factors are related to one another. (page 25)

Experimental method: A research method used to demonstrate cause-and-effect relationships. (page 27)

Experimental group: A group of subjects who are exposed to all experimental conditions, including the independent variable. (page 28)

Control group: A group of subjects who are exposed to all the experimental conditions, except for the independent variable. (pages 28–29)

Placebo: A fake substance or treatment that has no known effects. (page 32)

Placebo effect: The phenomenon in which a subject receiving a fake treatment has, or reports to have, the same results as the subject's real treatment. (page 32)

Pseudoscience: A fake or false science that makes claims based on little or no scientific evidence. (pages 34–35)

Double-blind experiment: A research procedure wherein neither the researcher nor the subject is aware who is receiving the treatment and who is not receiving the treatment. (page 33)

Study Activities

The following self-tests are designed as a study exercise to aid you in understanding the most important terms and concepts in this lesson. To ensure that you have an accurate understanding of the key terms and concepts in the lesson, please check your answers with the Answer Key provided at the end of this lesson.

Multiple-Choice Questions

1. The four basic goals of psychology are to

    a. describe, explain, predict, and research behavior.

    b. explain, research, control, and influence behavior.

    c. describe, explain, predict, and control or influence behavior.

    d. discover, understand, research, and explain behavior.

2. Like all scientists, psychologists assume that

    a. all data is scientifically important.

    b. certain phenomena will never be understood.

    c. events are lawful and ultimately explainable.

    d. all myths are false.

3. Critical thinking refers to the practice of

    a. criticizing other people.

    b. assuming new ideas are wrong until proven.

    c. actively questioning statements or beliefs.

    d. using personal opinion to help in determining conclusions.

4. Which is NOT a step in the scientific method?

    a. formulate a hypothesis.

    b. design a study and collect data.

    c. analyze the data and draw conclusions.

    d. apply the findings to solve human problems.

5. The basic goal of the descriptive methods of research is to

    a. explain, predict, and control behavior.

    b. manipulate variables to control experimental results.

    c. generate new theories.

    d. observe and describe behavior.

6. Naturalistic research refers to research that is

   a. conducted in a natural setting.

   b. conducted on animals.

   c. used to determine if a natural event has occurred.

   d. used to prove a theory outside a laboratory setting.

7. In a case study,

   a. each subject must be interviewed and given a questionnaire.

   b. each case must be reviewed by two independent researchers.

   c. is used when other methods of research are impractical.

   d. is only used if correlation cannot be established.

8. The survey method of research is used

   a. only when questionnaires can be given to a specific group of subjects.

   b. when researchers need to gather information from a large group of subjects.

   c. when no researchers are available to conduct interviews.

   d. if a random sample is needed to verify experimental results.

9. A correlational study

   a. examines how strongly two variables are related to one another.

   b. can be used to establish a cause-and-effect relationship.

   c. is no longer allowed due to ethical guidelines.

   d. is the best method to use to determine if a hypothesis is valid.

10. In an experiment, the independent variable is the variable that is

    a. unknown.

    b. used as a substitute for the dependent variable in the control group.

    c. deliberately manipulated by the researcher.

    d. not used unless the control group and experimental groups are randomly selected.

11. A placebo is

    a. is a treatment or substance that has no known effects.

    b. must be used to verify a hypothesis in all drug studies.

    c. cannot be used in double-blind studies.

    d. is a way of controlling the dependent variable.

12. A double-blind study is

    a. only used in research experiments using two or more groups.

    b. a method to eliminate experimenter bias.

    c. required of all studies using placebos.

    d. the best method to ensure a hypothesis is proven.

13. The experimental method is used

    a. to demonstrate a cause-and-effect relationship.

    b. to verify that two factors are related.

    c. when there is one control group and one experimental group.

    d. by researchers when they need to establish a hypothesis as valid.

14. In the video, researchers Anderson and Dill explained that in addition to gathering empirical data, there are other ways of knowing information, such as

    a. trial and error, logical reasoning, and advice received from an authority.

    b. rational thinking, advice from an authority, and personal anecdotes.

    c. reading, listening, and forming a hypothesis.

    d. asking others, checking research data, and drawing your own conclusions.

15. In the video, the main hypothesis of the first Anderson and Dill research experiment on video games and aggression was that people who played video games in real life would

    a. display less aggressive behaviors after playing the game.

    b. be equal in aggressive behavior as other people after playing the game.

    c. display more aggressive behaviors after playing the game.

    d. be more aggressive in game playing, but not more aggressive in real life.

16. In the video, a loud burst of noise delivered to other people was used

    a. as a display of aggression.

    b. as a notice to stop playing the game.

    c. as a method to increase aggression.

    d. to stop aggressive behavior.

17. In the video, what methods of research did Anderson and Dill use to study video games and aggressive behavior?

    a. naturalistic method and case study methods

    b. case study and the experimental method

    c. correlational and experimental methods

    d. survey method and random assignment methods

18. In the video, the three characteristics of the experimental method that were introduced were the manipulation of variables, the use of control groups, and

    a. the need for a hypothesis.

    b. the importance of random assignment.

    c. the need for strict adherence to research guidelines.

    d. the importance of not telling test subjects about the experiment.

19. In the Anderson and Dill experimental study, the main independent variable was

    a. aggressive behavior.

    b. violent vs. nonviolent game playing.

    c. the length of time the subject played the video game.

    d. the subject's behavior prior to playing the violent video game.

Short-Answer Questions

20. List the steps of the scientific method.

_____

_____

_____

21. Describe the three types of descriptive studies.

_____

_____

_____

22. Explain the difference between an independent variable and a dependent variable as used in the experimental method.

_____

_____

_____

23. Discuss the difference between correlation and cause and effect.

_____

_____

_____

24. What is naturalistic observation and what are some of its advantages and limitations?

_____

_____

_____

25. Describe and give an example of the placebo effect.

_____

_____

_____

26. What does it mean if some data are referred to as being statistically significant?

_____

_____

_____

Matching Exercises

Match the following terms and concepts with the correct definition.

scientific method	critical thinking	case study
naturalistic research	empirical evidence	placebo
pseudoscience	experimental method	double-blind experiment

27. _____ The rational method of evaluating evidence while trying to minimize the influence of preconceptions and biases.

28. _____ A set of assumptions, attitudes and procedures that guide researchers.

29. _____ Evidence that is based on observation and measurement.

30. _____ Research study in which neither the researcher nor the participants are aware of which group the participant belongs.

31. _____ Science that makes claims with little or no evidence.

32. _____ A method of investigation used to demonstrate cause-and-effect relationships.

33. _____ A highly detailed description of a single individual or event.

34. _____ The systemic observation and recording of events as they occur in their natural setting.

35. _____ A fake treatment or substance that has no known effects.

Completion Exercises

Fill in each blank with the most appropriate term or terms from the list of answers provided.

cause and effect	placebo effect
control group	predict
correlational studies	random selection
descriptive	scientific method
descriptive research method	statistics
empirical research	survey method
experimental group	

36. The four basic goals of psychology are to describe, explain, _____, and control or influence behavior and mental processes.

37. _____ means that every member has an equal chance of being selected.

38. When psychologists systemically observe and record behaviors as they occur in their natural settings, they are using a _____.

39. The research method that uses questionnaires or interviews to investigate opinions and behaviors is called the _____.

40. _____ refers to a research strategy that investigates how two factors are related to one another.

41. During research using the experimental method, one group of subjects is exposed to the experimental conditions. This group is called the _____.

42. During research using the experimental method, one group of subjects is exposed to all the experimental conditions, except the independent variable. This group is called the _____.

43. Changes that occur simply because the subjects expect a change to occur is called the _____.

44. Psychologists and other researchers use _____ to summarize data and draw conclusions based on the data.

45. In the video, psychological researcher Craig Anderson explained that scientifically valid information is based on _____ that is publicly observable.

46. In the video, Dr. Elaine Vaughn explained that the _____ should really be thought of as a way of thinking about problems.

47. In the video, researcher Karen Dill explained that one of the main advantages of _____ methodologies involves the fact that it is very natural and can lead to some real insights.

48. As Dr. Vaughn explained in the video, correlational studies do not prove _____, and caution must always be exercised in interpreting the results of these type of studies.

Multiple-Choice Questions

1. c	6. a	11. a	16. a
2. c	7. c	12. b	17. c
3. c	8. b	13. a	18. b
4. d	9. a	14. b	19. b
5. d	10. c	15. c	

Short-Answer Questions

20. Your answer should include these four steps: (1) formulate a question that can be tested (hypothesis), (2) design a study and collect data, (3) analyze the data and draw a conclusion, and (4) report the results. (pages 18–21)

21. The three types of descriptive studies are (1) naturalistic observation, (2) case studies, and (3) the survey method. (pages 22–23)

22. Your answer should include that conducting an experiment using the experimental method involves deliberately varying one factor, which is called the independent variable. Changes produced by varying the independent variable are called the dependent variable. The dependent variable is so named because changes in it depend on variations in the independent variable. (pages 27–28)

23. Your answer should point out that correlation refers to the relationship between to factors. Cause and effect refers to one specific factor producing a change in another factor. (pages 25–26)

24. Your answer should include that naturalistic observation is a descriptive type of research that involves systematically observing and recording behaviors in their natural setting. The advantage of naturalistic observation is that it tends to be more accurate than studies that are artificially staged or manipulated. A major disadvantage of naturalistic observation is that many behaviors cannot be studied using this type of research. (pages 22–23)

25. Your answer should include that the placebo effect refers to phenomenon wherein some subjects experience changes not due to some test variable, but solely because they expected a change to occur. The most common form of placebo experiments involving giving a test pill to some subjects while other subjects a fake pill or placebo. The two groups, those taking the real pill and those taking the fake pill (placebo) are then compared. (page 32)

26. Your answer should include that if a research finding is statistically significant, it means that these results are not very likely to have occurred by chance. (page 19)

Matching Exercises

27. critical thinking

28. scientific method

29. empirical evidence

30. double-blind experiment

31. pseudoscience

32. experimental method

33. case study

34. naturalistic research

35. placebo

Completion Exercises

36. predict

37. random selection

38. descriptive research method

39. survey method

40. correlational studies

41. experimental group

42. control group

43. placebo effect

44. statistics

45. empirical research

46. scientific method

47. descriptive

48. cause and effect

Study Matrix

Lesson 2

Research Methods in Psychology

Please Note: Use this matrix to guide your study and achieve the learning objectives of this lesson. It will also help you to view the video, which defines and demonstrates important concepts and objectives as they relate to everyday life and actual case studies.

Learning Objective	Textbook	Telecourse Student Guide
List the four goals of psychology.	p. 16	Study Activities 1, 2, 36.
List the steps that comprise the scientific method.	p. 18	Key Terms and Concepts; Study Activities 4, 20, 28, 46.
Define the concepts hypothesis, empirical evidence, and critical thinking.	pp. 16–19	Key Terms and Concepts; Study Activities 3, 14, 15, 27, 29, 45.
Define what is meant by the concept of descriptive methods of research.	pp. 22–23	Key Terms and Concepts; Study Activities 5, 33, 34, 38, 47.
Compare and contrast the three categories of descriptive research.	pp. 22–25	Key Terms and Concepts; Study Activities 6, 8, 21, 24, 37, 39.
Define what is meant by the concept of correlational method of research.	p. 25	Key Terms and Concepts; Study Activities 9, 40.
Explain the difference between correlation and cause-and-effect.	pp. 26–27	Key Terms and Concepts; Study Activities 16, 17, 23, 48.
Define what is meant by the concept of experimental method of research.	pp. 27–28	Key Terms and Concepts; Study Activities 13, 17, 18, 32, 41.
Explain the difference between an independent variable and a dependent variable as used in the experimental method.	p. 28	Key Terms and Concepts; Study Activities 10, 19, 22.
Explain the difference between an experimenter group and a control group as used in the experimental method.	pp. 28–29	Key Terms and Concepts; Study Activities 11, 25, 30, 35, 42, 43.
Describe how statistics are used in research.	pp. 19–20	Key Terms and Concepts; Study Activities 26, 31, 44.

Use the Course Compass to orient yourself in the road that you are taking to explore branches and aspects of psychology. The branch and aspects that are covered in this lesson are highlighted in the compass.

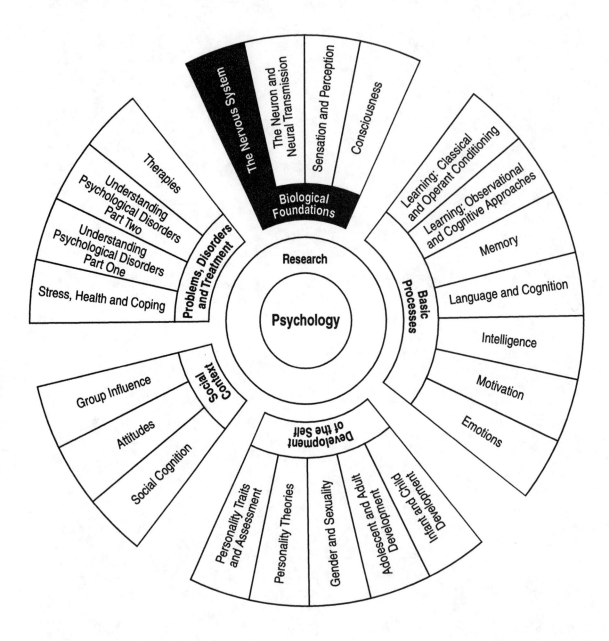

Please note: This compass does not represent the full range of topics comprising the field of psychology; it represents a map for this course only. Each of the five branches represented above has many aspects and subjects that are covered in the 26 lessons of this telecourse. You should remember that these branches and subjects all interrelate.

Lesson

The Nervous System

Questions to Consider

What is the primary function of the nervous system?

What parts of the body make up the nervous system?

How does our brain control what we feel, think, and do?

What are the methods researchers use to study the brain?

What would happen if it were necessary to remove half of a person's brain?

Lesson Assignments

Before viewing the video program

Read the Questions to Consider, Lesson Preview, and Learning Objectives for this lesson. Use this information to guide your reading, viewing, and thinking.

Read Chapter 2, "Neuroscience and Behavior," pages 55–85, in the textbook.

View the video program, "The Nervous System"

After viewing the video program

Review the vocabulary listed in the Key Terms and Concepts section. (Page references are keyed to the Hockenbury textbook, *Psychology*. Remember: there is a complete Glossary at the end of the textbook.)

Review the reading assignments for this lesson.

Complete the exercises found in the Study Activities section and check your answers with the Answer Key at the end of this lesson.

Use the Study Matrix found at the end of this lesson to review and assess your knowledge of each Learning Objective.

Lesson Preview

Every emotion you feel, every thought you think, every action you take, every memory you have, and every sensation you feel is rooted in your nervous system. When you study behavior, you are also studying biology—for all behavior can ultimately be traced back to some biological connection.

The nervous system is comprised of the central nervous system and the peripheral nervous system. Of all the components of the nervous system, the brain is, by far, the most complex and fascinating. The brain is the place from which all learning, memory, awareness, and reason emanate. Comprised of billions of interconnected neurons the human brain is the most complex communication structure in the known universe.

What would life be like if your brain were damaged or did not function properly? Who would you be and what would you be able to do? In this video lesson you will meet Guy Gabelich, who at age six underwent a rare operation called a hemispherectomy. Half of Guy's brain was surgically removed.

Guy was facing the rest of his life with only half his brain intact. How would this incredible event affect his future? What behaviors would change? Would Guy still be able to walk, talk, learn, and rely on his memory?

By following the remarkable story of Guy Gabelich, you will discover how the human brain adapts and changes. You will learn the basic structures and functions of the brain by going on a tour of the brain guided by UCLA neurobiologist Arnold Scheibel. You will also learn about how new and more advanced brain-imaging techniques are dramatically changing our understanding of the human brain.

Pediatric neurologist Donald Shields will explain risks and the recovery of Guy Gabelich, including the very important part played by his mother and his environment.

This lesson concludes with a discussion by Dr. Marian Diamond on the important role that enriched environments play in the development and maintenance of our mental capacities.

Learning Objectives

When you have completed this lesson, you should be able to:

1. Define biological psychology, neurogenesis, and explain why psychologists are concerned with human biology.

2. List the major components of the nervous system and describe their functions.

3. Distinguish between the basic components that make up the central nervous system and the peripheral nervous system.

4. Explain the difference between sympathetic and parasympathetic reactions as they occur in the autonomic nervous system.

5. Identify and describe the primary functions of the hindbrain, midbrain, and forebrain.

6. Discuss the location and function of the cerebral cortex.

7. Identify several different brain-imaging techniques.

8. Discuss specialization in the right and left hemispheres of the brain, including the concept of lateralization of function.

9. Discuss the concept of structural plasticity.

10. Describe the endocrine system and discuss how it interacts with the nervous system.

Key Terms and Concepts

Page references are keyed to the Hockenbury textbook, *Psychology.*

Biological psychology: A specialized branch of psychology that studies the relationship between behavior and bodily systems. (pages 44–45)

Nervous system: The primary communication system of the body comprised of the central nervous system and the peripheral nervous system. (page 55)

Central nervous system: Division of the nervous system that consists of the brain and the spinal cord. (page 56)

Peripheral nervous system: Division of the nervous system that includes all nerves lying outside the central nervous system. (page 57)

Somatic nervous system: A division of the peripheral nervous system that communicates sensory information between the muscles and the central nervous system. (page 57)

Autonomic nervous system: A division of the peripheral nervous system that regulates involuntary functions. (page 57)

Sympathetic nervous system: Part of the autonomic nervous system that produces rapid physical arousal, the body's emergency response system. (pages 58–59)

Parasympathetic nervous system: Part of the autonomic nervous system that produces the opposite effect of the sympathetic nervous system, calms the body down, and helps return the body to normal functioning. (page 59)

Hindbrain: A region at the base of the brain that regulates basic life functions. (page 70)

Midbrain: The middle and smallest region of the brain, involved in processing auditory and visual sensory information. (pages 70–71)

Forebrain: The largest and most complex region of the brain, controls complex behaviors and mental processes. (pages 70–71)

Cerebral cortex: The large outer portion of the forebrain, involved in controlling complex mental processes. (pages 70–72)

Cerebral hemispheres: The nearly identical and symmetrical two halves of the cerebral cortex. (pages 70, 77, and 82)

Brain-imaging techniques: A variety of advanced techniques (electroencephalograph, PET scans, CAT scans, MRI, fMRI) used to study the living brain. (pages 66–68)

Endocrine system: A system of glands that secrete hormones into the bloodstream. Not part of the nervous system, the endocrine system interacts with the nervous system. (page 59)

Hormones: Chemical messengers secreted into the bloodstream by endocrine glands. (page 59)

Lateralization of function: The notion that specific cognitive functions are processed primarily on one side of the brain. (pages 78 and 82)

Structural plasticity: A phenomenon in which brain structures physically change in response to environmental influences. (pages 83–84)

Neurogenesis: The development of new neurons. (pages 68–69)

Study Activities

These self-test questions are designed as a study exercise to aid you in understanding the most important terms and concepts in this lesson. To ensure that you have an accurate understanding of the key terms and concepts in this lesson, please check your answers with the Answer Key provided at the end of this lesson.

Multiple-Choice Questions

1. The nervous system is divided into two main parts. These are called the

    a. central and peripheral nervous systems.
    b. sensory and motor nervous systems.
    c. autonomic and skeletal nervous systems.
    d. spinal and reflexive nervous systems.

2. The somatic and autonomic nervous systems constitute the

    a. parasympathetic nervous system.
    b. peripheral nervous system.
    c. sympathetic nervous system.
    d. central nervous system.

3. The central nervous system is comprised of

    a. the brain.
    b. all the nerves lying outside the central nervous system.
    c. the brain and the spinal cord.
    d. motor neurons.

4. The sympathetic nervous system is a division of the _____ nervous system

    a. parasympathetic
    b. autonomic
    c. somatic
    d. central

5. After a stressful event, the _____ nervous system calms the body and returns the body to its normal functioning.

    a. sympathetic
    b. somatic
    c. parasympathetic
    d. central

6. Hormones are produced by the

   a. pituitary glands.

   b. pancreatic glands.

   c. endocrine glands.

   d. neurons.

7. Your _____ is most likely used when reading this question.

   a. forebrain

   b. midbrain

   c. hindbrain

   d. corpus callosum.

8. The branch of psychology that studies the relationship between behavior and bodily processes and systems is called

   a. clinical psychology.

   b. biological psychology.

   c. cognitive psychology.

   d. forensic psychology.

9. The notion that specific cognitive functions are processed primarily on one side of the brain is called

   a. structural plasticity.

   b. phrenology.

   c. cognitive displacement.

   d. lateralization of function.

10. Contrary to what was originally believed, scientists have discovered that people can grow new neurons. The development of new neurons is called

    a. action potential.

    b. neurogenesis.

    c. lateralization connecting.

    d. neural feedback.

11. The primary reason why Guy Gabelich's surgery became necessary was that

    a. he was unable to walk.

    b. his seizures were starting to interfere with normal brain development.

    c. without the operation he would not be able to speak.

    d. it lessened the chance of him having another stroke.

12. The video graphically displayed and explained that one area of the brain is primarily responsible for regulating basic life functions. This area is called the

    a. forebrain.
    b. midbrain.
    c. hindbrain.
    d. corpus callosum.

13. One basic skill that Guy Gabelich has **NOT** mastered is

    a. driving a car.
    b. counting money.
    c. reading.
    d. watching television.

14. In the video, Dr. Steward explained that over the past 30 years it has been learned that the brain is capable of substantial rewiring. This rewiring process is called

    a. structural cell regeneration.
    b. asphasia.
    c. plasticity.
    d. cerebral realignment.

Short-Answer Questions

15. Briefly describe the functions of the peripheral nervous system.

    _____
    _____
    _____

16. Briefly discuss the concept of neurogenesis.

    _____
    _____
    _____

17. What imaging methods are used to study the structures and activity of the brain?

    _____
    _____
    _____

18. Identify the three major regions of the brain. What is function of the cerebral cortex? In what region is the cerebral cortex located?

_____

_____

_____

19. Briefly describe the endocrine system and discuss how it interacts with the nervous system.

_____

_____

_____

20. Define biological psychology and explain why psychologists are concerned with human biology.

_____

_____

_____

21. Discuss specialization in the right and left hemispheres of the brain, including the concept of lateralization of function.

_____

_____

_____

22. Discuss the role that Guy's mother played in his recovery and the importance of being exposed to an enriched environment.

_____

_____

_____

Matching Exercises

Match the following terms and concepts with the correct definition.

autonomic nervous system	midbrain	cerebral cortex
biological psychology	hindbrain	cerebral hemispheres
structural plasticity	forebrain	central nervous system

23. _____ The middle and smallest region of the brain, involved in processing auditory and visual sensory information.

24. _____ A branch of psychology that studies the relationship between behavior and bodily systems.

25. _____ Division of the nervous system that consists of the brain and the spinal cord.

26. _____ A phenomenon in which brain structures physically change in response to environmental influences.

27. _____ A division of the peripheral nervous system that regulates involuntary functions.

28. _____ The largest and most complex region of the brain, involved in controlling complex behaviors and mental processes.

29. _____ A region at the base of the brain that regulates basic life functions.

30. _____ The nearly identical and symmetrical two halves of the cerebral cortex.

31. _____ The large outer portion of the forebrain, involved in complex mental processes.

Completion Exercises

Fill in each blank with the most appropriate term or terms from the list of answers provided.

auditory information

brain imaging

corpus callosum

endocrine system

functional magnetic resonance imaging (fMRI)

hormones

lateralization of function

left

nervous system

parasympathetic nervous system

somatic nervous system

sympathetic nervous system

synchronizing movement, balance, and posture

32. By interacting with the nervous system and affecting internal organs and body tissues, the _____ regulate physical processes and influence behavior in a variety of ways.

33. When someone is feeling afraid or anxious, the _____ produces rapid physical arousal.

34. Up to one trillion neurons are linked throughout your body in a complex communication network called the _____.

35. The discovery that the left hemisphere exerts greater control over speech and language is an example of the notion of _____.

36. The _____ is made up of glands located throughout the body that transmit information via chemical messengers.

37. The part of the autonomic nervous system that calms the body is called the _____.

38. PET scans, MRIs, and CAT scans are methods scientists and researchers use for _____.

39. The _____ communicates sensory information between muscles and the central nervous system.

40. In the video it was explained that the frontal lobe of the brain is associated with behavior and voluntary muscle movements and the temporal lobe is the primary area for receiving _____.

41. In the video Dr. Scheibel explained that the cerebellum, or little brain, is a large, two-sided structure located at the back of the brain that is responsible for _____.

42. In the video you were shown that the left and right hemispheres of the brain are connected by the _____.

43. As explained in the video, lateralization of function refers to the control and processing of an aspect of either motor or cognitive function to one side of the brain. Speech and language are lateralized to the _____ hemisphere.

44. As shown in the video, _____ maps brain activity by measuring changes in the blood supply of the brain during different mental activities.

Answer Key

Multiple-Choice Questions

1. a	6. c	11. b
2. b	7. a	12. c
3. c	8. b	13. b
4. a	9. d	14. c
5. c	10. b	

Short-Answer Questions

15. Your answer should include that the peripheral nervous system controls sensory information and muscle movement and regulates body functions, such as heartbeat, digestion, blood pressure, and breathing. (page 57)

16. The term neurogenesis means the development of new neurons. Until recently, it was commonly believed that humans could not grow new neurons. New research has now proved that humans can, in fact, grow new neurons. (pages 68–69)

17. Your answer should include two or more of the following brain-imaging methods: CAT scans, PET scans, MRI, fMRI, electroencephalograph. (pages 66–68)

18. Your answer should state the hindbrain, midbrain, and forebrain. The cerebral cortex functions as the center for our most sophisticated brain activity. The cerebral cortex is the large outer portion of the forebrain. (pages 69–71)

19. Your answer should state that the endocrine system is made up of glands that transmit information via hormones. The endocrine system interacts with the nervous system by secreting hormones that affect internal organs and body tissue, which then affect physical processes and influence behavior. (pages 59–61)

20. Your answer should include that biological psychology is the study of the relationship between biological activity and behavior and mental processes. Psychologists are concerned with human biology because ultimately all behavior and mental processes can be traced back to some biological event. (page 44)

21. Your answer should include that specialization in cerebral hemispheres refers to the notion that specific psychological and cognitive functions are located in either the left or right hemispheres. Lateralization of function is the notion that specific psychological or cognitive functions are processed primarily on one side of the brain. (pages 77–78)

22. Your answer should include that his mother's dedication was one of the primary reasons why Guy progressed as well as he did. An enriched environment is critical to give the maximum opportunity for any child to do his or her best; it is especially important for someone who faced the many obstacles that confronted Guy Gabelich. (video)

Matching Exercises

23. midbrain

24. biological psychology

25. central nervous system

26. structural plasticity

27. autonomic nervous system

28. forebrain

29. hindbrain

30. cerebral hemispheres

31. cerebral cortex

Completion Exercises

32. hormones

33. sympathetic nervous system

34. nervous system

35. lateralization of function

36. endocrine system

37. parasympathetic nervous system

38. brain imaging

39. somatic nervous system

40. auditory information

41. synchronizing movement, balance, and posture

42. corpus callosum

43. left

44. functional magnetic resonance imaging (fMRI)

Study Matrix

Lesson 3
The Nervous System

Please Note: Use this matrix to guide your study and achieve the learning objectives of this lesson. It will also help you to view the video, which defines and demonstrates important concepts and objectives as they relate to everyday life and actual case studies.

Learning Objective	Textbook	Telecourse Student Guide
Define biological psychology, neurogenesis, and explain why psychologists are concerned with human biology.	p. 44	Key Terms and Concepts; Study Activities 8, 10, 11, 16, 20, 24, 32, 44.
List the major components of the nervous system and describe their functions.	pp. 55–59	Key Terms and Concepts; Study Activities 1, 34.
Distinguish between the basic components that make up the central nervous system and the peripheral nervous system.	pp. 56–57	Key Terms and Concepts; Study Activities 3, 15, 25, 39, 40.
Explain the difference between sympathetic and parasympathetic reactions as they occur in the autonomic nervous system.	pp. 57–59	Key Terms and Concepts; Study Activities 2, 4, 5, 27, 33, 37.
Identify and describe the primary functions of the hindbrain, midbrain, and forebrain.	pp. 69–71	Key Terms and Concepts; Study Activities 7, 12, 18, 23, 28, 29, 41.
Discuss the location and function of the cerebral cortex.	pp. 71–75	Key Terms and Concepts; Study Activities 18, 30, 31.
Identify several different brain-imaging techniques.	pp. 66–68	Key Terms and Concepts; Study Activities 17, 38, 44.
Discuss specialization in the right and left hemispheres of the brain, including the concept of lateralization of function.	pp. 77–82	Key Terms and Concepts; Study Activities 9, 21, 35, 42, 43.
Discuss the concept of structural plasticity.	pp. 83–84	Key Terms and Concepts; Study Activities 14, 22, 26.
Describe the endocrine system and discuss how it interacts with the nervous system.	pp. 59–61	Key Terms and Concepts; Study Activities 6, 19, 36.

Use the Course Compass to orient yourself in the road that you are taking to explore branches and aspects of psychology. The branch and aspects that are covered in this lesson are highlighted in the compass.

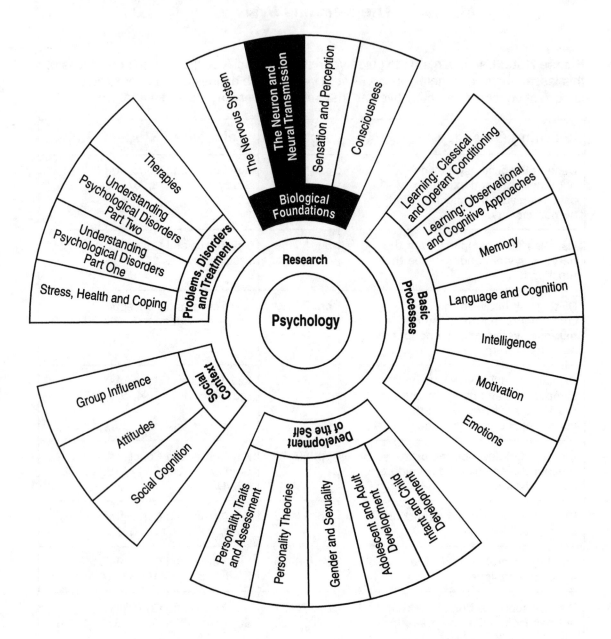

Please note: This compass does not represent the full range of topics comprising the field of psychology; it represents a map for this course only. Each of the five branches represented above has many aspects and subjects that are covered in the 26 lessons of this telecourse. You should remember that these branches and subjects all interrelate.

Lesson 4

The Neuron and Neural Transmission

Questions to Consider

What are neurons?

What are the basic components of neurons, and what are their functions?

How does the brain control what we think, feel, and do?

How is information transmitted within and between neurons?

What happens if brain communication becomes disrupted?

How do drugs affect how the brain functions?

Lesson Assignments

Before viewing the video program

Read the Questions to Consider, Lesson Preview, and Learning Objectives for this lesson. Use this information to guide your reading, viewing, and thinking.

Read Chapter 2, "Neuroscience and Behavior," pages 43–55, in the textbook.

View the video program, "The Neuron and Neural Transmission"

After viewing the video program

Review the vocabulary listed in the Key Terms and Concepts section. (Page references are keyed to the Hockenbury textbook, *Psychology*. Remember: there is a complete Glossary at the end of the textbook.)

Review the reading assignments for this lesson.

Complete the exercises found in the Study Activities section and check your answers with the Answer Key at the end of this lesson.

Use the Study Matrix found at the end of this lesson to review and assess your knowledge of each Learning Objective.

Lesson Preview

In this lesson, you will be studying neurons and neural transmission. By watching the dramatic story of Dr. Susie Curtiss in a groundbreaking fight with a severe neurological disorder, you will see how faulty neural transmission can deprive anyone of their ability to live a normal life.

All of our thoughts, senses, feelings, and behavior can ultimately be traced to the activity of the basic building block of the nervous system, the neuron. As you will learn, neurons are the highly specialized cells that receive and send information throughout our bodies. Most experts agree that there are as many as one trillion neurons throughout our nervous system and in excess of 100 billion neurons in the brain.

In this lesson, you will learn to identify the components of a neuron and understand how each component functions. You will learn how messages are transmitted *within* neurons and how messages are transmitted *between* neurons. You will also learn about the essential role played by very specialized chemicals called neurotransmitters.

This lesson tells the story of Susie Curtiss, a professor of linguistics at UCLA who, without any warning, was stricken with a debilitating neurological disease called dystonia. Although the exact cause of dystonia is not known, it is known that this disease is the result of malfunctions in neural transmission.

Dr. Curtiss' neurological symptoms began gradually, but soon her symptoms became severe and she lost her ability do such simple things as drive a car or sing a song. With the support of her family, and because of her heroic determination, Dr. Curtiss remained determined to find a solution to her problem.

Neurosurgeon Dr. Jeffrey Schweitzer came up with a possible solution. It was an experimental surgery—but it did offer Susie Curtiss a chance to regain her ability to have a normal life.

As you learn about neurons and neural transmission, you will also learn about the remarkable progress science is making in understanding and treating neurological disorders. Within the past 10 to 15 years, science has made incredible progress in learning more about neurons, neural transmission, and neurotransmitters. What is so exciting is the flood of new information that is being gained by studying and treating people such as Susie Curtiss.

By understanding neurons and neural transmission, you will better appreciate how the nervous system interacts to create the uniqueness of every human being.

Learning Objectives

When you have completed this lesson, you should be able to:

1. Describe the functions of neurons and glial cells.

2. List the three types of neurons, and explain their respective functions.

3. Identify the basic components of a neuron, and describe their functions.

4. Explain the processes that take place within the neuron when it is activated.

5. Explain what is meant by action potential, stimulus threshold, and resting potential.

6. Describe the all-or-none principle as it applies to neural transmission.

7. Describe the role neurotransmitters play in communication between neurons.

8. Identify several neurotransmitters, and discuss their known or suspected effects.

Key Terms and Concepts

Page references are keyed to the Hockenbury textbook, *Psychology*.

Neurons: Highly specialized cells that communicate information in electrical and chemical form. (page 45)

Glial cells: Support cells that assist neurons by providing structure and nutrition, removing waste, and manufacturing myelin. (page 45)

Sensory neurons: Neurons that convey sensory information from organs to the brain. (pages 46–47)

Motor neurons: Neurons that convey information to muscles causing muscles to relax or contract. (pages 46–47)

Interneurons: The most common type of neuron, interneurons communicate information between neurons. (pages 46–47)

Cell body: Part of a neuron, the cell body contains the nucleus and other structures found in most body cells. (pages 46–47)

Dendrites: Part of a neuron, dendrites are fibers that extend from the cell body and receive information from other neurons and sensory receptors. (pages 46–47)

Axon: Part of a neuron, the axon is a long, fluid-filled tube that carries messages to other areas of the body. (page 47)

Nucleus: Provides energy for the neuron to carry out its function. (page 46)

Myelin sheath: A white, fatty covering wrapped around the axons of some neurons that increase their communication speed. (page 47)

Action potential: A brief electrical impulse by which information is transmitted. (page 47)

Stimulus threshold: The minimum level of stimulation required to activate a particular neuron. (page 47)

Resting potential: A state in which a neuron is prepared to activate if it receives sufficient stimulation. (page 48)

All-or-none law: The principle that either a neuron is sufficiently stimulated and an action potential occurs or a neuron is not sufficiently stimulated and no action potential occurs. (page 48)

Synaptic gap: A minuscule space between the axon terminal of one neuron and the dendrite of an adjoining neuron. (page 50)

Neurotransmitters: Chemical messengers manufactured by a neuron. (page 50)

Acetylcholine: A neurotransmitter that causes muscle contraction and is involved in memory and learning. Associated disorder: Alzheimer's disease. (pages 52–53)

Dopamine: A neurotransmitter involved in the regulation of movement, attention, learning, and pleasure. Associated disorders: Parkinson's disease and schizophrenia. (pages 52–53)

Serotonin: A neurotransmitter involved in sleep, moods, and emotion. Associated disorder: depression. (pages 52–53)

Norepinephrine: A neurotransmitter involved in learning and memory. Associated disorder: depression. (pages 52–53)

Gamma-aminobutyric acid (GABA): A neurotransmitter involved in slowing brain activity. Associated disorder: anxiety. (pages 52–53)

Endorphins: A neurotransmitter involved in regulating pain perception and producing positive moods. Associated disorder: chemical addiction. (page 54)

Study Activities

These self-test questions are designed as a study exercise to aid you in understanding the most important terms and concepts in this lesson. To ensure that you have an accurate understanding of the key terms and concepts in this lesson, please check your answers with the Answer Key provided at the end of this lesson.

Multiple-Choice Questions

1. The basic building blocks of the nervous system are

    a. nerves.

    b. dendrites.

    c. neurons.

    d. axons.

2. Neurons are held in place by

    a. axons.

    b. nerves.

    c. dendrites.

    d. glial cells.

3. The three basic types of neurons are

    a. sensory neurons, motor neurons, and glial neurons.

    b. brain neurons, body neurons, and support neurons.

    c. interneurons, communication neurons, and support neurons.

    d. sensory neurons, motor neurons, and interneurons.

4. The main function of neurons is

    a. communication.

    b. to support the nervous system.

    c. metabolism.

    d. learning and memory.

5. Data enters the neuron at the

    a. cell body.

    b. dendrites.

    c. axon.

    d. synapses.

6. The myelin sheath's function is to

   a. extend the life of the neuron.

   b. protect the neuron from antibodies.

   c. insulate the axon from interference.

   d. slow down the speed of transmission.

7. The space between neurons across which chemical messages pass is called the

   a. chemical receptor site.

   b. synaptic gap.

   c. axon-dendrite gap.

   d. neurotransmitter.

8. Transmission *within* a neuron is electrical. Transmission *between* neurons is

   a. chemical.

   b. electrochemical.

   c. synaptic.

   d. based on the type of neuron.

9. Endorphins have similar effects to opiates because they

   a. can cause personality change.

   b. can cause anxiety and depression.

   c. reduce the perception of pain and often produce a state of euphoria.

   d. make the body more sensitive to both pain and pleasure.

10. In general, messages are gathered by the dendrites and cell body and then transmitted along the axon in the form of a brief electrical impulse called

    a. a communication impulse.

    b. a nerve impulse.

    c. an action potential.

    d. a neurotransmitter discharge.

11. The neurological disorder suffered by Dr. Susie Curtiss is called dystonia. Dystonia is primarily associated with

    a. problems with language development.

    b. rapid heartbeats and sleep disruption.

    c. difficulty in controlling motor functions and coordination.

    d. problems with short-term memory.

12. In the video, Dr. Schweitzer explained that neurological disorders such as dystonia, multiple sclerosis, and Parkinson's disease are caused primarily by

   a. accidents or injuries.

   b. childhood trauma.

   c. malfunctions in neural transmission.

   d. nutritional deficiencies.

13. Information between neurons is received and transmitted by means of

   a. electrical impulses.

   b. electrical and chemical impulses.

   c. chemical impulses.

   d. intercellular reactions.

14. In the video, Dr. Oswald Steward explained that the centerpiece of the neuron, the place where all of the metabolic activity takes place, is the

   a. cell body.

   b. dendrite.

   c. axon.

   d. synaptic gap.

15. In the video, you were graphically shown that communication within a neuron occurs when one neuron is sufficiently stimulated and produces a brief electrical impulse. This impulse is called

   a. a neurotransmitter.

   b. an action potential.

   c. a cellular transmission message.

   d. a neural electrical discharge.

16. In the video for Lesson 4, Dr. Schweitzer points out that _____ is one of the most common neurological illnesses and affects approximately one person in 50 over the age of 50.

   a. depression

   b. dystonia

   c. multiple sclerosis

   d. Parkinson's disease

17. A postsurgical complication experienced by Susie Curtiss was the result of the brain's amazing ability to heal itself, a phenomenon called

    a. neural balancing.
    b. plasticity.
    c. the neurotransmitter effect.
    d. electromagnetic equilibrium.

Short-Answer Questions

18. What are the three main types of neurons?

    _____
    _____
    _____

19. What are the basic components of the neuron?

    _____
    _____
    _____

20. What are glial cells, and what is their role in the nervous system?

    _____
    _____
    _____

21. Define an action potential, and describe how an action potential is produced.

    _____
    _____
    _____

22. How does the myelin sheath affect the speed at which a nerve impulse travels?

    _____
    _____
    _____

23. Describe how the all-or-none law applies to the action potential of neurons.

    _____
    _____
    _____

24. What are the general functions of some common neurotransmitters?

_____

_____

_____

25. Define endorphins and explain the common effects related to these chemicals.

_____

_____

_____

26. Describe Dr. Susie Curtiss' attitude about the results of her remarkable surgery.

_____

_____

_____

Matching Exercises

Match the following terms and concepts with the correct definition.

stimulus threshold	myelin sheath	resting potential
action potential	sensory neurons	cell body
synaptic gap	axon	all-or-none law

27. _____ The minimum level of stimulation required to activate a neuron.

28. _____ The long, fluid-filled tube that extends from the cell body and carries information from the neuron to other areas of the body.

29. _____ A type of neuron that conveys information about the environment, such as light and sound, from sense organs to the brain.

30. _____ A brief electrical impulse that is transmitted along the axon of a neuron.

31. _____ A minuscule space between the axon terminal of one neuron and the dendrite of an adjacent neuron.

32. _____ A state in which a neuron is prepared to activate and communicate its message if it receives sufficient stimulation.

33. _____ The part of the neuron that contains the nucleus.

34. _____ The principle that states that either a neuron is sufficiently stimulated and an action potential occurs, or the neuron is not sufficiently stimulated and no action potential occurs.

35. _____ A white, fatty substance that insulates one axon from adjoining axons and increases the speed of neural transmissions.

Completion Exercises

Fill in each blank with the most appropriate term or terms from the list of answers provided.

dopamine	gamma-aminobutyric acid (GABA)	neurons
electrodes	glial cells	nucleus
endorphins	interneurons	serotonin

36. Located at the center of a neuron, the _____ provides energy for the neuron to carry out its function.

37. The cells that provide nutrition, enhance communication between neurons, remove waste products, and provide structural support for neurons are called

    _____.

38. Most of the neurons in the nervous system are _____, whose function is to communicate information between neurons.

39. The body produces it own painkillers, morphine-like chemicals called

    _____.

40. Antianxiety medications, such as Valium and Xanax, work by increasing _____ activity, which inhibits action potential and slows brain activity.

41. Characterized by rigidity, muscle tremors, poor balance, and difficulty in initiating movements, Parkinson's disease has been linked to a lack of the neurotransmitter _____.

42. The neurotransmitter _____ is involved in sleep, moods, and emotional states, including depression.

43. Communication throughout the nervous system takes place via _____, specialized cells that receive and transmit information.

44. To control her dystonia, Susie Curtiss elected to undergo an experimental surgical operation to have _____ implanted deep with her brain.

Answer Key

Multiple-Choice Questions

1. c	6. c	11. c	16. d
2. d	7. b	12. c	17. b
3. d	8. a	13. b	
4. a	9. c	14. a	
5. b	10. c	15. b	

Short-Answer Questions

18. Your answer should state that the three main types of neurons are sensory neurons, motor neurons, and interneurons. (page 46)

19. Your answer should state that most neurons have three basic components: a cell body, dendrites, and an axon. (page 46)

20. Your answer should include that glial cells primary function is to provide structural support for neurons. Glial cells also provide nutrition, enhance the speed of communication between neurons, and remove waste products. (page 45)

21. Your answer should include that an action potential is a brief, electrical impulse by which information is transmitted along the axon of a neuron. An action potential is produced by the movement of electrically charged particles, called ions, across the membrane of the axon. (pages 47–48)

22. Your answer should include that the myelin sheath increases the rate at which neurons transmit their messages by coating the axon and insulating it from other adjoining axons. (page 47)

23. Your answer should include that there is no such thing as a partially stimulated neuron. Either a neuron is sufficiently stimulated and an action potential occurs, or a neuron is not sufficiently stimulated and no action potential occurs. This principle is referred to as the all-or-none law. (page 48)

24. Your answer should include more than one of the following: (pages 52–54)

Acetylcholine	Learning, memory, muscle contractions
Dopamine	Movement, thought, rewarding sensations
Serotonin	Sleep, emotional states, depression
Norepinephrine	Physical arousal, learning, memory
GABA	Inhibition of brain activity, anxiety
Endorphins	Pain perception, positive emotions

25. Your answer should include that endorphins are chemicals manufactured by the brain that mimic the effects of opiates, such as morphine, heroin, and codeine.

Endorphins reduce the perception of pain and produce a state of euphoria. (page 54)

26. Your answer should include that, as shown in the video, the results were positive overall. "I think I have my life back. I can do things with so much ease. I hope I never forget how hard it was," says Dr. Susie Curtiss. (video)

Matching Exercises

27. stimulus threshold

28. axon

29. sensory neuron

30. action potential

31. synaptic gap

32. resting potential

33. cell body

34. all-or-none law

35. myelin sheath

Completion Exercises

36. nucleus

37. glial cells

38. interneurons

39. endorphins

40. gamma-aminobutyric acid (GABA)

41. dopamine

42. serotonin

43. neurons

44. electrodes

Study Matrix

Lesson 4

The Neuron and Neural Transmission

Please Note: Use this matrix to guide your study and achieve the learning objectives of this lesson. It will also help you to view the video, which defines and demonstrates important concepts and objectives as they relate to everyday life and actual case studies.

Learning Objective	Textbook	Telecourse Student Guide
Describe the functions of neurons and glial cells.	p. 45	Key Terms and Concepts; Study Activities 1, 2, 8, 13, 19, 20, 37.
List the three types of neurons, and explain their respective functions.	p. 46	Key Terms and Concepts; Study Activities 3, 18, 29, 38.
Identify the major parts and functions of a neuron.	pp. 46–47	Key Terms and Concepts; Study Activities 4, 19, 33, 36.
Explain the processes that take place within the neuron when it is activated.	pp. 47–48	Key Terms and Concepts; Study Activities 5, 6, 22, 27, 29.
Explain what is meant by action potential, stimulus threshold, and resting potential.	pp. 47–48	Key Terms and Concepts; Study Activities 10, 14, 21, 30, 32.
Describe the all-or-none principle as it applies to neural transmission.	p. 47	Key Terms and Concepts; Study Activities 7, 23, 31, 34.
Describe the role neurotransmitters play in communication between neurons.	pp. 50–52	Key Terms and Concepts; Study Activities 11, 24, 35, 38, 43.
Identify several neurotransmitters, and discuss their known or suspected effects.	pp. 52–54	Key Terms and Concepts; Study Activities 9, 12, 16, 17, 40, 41, 42.

Use the Course Compass to orient yourself in the road that you are taking to explore branches and aspects of psychology. The branch and aspects that are covered in this lesson are highlighted in the compass.

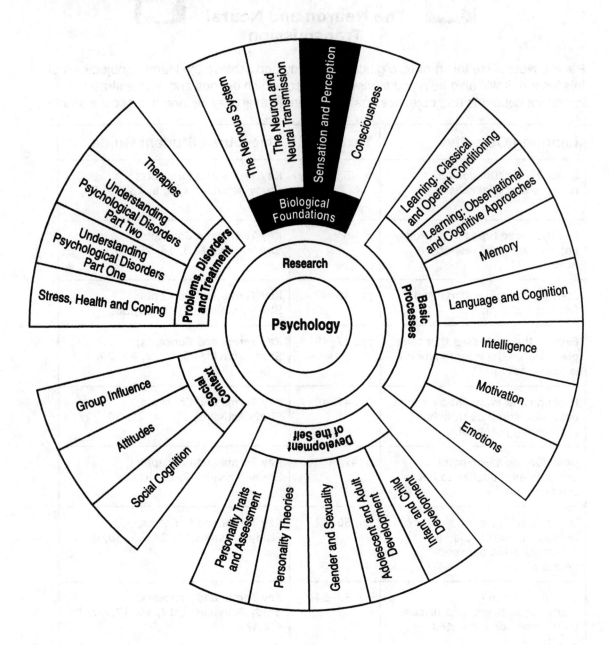

Please note: This compass does not represent the full range of topics comprising the field of psychology; it represents a map for this course only. Each of the five branches represented above has many aspects and subjects that are covered in the 26 lessons of this telecourse. You should remember that these branches and subjects all interrelate.

Sensation and Perception

Questions to Consider

How do we take physical energy, like light or sound waves, and change it into something we can experience?

When we see a color, does everyone see the same color?

What happens if we are overloaded with sensory information?

Can our emotions and expectations affect our senses and our perceptions?

How do education, culture, and life experiences affect how we perceive the world around us?

How can virtual reality help us learn more about human perception?

Lesson Assignments

Before viewing the video program

Read the Questions to Consider, Lesson Preview, and Learning Objectives for this lesson. Use this information to guide your reading, viewing, and thinking.

Read Chapter 3, "Sensation and Perception," in the textbook.

View the video program, "Sensation and Perception"

After viewing the video program

Review the vocabulary listed in the Key Terms and Concepts section. (Page references are keyed to the Hockenbury textbook, *Psychology*. Remember: there is a complete Glossary at the end of the textbook.)

Review the reading assignments for this lesson.

Complete the exercises found in the Study Activities section and check your answers with the Answer Key at the end of this lesson.

Use the Study Matrix found at the end of this lesson to review and assess your knowledge of each Learning Objective.

Lesson Preview

The senses gather information about the world by detecting various forms of physical energy, such as sound, light, heat, and pressure. If it were not for your senses you would exist in a void of darkness. Your world would be silent. You would feel nothing. You would not know if you were standing still or moving, wet or dry, hot or cold. Your senses allow you to experience life. Without your senses, you would not survive.

In this video, you will see how food critic Kelly Von Hemert uses her senses to form perceptions that lead to judgments—judgments that can affect the success or failure of a restaurant.

Psychologists have traditionally distinguished between sensation—the process of detecting a physical stimulus—and perception, the process of integrating, organizing and interpreting what you sense. But, as cognitive scientist Dr. Donald Hoffman explains in the video, it is often very difficult to distinguish between what we sense and what we perceive.

Ordinarily our experience of external reality is relatively accurate and error-free. Most of the time sensing and perceiving occur so effortlessly, continuously and automatically we forget about them. However, as you will see in this video, the sensation-perception process can easily go awry—and the results can vary from humorous to dangerous.

In this lesson you will learn the key components of the main senses—vision, hearing, taste, smell, and touch. You will also explore how the brain creates perception, and how emotions, needs, and past experiences influence how each of us perceives the world around us.

Learning Objectives

When you have completed this lesson, you should be able to:

1. Define sensation and explain the process of transduction.

2. Discuss absolute and difference thresholds, and describe how Weber's law explains the just noticeable difference.

3. Describe the process of sensory adaptation.

4. Discuss the key senses of vision, hearing, taste, smell, and touch.

5. Define perception and describe the differences between bottom-up processing and top-down processing.

6. Define and give an example of perceptual constancy.

7. Define and give an example of perceptual grouping.

8. Define and explain the process of depth perception.

9. Discuss the Gestalt laws of organization, including the concept of figure-ground reversal.

10. Explain perceptual set and discuss how prior assumptions and expectations can influence our perceptions.

Key Terms and Concepts

Page references are keyed to the Hockenbury textbook, *Psychology*.

Sensation: The process of detecting a physical stimulus, such as light, sound, heat, or pressure. (page 91)

Perception: The process of integrating, organizing, and interpreting sensory information in a way that is meaningful. (pages 91 and 116)

Sensory receptors: Specialized cells that respond to a particular form of physical energy. (page 91)

Transduction: The process by which a form of physical energy is converted into a neural signal. (page 91)

Absolute threshold: The smallest possible strength of a stimulus that can be detected half the time. (page 92)

Difference threshold: The smallest possible difference between two stimuli that can be detected half the time; also called the just noticeable difference. (page 92)

Weber's law: A principle of sensation that holds that the size of the just noticeable difference will vary depending on its relation to the strength of the original stimulus. (page 92)

Sensory adaptation: The decline in sensitivity to a constant stimulus. (page 92)

Light: One of the many different kinds of electromagnetic energy that travel in the form of waves. (page 94)

Optic nerve: A thick bundle of axons that carries information from the back of the eye to the brain. (page 99)

Hearing: The process of collecting, amplifying and transforming sound wave vibrations into the sensation of sound; technically called audition. (page 104)

Smell: The process of detecting airborne chemical molecules through the use of olfactory receptors cells located in the nasal cavity; technically called olfaction. (page 107)

Taste: The process of detecting dissolvable chemicals through the use of specialized receptors located in the mouth; technically called gustation. (page 110)

Taste buds: The specialized sensory receptors for taste that are located on the tongue and inside the mouth. (pages 110–111)

Bottom-up processing: Information processing that emphasizes the importance of sensory data in forming perceptions; analysis that moves from the parts to the whole. (page 115)

Top-down processing: Information processing that emphasizes the importance of the observer's knowledge and expectations in forming perceptions; analysis that moves from the whole to the parts. (page 115)

Figure-ground relationship: A Gestalt principle that states that we automatically separate perception into features that clearly stand out (the figure) and it less distinct background (the ground). (pages 116–118)

Gestalt principles of organization: Basic principles that explain how perception becomes organized. These principles include similarity, closure, good continuation and proximity. (page 118)

Perceptual constancies: Refers to the tendency to perceive objects as unchanging in size, shape and brightness despite changes in sensory input. (pages 124–125)

Perceptual illusions: The misperception of the true characteristics of an object or image. (page 125)

Perceptual set: The influence of prior assumptions and expectations on perceptual interpretations. (page 129)

Depth perception: The use of visual cues to perceive the distance or three-dimensional characteristics of objects. (page 119)

Perceptual grouping: The tendency to group different elements together in order to produce stable, well-defined perceptions. (page 118)

Study Activities

These self-test questions are designed as a study exercise to aid in understanding the most important terms and concepts in this lesson. To ensure that you have an accurate understanding of the key terms and concepts in this lesson, please check your answers with the Answer Key provided at the end of this lesson.

Multiple-Choice Questions

1. The process of detecting a physical stimulus, such as light, sound, heat, or pressure, is called

   a. perception.

   b. sensory reception.

   c. sensation.

   d. the sensation-perception process.

2. Sensation begins in the

   a. muscles.

   b. brain.

   c. sense receptors.

   d. nerves.

3. The process of transduction

   a. occurs in the brain.

   b. is the process by which a form of physical energy is converted into a signal that can be processed by the nervous system.

   c. takes place in sensory neurons.

   d. occurs only if the difference threshold is stimulated.

4. Music is constantly playing and, after a while, you become unaware that the music is still playing. This is an example of

   a. selective attention.

   b. sensory deprivation.

   c. auditory blending.

   d. sensory adaptation.

5. How is the lens of the eye different from the lens of a camera?

   a. The camera lens focuses by changing shape.

   b. The eye lens focuses by changing shape.

   c. The camera lens controls the amount of light entering the camera.

   d. The eye lens controls the amount of light entering the camera.

6. The receptor cells for smell and taste respond to

    a. the electromagnetic spectrum.

    b. neural stimulation in the same way as other sensory receptors.

    c. chemical stimulation.

    d. airborne, water-based chemicals.

7. Olfactory receptor cells respond to

    a. vibrations in the air.

    b. wavelengths of light.

    c. chemical molecules in the air.

    d. chemical molecules in the mouth.

8. Which sense lets you know if you are moving?

    a. equilibrium

    b. kinesthesis

    c. olfaction

    d. somatic nervous system

9. As you walk down a street, the shape, size, and location of everything around you keeps changing. Yet you experience your surroundings as stable. This stability is called

    a. the perceptual law of similarity.

    b. figure-ground.

    c. binocular cues.

    d. perceptual constancy.

10. Information processing that emphasizes the importance of the observer's knowledge and expectations in forming perceptions is called

    a. bottom-up processing.

    b. top-down processing.

    c. perceptual set.

    d. perceptual constancy.

11. As explained in the video lesson, the specialized nerve cells that allow us to extract information from the environment are called

    a. neurons.

    b. glial cells.

    c. sensory receptors.

    d. transduction nerves.

12. In the video, Dr. Bagrash discussed that the transforming, or recoding, of information from the language of the physical world into the language of the nervous system is called

    a. recoding phenomenon.

    b. transduction.

    c. sensory reorganization.

    d. the physical-neural connection.

13. When food critic Kelly Von Hemert inhaled odor molecules, they stimulated her

    a. olfactory receptors.

    b. nasal cavity.

    c. taste buds.

    d. neural pathways.

14. In the video, a Christmas tree was used to help explain the concept of

    a. bottom-up processing.

    b. top-down processing.

    c. visual discrimination.

    d. the Gestalt principle of organization.

15. In the video, you saw that a computer could be used to simulate various sensations. This process is called

    a. virtual reality.

    b. figure-ground.

    c. the computer-generated sensory input model.

    d. fourth-dimensional production.

16. The very important aspect of perception that explains how we can filter out things that are not important to us and attend to things that are important to us is called

    a. figure-ground.

    b. top-down processing.

    c. bottom-up processing.

    d. selective attention.

Short-Answer Questions

17. Distinguish between sensation and perception, and explain the how they interrelate.

    _____

    _____

    _____

18. Describe the role of sensory receptors and transduction in the sensory process.

_____

_____

_____

19. Define sensory adaptation, and explain the effects of sensory adaptation.

_____

_____

_____

20. Describe the process of hearing and the primary role of the outer ear, middle ear, and inner ear.

_____

_____

_____

21. Explain absolute threshold, difference threshold, and discuss Weber's law.

_____

_____

_____

22. Distinguish between bottom-up perceptual processing and top-down perceptual processing.

_____

_____

_____

23. Define and give an example of perceptual constancy.

_____

_____

_____

24. Define and give an example of the Gestalt perceptual principle of figure-ground relationship.

_____

_____

_____

Matching Exercises

Match the following terms and concepts with the correct definition.

pupil   hearing   taste buds

middle ear   perception   Gestalt principles of organization

optic nerve   smell   bottom-up processing

25. _____ The process of integrating, organizing, and interpreting sensory information in a way that is meaningful.

26. _____ The opening in the middle of the iris that changes size to let in different amounts of light.

27. _____ A thick bundle of axons that carries information from the back of the eye to the brain.

28. _____ The process of detecting airborne chemical molecules through the use of olfactory receptors cells.

29. _____ Information processing that emphasizes the importance of sensory data in forming perceptions.

30. _____ The specialized sensory receptors that are located on the tongue and inside the mouth.

31. _____ Amplifies sound waves and consists of three small bones, the hammer, the anvil, and the stirrup.

32. _____ Explains how perceptions become organized, and includes the principles of similarity, closure, good continuation, and proximity.

33. _____ The process of collecting, amplifying, and transforming sound wave vibrations, technically called audition.

Completion Exercises

Fill in each blank with the most appropriate term or terms from the list of answers provided.

absolute threshold   perceptual illusion

depth perception   perceptual set

figure-ground reversal   sensation

Gestalt   sensory receptors

perception   top-down processing

perceptual constancies   Weber's law

perceptual grouping

34. The principle of sensation that holds that the size of the just noticeable difference will vary depending on its relation to the strength of the original stimulus is called _____.

35. If a person wearing a white shirt goes into the shade, the white shirt still appears white, though it is actually darker in color. This is an example of _____, the phenomenon that allows us to perceive objects as constant and unchanging despite changes in sensory input.

36. When viewed on the horizon, the moon appears considerably larger than when it is viewed higher in the sky. This is an example of a _____.

37. Our _____ usually lead us to reasonably accurate conclusions. If they didn't, we would soon develop new ones so that the world would make sense to us.

38. Sensation is the result of stimulation of _____ by some form of physical energy.

39. The ability to perceive the distance of an object as well as the three-dimensional characteristics of an object is called _____.

40. As we interact with our environment, many of our perceptions are shaped by _____, which is also referred to as conceptually driven processing.

41. _____ refers to the smallest possible strength of a stimulus that can be detected, for example one teaspoon of sugar in two gallons of water or the tick of a watch at 20 feet.

42. As discussed in the video, in the last half of the twentieth century, research began to blur the lines of delineation between _____ and perception.

43. From looking down over a sheer cliff to peeling an exotic fruit, in the video there were several examples of the key role _____ plays in our lives.

44. In the video, the narrator explained that the German word _____, roughly translated, means unified whole, form, or shape.

45. As seen in the video, sometimes a single image can be seen in two different ways, a phenomenon called _____.

46. According to the laws or principles of _____, we tend to group elements together to arrive at the perception of forms, shapes, and figures.

Answer Key

Multiple-Choice Questions

1. c	5. b	9. d	13. a
2. c	6. c	10. b	14. a
3. b	7. c	11. c	15. a
4. d	8. b	12. b	16. d

Short-Answer Questions

17. Your answer should include that sensation refers to the detection and basic sensory experience of environmental stimuli, such as sounds, objects, and odors and that perception occurs when we integrate, organize, and interpret sensory information in a way that is meaningful. (page 90)

18. Your answer should include that sensation is the result of the stimulation of sensory receptors, specialized cells unique to each sense organ that respond to a particular form of physical energy. Transduction is the process by which physical energy is converted into a coded neural signal that can be processed by the nervous system. (page 91)

19. Your answer should state that sensory adaptation refers to the gradual decline in sensitivity to a constant stimulus. Because of sensory adaptation, we become accustomed to constant stimuli, which allows us to quickly notice new or changing stimuli. (page 92)

20. Your answer should include that sound waves are the physical stimuli that produce sound. Hearing is the result of the transduction of sound waves into coded neural signals that can be processed by the nervous system. The primary role of the outer ear is collecting sound waves, the primary role of the middle ear is amplifying sound waves, and the primary role of the inner ear is the transduction of sound waves into neural messages. (pages 104–106)

21. Your answer should include that absolute threshold refers to the smallest possible strength of a stimulus that can be detected. Difference threshold is the smallest possible difference between two stimuli that can be detected; also called the just noticeable difference. Weber's law holds that for each sense, the size of the difference threshold is a constant proportion of the size of the initial stimulus. Weber's law underscores that our psychological experience of sensation is relative. (page 92)

22. Your answer should include that bottom-up processing emphasizes the importance of the raw sensory data in detecting a perception. Top-down processing emphasizes the importance of the observer's knowledge, expectations, and other cognitive processes in arriving at meaningful perceptions. Bottom-up processing analysis moves from the parts to the whole, while top-down processing moves from the whole to the parts. (page 115)

23. Your answer should include that perceptual constancy refers to the tendency to perceive objects as unchanging despite changes in sensory input. Perceptual constancy promotes a stable view of the world. There are many examples of perceptual constancies. You may select any example that shows how size, shape, or brightness tend to appear unchanging even when, in reality, they are changing. (pages 124–125)

24. Your answer should include that figure-ground relationship refers to the perceptual principle that states that we automatically separate the elements of a perception into the feature that clearly stands out (the figure) and its less distinct background (the ground). An example of figure-ground separation would be when looking at a group of people (ground) you recognize a person you know, the person you know will tend to stand out (figure). (pages 117–118)

Matching Exercises

25. perception

26. pupil

27. optic nerve

28. smell

29. bottom-up processing

30. taste buds

31. middle ear

32. Gestalt principles of organization

33. hearing

Completion Exercises

34. Weber's law

35. perceptual constancies

36. perceptual illusion

37. perceptual sets

38. sensory receptors

39. depth perception

40. top-down processing

41. absolute threshold

42. sensation

43. perception

44. Gestalt

45. figure-ground reversal

46. perceptual grouping

Study Matrix

Lesson 5

Sensation and Perception

Please Note: Use this matrix to guide your study and achieve the learning objectives of this lesson. It will also help you to view the video, which defines and demonstrates important concepts and objectives as they relate to everyday life and actual case studies.

Learning Objective	Textbook	Telecourse Student Guide
Define sensation and explain the process of transduction.	pp. 90–91	Key Terms and Concepts; Study Activities 1, 2, 3, 12, 17, 18, 38, 42.
Discuss absolute and difference thresholds, and describe how Weber's law explains the just noticeable difference.	p. 92	Key Terms and Concepts; Study Activities 11, 21, 34, 41.
Describe the process of sensory adaptation.	p. 92	Key Terms and Concepts; Study Activities 4, 7, 13, 19.
Discuss the key senses of vision, hearing, taste, smell, and touch.	pp. 94–113	Key Terms and Concepts; Study Activities 5, 6, 20, 26, 27, 28, 30, 31, 33.
Define perception and describe the differences between bottom-up processing and top-down processing.	pp. 90, 115	Key Terms and Concepts; Study Activities 10, 14, 15, 16, 17, 22, 25, 29, 40, 42, 43.
Define and give an example of perceptual constancy.	pp. 124–125	Key Terms and Concepts; Study Activities 9, 23, 35.
Define and give an example of perceptual grouping.	p. 118	Key Terms and Concepts; Study Activity 46.
Define and explain the process of depth perception.	pp. 119–121	Key Terms and Concepts; Study Activities 8, 39.
Discuss the Gestalt laws of organization, including the concept of figure-ground reversal.	pp. 117–119	Key Terms and Concepts; Study Activities 24, 32, 44, 45.
Explain perceptual set and discuss how prior assumptions and expectations can influence our perceptions.	p. 129	Key Terms and Concepts; Study Activities 15, 36, 37.

Use the Course Compass to orient yourself in the road that you are taking to explore branches and aspects of psychology. The branch and aspects that are covered in this lesson are highlighted in the compass.

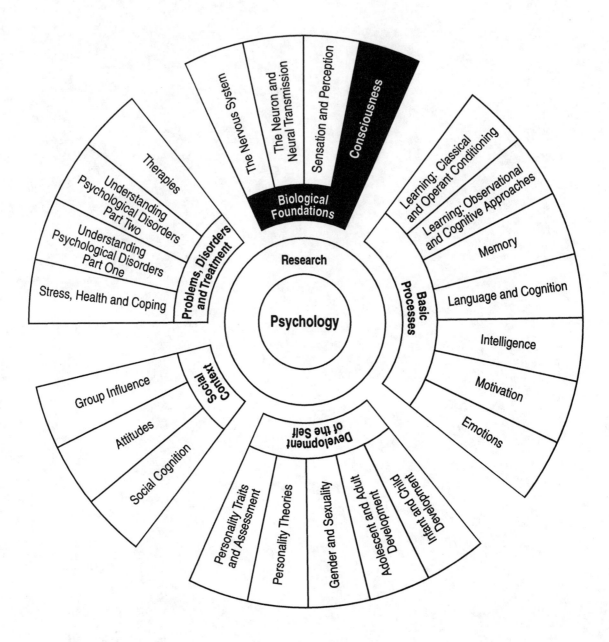

Please note: This compass does not represent the full range of topics comprising the field of psychology; it represents a map for this course only. Each of the five branches represented above has many aspects and subjects that are covered in the 26 lessons of this telecourse. You should remember that these branches and subjects all interrelate.

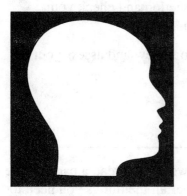

Lesson

Consciousness

Questions to Consider

What is the nature of human consciousness?

What causes us to dream and what do people usually dream about?

Is it true that each of us has a biological clock inside us that regulates our consciousness?

Can anyone be hypnotized? What does it feel like to be hypnotized?

Does meditation have proven psychological and physiological benefits?

What are psychoactive drugs and how do they alter consciousness?

Lesson Assignments

Before viewing the video program

Read the Questions to Consider, Lesson Preview, and Learning Objectives for this lesson. Use this information to guide your reading, viewing, and thinking.

Read Chapter 4, "Consciousness and Its Variations," in the textbook.

View the video program, "Consciousness"

After viewing the video program

Review the vocabulary listed in the Key Terms and Concepts section. (Page references are keyed to the Hockenbury textbook, *Psychology*. Remember: there is a complete Glossary at the end of the textbook.)

Review the reading assignments for this lesson.

Complete the exercises found in the Study Activities section and check your answers with the Answer Key at the end of this lesson.

Use the Study Matrix found at the end of this lesson to review and assess your knowledge of each Learning Objective.

Lesson Preview

Consider a typical day. You wake up and decide what to wear. You read a paper while having breakfast. You think about the day as you remember all the things you need to do. As you are driving in your car, you notice that you are daydreaming. Your mind begins to wander. You consciously try to refocus your mind on the task at hand. During lunch, you drink some coffee to stay alert. You concentrate and make some decisions. As the day moves along, you take a few minutes to meditate and relax. Later in the day, you catch yourself fantasizing about an upcoming vacation. During dinner, you talk about your plans for the future. Then you get tired. You fall asleep and experience the first of several dreams you will have before you wake—and the cycle of changes in consciousness starts all over again. Every 24 hours we all experience many distinct states of consciousness.

Consciousness is normal, something that is always present, ever-changing. To be conscious is to be human. To be conscious is to be aware of your thoughts, your emotions, your physical sensations. Consciousness is a stream of mental activities, from focused concentration to fleeting daydreams about the future.

Psychology has long been fascinated with the study of consciousness. Psychologists have recognized that a complete understanding of behavior is not possible without a complete understanding of consciousness. Although the experience of consciousness is personal and subjective, psychologists have discovered ways to study human consciousness. Psychologists generally study consciousness by studying altered states of consciousness, or variations of normal waking consciousness. Advances in the procedures used to study brain activity, such as functional magnetic resonance imaging (fMRI), now allow psychologists new and fascinating methods of studying human consciousness.

This video lesson explores human consciousness by exploring what happens to a firefighter and paramedic as he tries to cope with the demands of working 24-hour shifts. You will learn about circadian rhythms and the effects sleep interruptions can have on a person's ability to function normally. In this video, you will be introduced to the stages of sleep and the important distinction between REM and NREM sleep. You will learn about sleep and how it is related to memory and other cognitive functions.

In this video, you will also learn the four categories of psychoactive drugs. Psychologist Michael Stevenson will discuss the effects of several psychoactive drugs, including the most commonly used psychoactive drugs, caffeine and alcohol.

Our environment, the time of day, individual circumstances, and biology all play important roles in determining our state of consciousness. In this video, you will discover the problems that can arise when we try to control how and when we are at our peak of awareness—most conscious of the world around us.

Learning Objectives

When you have completed this lesson, you should be able to:

1. Define consciousness, and discuss the importance of understanding human consciousness and its variations.

2. Define circadian rhythms, and explain the function of the suprachiasmatic nucleus.

3. Specify the functions of sleep, and describe the four stages of sleep.

4. Describe the differences between REM and NREM sleep.

5. Identify and describe the main characteristics of the major sleep disorders.

6. Compare and contrast Freud's theory of dreams as fulfilled wishes to the activation-synthesis theory of dreams.

7. Define hypnosis and describe the characteristics of the hypnotic state.

8. Define meditation and describe the common goal of meditation.

9. Identify the categories and common properties of psychoactive drugs.

Key Terms and Concepts

Page references are keyed to the Hockenbury textbook, *Psychology*.

Consciousness: Personal awareness of mental activities, internal sensations, and the external environment. (page 136)

Circadian rhythm: An approximately 24-hour cycle of daily fluctuations in biological and psychological processes. (page 138)

Suprachiasmatic nucleus (SCN): A cluster of neurons in the brain that governs the timing of circadian rhythms. (pages 138–139)

Melatonin: A hormone that produces sleepiness. (pages 138–139)

REM sleep: Active sleep during which rapid eye movements and dreaming usually occur. (page 142)

NREM sleep: Quiet sleep that is absent of rapid eye movements and is typically dreamless. (page 142)

Sleep disorders: Serious disturbances in the normal sleep pattern that interfere with daytime functioning and cause subjective distress. (page 150)

Insomnia: The inability to fall asleep or to stay asleep. (page 150)

Sleep apnea: A sleep disorder in which the person repeatedly stops breathing during sleep. (pages 150–151)

Narcolepsy: A sleep disorder characterized by excessive daytime sleepiness and brief lapses into sleep throughout the day. (page 153)

Sleep thinking: Repetitive, bland, and uncreative ruminations about real-life events during sleep. (page 153)

Sigmund Freud's theory of dreams as fulfilled wishes: Freud believed that dreams have disguised psychological meanings. (page 158)

Activation-synthesis theory of dreams: The theory that brain activity during sleep produces dream images, which are synthesized by the brain into a story. (pages 158–159)

Hypnosis: A unique state of awareness in which a person responds to suggestions with changes in perception, memory, and behavior. (pages 160–161)

Meditation: Various sustained concentration techniques that focus awareness and heighten awareness. (pages 166–168)

Psychoactive drugs: Drugs that alter consciousness, perception, mood, and behavior. (pages 169–171)

Depressants: A category of psychoactive drugs that inhibit brain activity; includes alcohol, barbiturates, and tranquilizers. (pages 171–173)

Barbiturates: A class of depressant drugs that reduce anxiety and promote sleep. (page 173)

Tranquilizers: Depressant drugs that relieve anxiety. (page 173)

Opiates: Also called narcotics, opiates are a category of psychoactive drugs that have pain-relieving qualities. (page 174)

Stimulants: A category of psychoactive drugs that increase brain activity; includes caffeine, nicotine, amphetamines, and cocaine. (pages 174–176)

Amphetamines: A class of stimulant drugs that arouse the central nervous system. (pages 175–176)

Psychedelic drugs: A category of psychoactive drugs that create sensory and perceptual distortions, alter mood, and affect judgment; includes mescaline, LSD, and marijuana. (pages 176–179)

Study Activities

These self-test questions are designed as a study exercise to aid you in understanding the most important terms and concepts in this lesson. To ensure that you have an accurate understanding of the key terms and concepts in this lesson, please check your answers with the Answer Key provided at the end of this lesson.

Multiple-Choice Questions

1. Consciousness is best defined as

    a. all awareness other than sleep.

    b. thinking, sensing, feeling, and remembering.

    c. personal awareness of mental activities, internal sensations, and the environment.

    d. a "stream of thoughts and desires."

2. The suprachiasmatic nucleus, sunlight, and melatonin play a role in regulating

    a. biorhythms.

    b. circadian rhythms.

    c. consciousness.

    d. unconsciousness.

3. An example of circadian rhythms is

    a. REM and NREM sleep.

    b. loss of sleep.

    c. stimulus-response associations.

    d. jet lag.

4. Divided into four stages, this type of sleep is also called quiet sleep.

    a. NREM sleep

    b. REM sleep

    c. alpha-induced sleep

    d. electroencephalograph sleep

5. Changes in states of consciousness are most related to

    a. changes in mental activities.

    b. perceptual illusions.

    c. circadian rhythms.

    d. regular bodily cycles.

6. A sleep disorder characterized by excessive daytime sleepiness and brief lapses into sleep is called

    a. sleep apnea.

    b. insomnia.

    c. sleep thinking.

    d. narcolepsy.

7. The theory that dreams are the result of brain activity during sleep that produces images which are combined by the brain into a story is called the

    a. activation-synthesis model of dreaming.

    b. royal road to unconsciousness.

    c. neural stimulation-dream story theory of dreaming.

    d. wish-fulfillment theory of dreaming.

8. When individuals are hypnotized, they are

    a. under the control of another person.

    b. able to change any habits by following the suggestions of the hypnotist.

    c. in a suggestive state characterized by highly focused attention.

    d. experiencing hypermnesia.

9. Common to all forms of meditation is the goal of

    a. controlling attention.

    b. developing concentration by focusing awareness.

    c. opening up awareness of each passing moment.

    d. developing spiritually.

10. Psychoactive drugs alter consciousness by changing arousal, mood, thinking, sensation, and perception. The four broad categories of psychoactive drugs are

    a. depressants, barbiturates, opiates, and stimulants.

    b. psychedelics, stimulants, opiates, and depressants.

    c. stimulants, tranquilizers, opiates, and psychedelics.

    d. depressants, opiates, psychedelics, and amphetamines.

11. In the video, psychologist Michael Stevenson explained that when a person is asleep he or she is

    a. in a comatose state.

    b. unable to sense the external environment.

    c. in an altered state of consciousness.

    d. unconscious.

12. In the video, you were shown that circadian rhythms are not only responsible for when you go to sleep and when you wake but also affect

    a. how tired you are during the day.

    b. your mental alertness.

    c. your appetite.

    d. your perception of pain.

13. In the video, a survey from the National Sleep Foundation indicated that most people sleep about

    a. 8 hours.

    b. 7 to 8 hours.

    c. more than 8 hours.

    d. 6 hours and 50 minutes.

14. In the video, psychologist Margaret White explained that we spend approximately 5 percent of our sleep in

    a. stage 1.

    b. stage 2.

    c. stage 3.

    d. stage 4.

15. In the video, firefighter and paramedic Ray Casillas used a familiar thing to help him sleep. What he used was a

    a. a radio.

    b. a book.

    c. a fan.

    d. a candle.

16. In the video, it was explained that the most common sleep complaint is

    a. daytime tiredness.

    b. sleep apnea.

    c. insomnia.

    d. sleepwalking

17. In the video, the four categories of psychoactive drugs were graphically displayed. The four categories of psychoactive drugs are

    a. depressants, opiates, stimulants, and narcotics.

    b. depressants, stimulants, barbiturates, and opiates.

    c. depressants, opiates, stimulants, and psychedelics.

    d. psychedelics, opiates, stimulants, and narcotics.

18. In the video, Dr. Stevenson presented the point of view that probably the most commonly used psychoactive drug is

    a. alcohol.
    b. caffeine.
    c. aspirin.
    d. cigarettes.

19. In the video, Dr. White explained that a major problem with using alcohol as a sleep aid is that it causes

    a. wild and upsetting dreams.
    b. a great deal of fragmentation of sleep.
    c. morning headaches.
    d. the lack of REM sleep.

20. In the video, you learned that Ray and his family did many things to help them sleep, including

    a. using calming routines and familiar objects.
    b. the use of depressants.
    c. drinking something just before retiring.
    d. securing the home so that everyone feels safe and protected.

Short-Answer Questions

21. Define consciousness, and explain what William James meant when he described conscious "stream of thought."

    _____

    _____

    _____

22. Define circadian rhythms, and explain how bright light affects the body.

    _____

    _____

    _____

23. Specify the functions of sleep, and describe the difference between REM and NREM sleep.

    _____

    _____

    _____

24. Identify the main symptoms of the following sleep disorders: insomnia, sleep apnea, and narcolepsy.

_____

_____

_____

25. Define hypnosis, and describe the characteristics of the hypnotic state.

_____

_____

_____

26. Describe the two general types of meditation.

_____

_____

_____

27. Identify the common properties of the following categories of psychoactive drugs: depressants, opiates, stimulants, and psychedelics.

_____

_____

_____

Matching Exercises

Match the following terms and concepts with the correct definition.

psychedelics   REM sleep   insomnia

sleep disorders   hypnosis   suprachiasmatic nucleus

dreams as fulfilled wishes   narcolepsy   consciousness

28. _____ A theory by Sigmund Freud that dreams have disguised psychological meanings.

29. _____ A cooperative social interaction in which a person responds to suggestions with changes in perception, memory, and behavior.

30. _____ Personal awareness of mental activities, internal sensation, and the external environment.

31. _____ Accompanied by considerable physical arousal, dreams usually occur during this event.

32. _____ Located in the hypothalamus in the brain and governs the timing of circadian rhythms.

33. _____ A common disorder affecting more than 40 percent of adults.

34. _____ Categories of drugs that alter mood, create perceptual distortions, and affect thinking.

35. _____ Disturbances that interfere with daytime functioning and cause subjective distress.

Completion Exercises

Fill in each blank with the most appropriate term or terms from the list of answers provided.

activation-synthesis theory   meditation

barbiturates   melatonin

biological   NREM sleep

circadian rhythms   opiates

consciousness   sunlight

depressants

36. A form of sleep that is typically quiet and dreamless, _____ is divided into four stages.

37. Increased blood levels of _____ make you sleepy and reduce activity levels.

38. Changes in mental alertness and the sleep-wake cycle are two examples of _____.

39. A common goal of all forms of _____ is controlling or retraining attention.

40. The dream story is derived from a hodgepodge of memories, emotions, and sensations according to the _____ of dreaming.

41. Also called narcotics, _____ are a category of psychoactive drugs that have pain-relieving qualities.

42. Inhibiting brain activity, alcohol belongs to the category of psychoactive drugs known as _____.

43. Sometimes called downers, _____ reduce anxiety and promote sleep.

44. In the video, textbook author Don Hockenbury explained that circadian rhythms refer to the psychological and _____ process that oscillate over the course of a day.

45. In the video, it was explained that _____ is probably the most important timing mechanism for the circadian rhythms.

46. In the video, psychologist Michael Stevenson explained that any substance that can be used to alter _____ is called a psychoactive drug.

Answer Key

Multiple-Choice Questions

1. c	6. d	11. c	16. c
2. b	7. a	12. b	17. c
3. d	8. c	13. d	18. b
4. a	9. a	14. a	19. b
5. a	10. b	15. c	20. a

Short-Answer Questions

Your answers should include the following:

21. Consciousness is defined as the personal awareness of mental activities, internal sensations, and the external environment. William James' "stream of thought" refers to the idea that consciousness is not chopped up in bits and pieces, but rather continuously flows and is unified and unbroken, much like a stream or river. (page 137)

22. Circadian rhythms are biological processes that systematically vary over a 24-hour period. Bright light is the most important cure affecting circadian rhythms. (pages 138–139)

23. Sleep is a biological need and functions to restore and rejuvenate the body and the mind. However, the exact function of sleep is unknown. REM sleep is a type of sleep during which rapid eye movements and dreaming typically occur. NREM sleep is typically a quiet and dreamless state in which rapid eye movements are absent. NREM sleep is divided into four stages. (pages 142–146)

24. Insomnia is a condition in which a person regularly experiences an inability to fall asleep, to stay asleep, or to feel adequately rested. Sleep apnea is a sleep disorder in which the person repeatedly stops breathing during sleep. Narcolepsy is a sleep disorder characterized by excessive daytime sleepiness and brief lapses into sleep throughout the day. (pages 150–153)

25. Hypnosis is a unique state of consciousness in which a person responds to suggestions with changes in perception, memory, and behavior. (pages 160–163)

26. The two types of meditation are opening-up techniques, which involve focusing awareness on the present moment, and concentration techniques, which involve focusing awareness on a specific item, word, or thought. (pages 166–168)

27. Depressants inhibit brain activity. Opiates relieve pain and produce euphoria. Stimulants excite, or stimulate brain activity. Psychedelic drugs distort perceptions. (page 169)

Matching Exercises

28. dreams as fulfilled wishes

29. hypnosis

30. consciousness

31. REM sleep

32. suprachiasmatic nucleus

33. insomnia

34. psychedelics

35. sleep disorders

Completion Exercises

36. NREM sleep

37. melatonin

38. circadian rhythms

39. meditation

40. activation-synthesis theory

41. opiates

42. depressants

43. barbiturates

44. biological

45. sunlight

46. consciousness

Study Matrix

Lesson 6

Consciousness

Please Note: Use this matrix to guide your study and achieve the learning objectives of this lesson. It will also help you to view the video, which defines and demonstrates important concepts and objectives as they relate to everyday life and actual case studies.

Learning Objective	Textbook	Telecourse Student Guide
Define consciousness, and discuss the importance of understanding human consciousness and its variations.	pp. 137–138	Key Terms and Concepts; Study Activities 1, 5, 21, 30.
Define circadian rhythms, and explain the function of the suprachiasmatic nucleus.	pp. 138–139	Key Terms and Concepts; Study Activities 2, 3, 12, 22, 32, 37, 38, 44, 45.
Specify the functions of sleep, and describe the four stages of sleep.	pp. 142–146	Key Terms and Concepts; Study Activities 4, 11, 13, 14, 15, 20, 23.
Describe the differences between REM and NREM sleep.	pp. 143–146	Key Terms and Concepts; Study Activities 23, 31, 36.
Identify and describe the main characteristics of the major sleep disorders.	pp. 150–153	Key Terms and Concepts; Study Activities 6, 16, 24, 33, 35.
Compare and contrast Freud's theory of dreams as fulfilled wishes to the activation-synthesis theory of dreams.	pp. 158–159	Key Terms and Concepts; Study Activities 7, 28, 40.
Define hypnosis and describe the characteristics of the hypnotic state.	pp. 160–164	Key Terms and Concepts; Study Activities 8, 25, 29.
Define meditation and describe the common goal of meditation.	pp. 166–168	Key Terms and Concepts; Study Activities 9, 26, 39.
Identify the categories and common properties of psychoactive drugs.	pp. 169–179	Key Terms and Concepts; Study Activities 10, 17, 18, 19, 27, 34, 41, 42, 43, 46.

Use the Course Compass to orient yourself in the road that you are taking to explore branches and aspects of psychology. The branch and aspects that are covered in this lesson are highlighted in the compass.

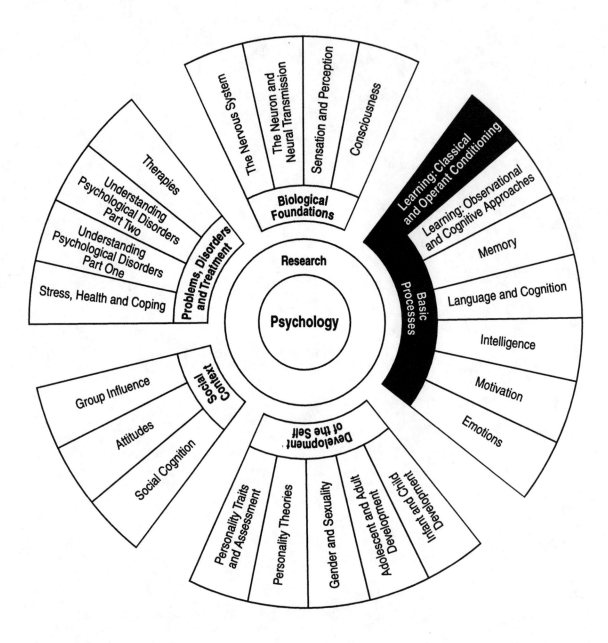

Please note: This compass does not represent the full range of topics comprising the field of psychology; it represents a map for this course only. Each of the five branches represented above has many aspects and subjects that are covered in the 26 lessons of this telecourse. You should remember that these branches and subjects all interrelate.

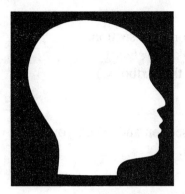

Lesson 7

Learning: Classical and Operant Conditioning

Questions to Consider

How do human beings learn?

What is the major difference between classical conditioning and operant conditioning?

What was Ivan Pavlov's famous experiment?

Are emotions learned or are we born with our emotions intact?

What was B. F. Skinner's major contribution to psychology?

Should punishment be used to control behavior?

Is there a limit on how much a human being can learn?

Lesson Assignments

Before viewing the video program

Read the Questions to Consider, Lesson Preview, and Learning Objectives for this lesson. Use this information to guide your reading, viewing, and thinking.

Read Chapter 5, "Learning," pages 185–220, in the textbook.

View the video program, "Learning: Classical and Operant Conditioning"

After viewing the video program

Review the vocabulary listed in the Key Terms and Concepts section. (Page references are keyed to the Hockenbury textbook, *Psychology*. Remember: there is a complete Glossary at the end of the textbook.)

Review the reading assignments for this lesson.

Complete the exercises found in the Study Activities section and check your answers with the Answer Key at the end of this lesson.

Use the Study Matrix found at the end of this lesson to review and assess your knowledge of each Learning Objective.

Lesson Preview

Consider this scenario. Suppose you are driving, and you turn on the radio. On your favorite station, they are playing one of your favorite songs. You start to sing aloud. You feel inspired, uplifted. Then you look behind you and see a police car following you. You tense up, and your mood changes. How can your response to what happened be explained? Psychologists can help you understand your reactions by using the principles of learning.

Most people equate learning with school, classrooms, reading, and studying. Yet, psychologists have a much broader definition of learning. As you will discover in this lesson, learning is involved in virtually all human behavior. For example, we learn to drive a car, we turn off the lights when we leave a room, we learn to throw a ball, to dance and play—and we learn to get upset at the flashing lights of a police car.

In this lesson, you will be introduced to the two most basic forms of learning, classical conditioning and operant conditioning.

More than anything else, it is our capacity to learn that separates us from other creatures. Learning allows us free choice, the ability to shape our lives and create ourselves in an image of our choosing.

In this video, you will discover how learning principles are used by way of example in the training of military recruits.

Learning is the heart of psychology, for it is our capacity and willingness to learn that gives each of us the ability to change and grow.

Learning Objectives

When you have completed this lesson, you should be able to:

1. Define learning, and name the two forms of conditioning.

2. Describe the general procedures used in classical conditioning as demonstrated by Pavlov's experiments.

3. Explain the processes of generalization, extinction, and shaping as they occur in classical conditioning.

4. Discuss the role of cognition and biological predisposition in classical conditioning.

5. Describe the procedures used in operant conditioning as demonstrated by the Skinner experiments.

6. Compare and contrast positive and negative reinforcement in operant conditioning.

7. Discuss the effects of punishment on behavior.

8. Describe the shaping procedure used in operant conditioning.

9. Explain the difference between continuous and partial reinforcement.

Key Terms and Concepts

Page references are keyed to the Hockenbury textbook, *Psychology*.

Learning: The relatively enduring change in behavior or knowledge as a result of past experience. (page 186)

Classical conditioning: The basic learning process that involves repeatedly pairing a neutral stimulus with a response-producing stimulus until the neutral stimulus elicits the same response. (pages 187–188)

Ivan Pavlov: A Russian scientist who discovered classical conditioning by showing how dogs can be conditioned to respond to a ringing bell. (pages 187–188)

Unconditioned stimulus: The natural stimulus that reflexively elicits a response without the need for prior learning. (page 188)

Conditioned stimulus: A formerly neutral stimulus that acquires the capacity to elicit a reflexive response. (page 189)

Unconditioned response: The unlearned, reflexive response that is elicited by an unconditioned stimulus. (page 188)

Conditioned response: The learned, reflexive response to a conditioned stimulus. (page 189)

Stimulus generalization: The occurrence of a learned response not only to the original stimulus but also to other similar stimuli. (page 190)

Extinction: The gradual weakening of a conditioned behavior. (page 191)

Cognitive aspects of classical conditioning: The contemporary view that mental processes, such as thinking, anticipating and deciding, play an important role in classical conditioning. (pages 200–201)

Behaviorism: School of psychology and theoretical viewpoint that emphasizes the scientific study of observable behaviors. (page 192)

Biological preparedness: The idea that an organism can be innately predisposed to form association between certain stimuli and responses. (page 204)

Operant conditioning: The basic learning process in which behavior is shaped and maintained by its consequences; learning involving positive and negative reinforcement. (page 207)

B. F. Skinner: An American psychologist who developed many of the principles of operant conditioning. (page 207)

Positive reinforcement: A situation in which a response is followed by the addition of a reinforcing stimulus, increasing the likelihood that the response will be repeated in similar situations. (page 208)

Negative reinforcement: A situation in which a response results in the removal, avoidance, or escape from a punishing stimulus, increasing the likelihood that the response will be repeated in similar situations. (page 209)

Punishment: The presentation of a stimulus following a behavior that acts to decrease the likelihood of the behavior being repeated. (page 210)

Shaping: The operant conditioning procedure of selectively reinforcing closer approximations of a goal behavior. (page 216)

Continuous reinforcement: A schedule of reinforcement in which every occurrence of a particular response is reinforced. (page 218)

Partial reinforcement: A schedule of reinforcement in which only some occurrences of a particular response is reinforced. (page 218)

Behavior modification: The application of learning principles to help people develop more effective or adaptive behaviors. (page 220)

Study Activities

These self-test questions are designed as a study exercise to aid in understanding the most important terms and concepts in this lesson. To ensure that you have an accurate understanding of the key terms and concepts in this lesson, please check your answers with the Answer Key provided at the end of this lesson.

Multiple-Choice Questions

1. A psychologist would broadly define learning as

    a. any permanent change in behavior.

    b. a relatively enduring change in behavior or knowledge as a result of experience.

    c. the acquisition of knowledge.

    d. a relatively enduring change in the amount of knowledge acquired.

2. You go into the kitchen and open a can with the electric can opener. Your dog comes running in looking for food. This is an example of

    a. classical conditioning.

    b. operant conditioning.

    c. biological drift.

    d. observational learning.

3. In classical conditioning, extinction should occur if the

    a. conditioned stimulus is presented repeatedly without the unconditioned stimulus.

    b. unconditioned stimulus is presented repeatedly without the conditioned stimulus.

    c. conditioned stimulus is presented repeatedly without the conditioned response.

    d. unconditioned stimulus is presented repeatedly without the unconditioned response.

4. Responding to a stimulus that is similar to the conditioned stimulus is referred to as

    a. stimulus discrimination.

    b. extinction.

    c. classical conditioning.

    d. stimulus generalization.

5. The type of conditioning that depends on the consequences of behavior is called

    a. stimulus-response.

    b. operant.

    c. classical.

    d. reinforcement.

6. If a stimulus provided reinforcement for you, then you can expect that stimulus to

    a. generalize to other stimulus.

    b. have a biological component.

    c. be pleasing and positive to other people.

    d. increase the likelihood of your repeating a behavior.

7. Punishment is a process that decreases the occurrence of a behavior. The two types of punishment are

    a. punishment by demanding and punishment by request.

    b. punishment by application and punishment by removal.

    c. punishment by removal and punishment by negative reinforcement.

    d. punishment by aversion and punishment by negative reinforcement.

8. The operant conditioning procedure of selectively reinforcing successively closer approximations of a goal behavior until the goal behavior is displayed is called

    a. fixed-ratio reinforcement.

    b. continuous reinforcement.

    c. shaping.

    d. reinforcement by consequence.

9. Positive reinforcement involves following an operant with the

    a. removal of negative reinforcement.

    b. removal of the positive reinforcement.

    c. addition of a reinforcing stimulus.

    d. addition of a reinforcing response.

10. Ivan Pavlov's famous experiment involved

    a. pairing a dog with food.

    b. teaching a dog to salivate.

    c. paring a neutral stimulus with a natural reflex.

    d. the principles of operant conditioning.

11. In the video, the learning principle of classical conditioning was presented by the example of Laura associating

    a. pain with getting an injection.

    b. getting upset with being forced to go to a doctor's office.

    c. a nurse's white uniform with the pain of getting an injection.

    d. the doctor's office with an unpleasant experience.

12. In the video, it was explained that classical conditioning is used to explain how we learn many of our

    a. defense mechanisms.

    b. reflexive responses.

    c. unconscious reactions.

    d. social skills.

13. In the video, Ivan Pavlov tested his discovery by pairing a neutral stimulus, a metronome, with an unconditioned stimulus, food. After repeatedly pairing the metronome with food, the metronome became

    a. a conditioned stimulus.

    b. a conditioned response.

    c. an unconditioned stimulus.

    d. an unconditioned response.

14. In the video, the Marine Corps drill instructors use yelling to elicit the unconditioned response of

    a. obedience.

    b. attention.

    c. fear.

    d. respect.

15. In the video, the concept of stimulus generalization was introduced by showing

    a. Marine Corps recruits making beds.

    b. Ivan Pavlov using high-and-low pitched tones with dogs.

    c. Laura becoming afraid of nurses and doctor's offices.

    d. drill instructors wearing distinctive campaign covers.

16. In the video, you learned that American psychologist B. F. Skinner became famous for defining the principles of

    a. classical conditioning.

    b. learning from positive reinforcement.

    c. operant conditioning.

    d. learning that control all animal behavior.

Short-Answer Questions

17. Describe Ivan Pavlov's famous experiment.

_____

_____

_____

18. Discuss the role of cognition in classical conditioning.

_____

_____

_____

19. Describe the operant conditioning process of shaping.

_____

_____

_____

20. Compare and contrast positive and negative reinforcement.

_____

_____

_____

21. Discuss the effects of punishment on behavior.

_____

_____

_____

22. Explain the difference between partial and continuous reinforcement.

_____

_____

_____

Matching Exercises

Match the following terms and concepts with the correct definition.

learning   unconditioned stimulus   stimulus generalization

extinction   conditioned stimulus   continuous reinforcement

punishment   negative reinforcement   operant conditioning

23. _____ The basic learning process that involves changing the probability of a response being repeated by manipulating the consequences of that response.

24. _____ A gradual weakening of a conditioned response.

25. _____ A schedule of reinforcement in which every occurrence of a particular response is reinforced.

26. _____ A situation in which a response results in the removal, avoidance, or escape from a punishing stimulus, increasing the likelihood that the response will be repeated in similar situations.

27. _____ The natural stimulus that reflexively elicits a response without the need for prior learning.

28. _____ A formerly neutral stimulus that acquires the capacity to elicit a reflexive response.

29. _____ The occurrence of a learned response not only to the original stimulus but also to other stimulus as well.

30. _____ The presentation of a stimulus following a behavior that acts to decrease the likelihood of the behavior being repeated.

31. _____ The relatively enduring change in behavior or knowledge as a result of past experience.

Completion Exercises

Fill in each blank with the most appropriate term or terms from the list of answers provided.

behavior

classical conditioning

cognitive aspects of classical
  conditioning

conditioned response

negative reinforcement

operant conditioning

partial reinforcement

positive reinforcement

shaped

shaping

unconditioned response

32. In Pavlov's experiment, a dog's natural tendency to salivate was the
    _____.

33. In Pavlov's experiment, the dog's salivation to a ringing bell is an example of a
    _____.

34. In operant conditioning, new behaviors can be acquired through
    _____ and maintained through different patterns of reinforcement.

35. _____ refers to the contemporary view that mental
    processes, such as thinking, anticipating, and deciding, play an important type
    of learning.

36. One important consequence of behaviors that were acquired using
    _____ _____ is that these behaviors tend to be more
    resistant to extinction than are behaviors acquired using continuous
    reinforcement.

37. In the video, textbook author Don Hockenbury explained that psychologists
    define learning as a relatively permanent change in
    _____ due to experience.

38. In the video, the classic experiment of Ivan Pavlov was shown. This famous
    experiment lead to the discovery of the principles of _____.

39. In the video, B. F. Skinner defined _____ as shaping and
    maintaining behavior by making sure that reinforcing consequences follow.

40. In the video, you learned that _____ increases
    probability we will repeat a behavior because we want to avoid the reinforcer.

41. As shown in the video, B. F. Skinner acknowledged that although punishment
    works to control behavior, he much preferred the use of
    _____ to control behavior.

42. The video ended with a story about how a professor's behavior was _____
    by his students to the point where he was lecturing facing the blackboard and
    talking over his shoulder.

Answer Key

Multiple-Choice Questions

1. b	5. b	9. c	13. a
2. a	6. d	10. c	14. c
3. a	7. b	11. c	15. b
4. d	8. c	12. b	16. c

Short-Answer Questions

Your answer should include the following:

17. Ivan Pavlov's experiment showed how a dog could be conditioned to salivate (conditioned response) at the sound of a ringing bell (conditioned stimulus) by pairing a natural stimulus with a natural reflex. This experiment lead to the principles of classical conditioning. (pages 187–188)

18. Initially, psychologists believed that classical conditioning resulted from a simple association of conditioned stimulus and the unconditioned stimulus. However, most psychologists now believe that classical conditioning also involves several mental processes, such as thinking, anticipating, and deciding. (pages 200–201)

19. Shaping involves reinforcing successively closer approximations of a behavior until the correct behavior is displayed. (pages 216–217)

20. Both positive and negative reinforcement increase the likelihood that a behavior will be repeated. The difference between positive and negative reinforcement is that positive reinforcement uses the addition of a reinforcing stimulus to increase behavior and negative reinforcement uses the removal, avoidance, or escape from a punishing stimulus to increase behavior. (pages 208–209)

21. Punishment is a process that decreases the occurrence of a behavior. Punishment works best if it consistently and immediately follows response. Punishment does not always work to control behavior. Two of the major drawbacks to using punishment are that is does not teach a proper or desired response and that it may produce undesired responses, such as fear or hostility. (page 210)

22. Continuous reinforcement is a schedule of reinforcement in which every occurrence of a particular response is reinforced. Partial reinforcement is a schedule of reinforcement in which reinforcement occurs sometimes. Partial reinforcement type conditioning is more resistant to extinction that conditioning than was acquired using continuous reinforcement. (page 218)

Matching Exercises

23. operant conditioning

24. extinction

25. continuous reinforcement

26. negative reinforcement

27. unconditioned stimulus

28. conditioned stimulus

29. stimulus generalization

30. punishment

31. learning

Completion Exercises

32. unconditioned response

33. conditioned response

34. shaping

35. cognitive aspects of classical conditioning

36. partial reinforcement

37. behavior

38. classical conditioning

39. operant conditioning

40. negative reinforcement

41. positive reinforcement

42. shaped

Study Matrix

Lesson 7

Learning: Classical and Operant Conditioning

Please Note: Use this matrix to guide your study and achieve the learning objectives of this lesson. It will also help you to view the video, which defines and demonstrates important concepts and objectives as they relate to everyday life and actual case studies.

Learning Objective	Textbook	Telecourse Student Guide
Define learning, and name the two forms of conditioning.	pp. 186–187	Key Terms and Concepts; Study Activities 1, 23, 31, 33, 37.
Describe the general procedures used in classical conditioning as demonstrated by Pavlov's experiments.	pp. 187–190	Key Terms and Concepts; Study Activities 2, 3, 10, 12, 13, 17, 27, 28, 29, 32.
Explain the processes of generalization and extinction as they occur in classical conditioning.	pp. 190–191	Key Terms and Concepts; Study Activities 4, 15, 24, 38.
Discuss the role of cognition and biological predisposition in classical conditioning.	pp. 200–204, 221–223	Key Terms and Concepts; Study Activities 11, 18, 35.
Describe the procedures used in operant conditioning as demonstrated by the Skinner experiments.	pp. 207, 216–217	Key Terms and Concepts; Study Activities 16, 39.
Compare and contrast positive and negative reinforcement in operant conditioning.	pp. 208–209	Key Terms and Concepts; Study Activities 5, 6, 20, 26, 40, 41.
Discuss the effects of punishment on behavior.	pp. 210–212	Key Terms and Concepts; Study Activities 7, 21, 30.
Describe the shaping procedure used in operant conditioning.	pp. 216–217	Key Terms and Concepts; Study Activities 8, 14, 19, 34, 42.
Explain the difference between continuous and partial reinforcement.	p. 218	Key Terms and Concepts; Study Activities 9, 22, 25.

Use the Course Compass to orient yourself in the road that you are taking to explore branches and aspects of psychology. The branch and aspects that are covered in this lesson are highlighted in the compass.

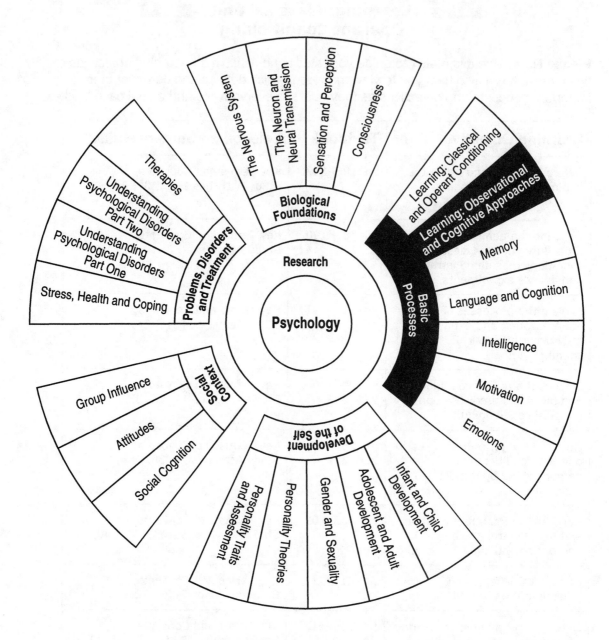

Please note: This compass does not represent the full range of topics comprising the field of psychology; it represents a map for this course only. Each of the five branches represented above has many aspects and subjects that are covered in the 26 lessons of this telecourse. You should remember that these branches and subjects all interrelate.

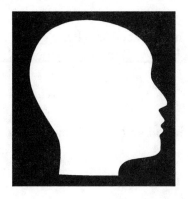

Lesson 8

Learning: Observational and Cognitive Approaches

Questions to Consider

Is all learning intentional or do we also learn unintentionally?

How does observation contribute to the learning process?

What is the role of practice in the learning of a skill?

How does insight and understanding affect learning?

How does watching television affect behavior?

How important are role models in teaching children new behaviors?

What is behavior modification and how do psychologists use it to help people develop new behaviors?

Lesson Assignments

Before viewing the video program

Read the Questions to Consider, Lesson Preview, and Learning Objectives for this lesson. Use this information to guide your reading, viewing, and thinking.

Read Chapter 5, "Learning," pages 221–232, in the textbook.

View the video program, "Learning: Observational and Cognitive Approaches"

After viewing the video program

Review the vocabulary listed in the Key Terms and Concepts section. (Page references are keyed to the Hockenbury textbook, *Psychology*. Remember: there is a complete Glossary at the end of the textbook.)

Review the reading assignments for this lesson.

Complete the exercises found in the Study Activities section and check your answers with the Answer Key at the end of this lesson.

Use the Study Matrix found at the end of this lesson to review and assess your knowledge of each Learning Objective.

Lesson Preview

During the first half of the twentieth century, psychologists tended to look at learning as the result of either classical or operant conditioning. Although human beings clearly learn through classical and operant conditioning, psychologists now recognize that there are many other important factors that affect learning. For example, much of what we learn is learned by watching what happens to other people and by hearing about things. In fact, as you will discover in this lesson, we can learn new behaviors without ever actually carrying them out or receiving any type of reinforcement.

Learning by listening, thinking, and observing is commonplace. By watching, listening and thinking we can learn a lot about the world we live in. We can learn about love, how to tie our shoes, play a guitar, make friends or change a flat tire. Much of what we learn comes from watching and modeling other people's behavior. When the government banned cigarette commercials on television, the idea was to stop people from observing and modeling a specific behavior—lighting up a cigarette. The government was discouraging smoking behavior by removing the model—in effect, trying to teach us not to smoke.

In this lesson, we will explore how observation and cognition affect learning. In the video, you will discover that much of what we learn happens unintentionally. You will follow Barbara Noel, a dance instructor, and her students as they prepare for a dance recital. As you watch the students preparing for a performance, you will discover the importance role models and motivation have in learning.

In this video, famed psychologist Albert Bandura will introduce his theory of observational learning, including original footage of his famous Bobo doll experiment. You will also learn about the concepts of latent learning and cognitive mapping.

Because of expectations, insight, information, modeling, and our personal sense of satisfaction and disappointment, humans can—and do—control much of what they learn. By understanding the role of observation and cognition in learning, you will not only broaden your understanding of how people learn skills and gain abilities but also better understand how emotions, attitudes, and values affect each of us as we learn and grow.

Learning Objectives

When you have completed this lesson, you should be able to:

1. Explain the roles played by cognitive processes in classical and operant conditioning.

2. Explain the concepts of latent learning and cognitive maps.

3. Discuss the concept of learned helplessness.

4. Define instinctive drift, and give an example of instinctive drift.

5. Define observational learning, and give an example of this form of learning.

6. Identify the four processes that must be present for imitation to occur.

7. Compare and contrast observational and cognitive learning to classical conditioning and operant conditioning.

8. Discuss the relationship between violence and exposure to aggressive media.

9. Discuss how individuals could use observational and cognitive learning to improve their lives.

Key Terms and Concepts

Page references are keyed to the Hockenbury textbook, *Psychology*.

Cognitive map: A mental representation of the layout of a familiar environment. (page 222)

Latent learning: Describes learning that occurs in the absence of reinforcement but is not behaviorally demonstrated until a reinforcer becomes available. (page 223)

Learned helplessness: A phenomenon in which exposure to inescapable and uncontrollable aversive events produces passive behavior. (pages 223–225)

Acquisition of knowledge: The idea that learning involves more than simply changes in outward behavior, that learning commonly involves the acquisition of new knowledge. (page 223)

Role models: Someone who serves as an example and influences the learner by displaying behaviors. (page 232)

Instinctive drift: The tendency of an animal to revert to instinctive behaviors that can interfere with the performance of an operantly conditioned response. (pages 225–226)

Observational learning: Learning that occurs through observing the action of others. (page 226)

Cognitive learning: Learning that involves higher mental processes, such as understanding, knowing, anticipating, and remembering. (pages 221–222)

Expectation of reinforcement: The concept that reinforcement is not essential for learning to occur, but rather the expectation of reinforcement is sufficient for learning to occur. (page 227)

Four processes required for imitation: Attention, memory, motor skills, and motivation. (pages 227 and 230)

Steps for improving self-control: Five suggested steps include: 1) Make a precommitment, 2) Self-reinforcement, 3) Stimulus control, 4) Focus on the delayed reinforcer, and 5) Observe good role models. (page 232)

Aggression and the media: The relationship between media exposure to violence and aggressive behavior. (pages 228–229)

Study Activities

These self-test questions are designed as a study exercise to aid you in understanding the most important terms and concepts in this lesson. To ensure that you have an accurate understanding of the key terms and concepts in this lesson, please check your answers with the Answer Key provided at the end of this lesson.

Multiple-Choice Questions

1. A cognitive map is

    a. a description of the route neural transmission takes during learning.

    b. a mental representation of the layout of a familiar environment.

    c. a term for a maze used in research experiments.

    d. a mental representation of how to solve a problem.

2. Learning that is not immediately demonstrated in overt behavior is called

    a. unexpressed learning.

    b. observational learning.

    c. latent learning.

    d. reinforcement-pending learning.

3. A phenomenon in which exposure to inescapable and uncontrollable aversive events produces passive behavior is referred to by psychologists as

    a. negative reinforcement.

    b. punishment.

    c. aversion-induced passivity.

    d. learned helplessness.

4. Operant conditioning can be influenced by an animal's natural behavioral patterns. This tendency to follow innate biological predispositions is called

    a. instinctive drift.

    b. the biological conditioning effect.

    c. cognitive map.

    d. evolutionary conditioning.

5. Observational learning is sometimes called

    a. cognitive learning.

    b. modeling.

    c. discovery learning.

    d. latent learning.

6. The idea that much learning occurs indirectly is a cornerstone of

   a. operant learning.
   b. classical learning.
   c. observation learning.
   d. cognitive learning.

7. Observing good role models is an important step in

   a. changing behavior.
   b. behavior modification.
   c. forming a new cognitive map.
   d. improving self-control.

8. As discussed in the video, a dancer may learn how to dance on a particular stage and then for another performance must move to a stage of a different size and shape. The ability to make the transition to different size and shape stages demonstrates the concept of

   a. latent learning.
   b. cognitive mapping.
   c. operant conditioning.
   d. learning by association.

9. As seen in the video, dancers can learn a behavior in the absence of reinforcement and not display that behavior until they are rewarded for it. Psychologist Edward Tolman called this type of learning

   a. unrewarded learning.
   b. instinctual learning.
   c. latent learning.
   d. delayed action learning.

10. In the video, it was explained that there are four processes that interact to make observational learning possible. These processes are

    a. pay attention, memory, motor skills, and cognition.
    b. cognition, memory, attention, and motivation.
    c. pay attention, memory, motor skills, and motivation.
    d. motivation, pay attention, cognition, and memory.

11. In the video, psychologist Albert Bandura explains that the three factors that increase the likelihood a model will be imitated are

    a. power, prestige, and motivation.
    b. prestige, attractiveness, and power.
    c. attractiveness, exposure time, and power.
    d. exposure time, prestige, and power.

12. In the video, an example of the detrimental effects of negative role models was

   a. terrorists learning to highjack airlines.

   b. Carlos dropping out of class to pursue a career in dancing.

   c. the aggression that children learned watching adults hit the Bobo doll.

   d. students getting into fights at political protests.

Short-Answer Questions

13. Explain the roles played by cognitive process in classical and operant conditioning.

   _____

   _____

   _____

14. Explain and give an example of a cognitive map.

   _____

   _____

   _____

15. Explain the concept of latent learning.

   _____

   _____

   _____

16. Define instinctive drift and discuss how this phenomenon can affect learning.

   _____

   _____

   _____

17. State the four processes that must be present for imitation to occur.

   _____

   _____

   _____

18. Define observational learning, and give an example of this form of learning.

   _____

   _____

   _____

19. Discuss the role modeling plays in teaching children new behaviors.

_____

_____

_____

20. Discuss the relationship between exposure to aggressive media and aggressive behavior.

_____

_____

_____

Matching Exercises

Match the following terms and concepts with the correct definition.

self-control   imitation

latent learning   instinctive drift

observational learning   cognitive map

discovery learning   learned helplessness

role model

21. _____ A phenomenon in which exposure to inescapable and uncontrollable aversive events produces passive behavior.

22. _____ A type of learning in which skills are gained by insight and understanding.

23. _____ Learning that occurs through observing the action of others.

24. _____ Learning that occurs in the absence of reinforcement but is not behaviorally demonstrated until a reinforcer is available.

25. _____ A person who is demonstrating a behavior that the learner wants to emulate.

26. _____ Requires fours factors: attention, memory, motor skills, and motivation.

27. _____ A mental representation of a familiar layout.

28. _____ Must have two types of reinforcers: a long-term reinforcer that will provide gratification in the future, and a short-term reinforcer that will provide immediate gratification.

29. _____ An animal's natural behavior pattern that can negatively influence the long-term effects of operant conditioning.

Completion Exercises

Fill in each blank with the most appropriate term or terms from the list of answers provided.

acquisition of knowledge

cognition

cognitive abilities

expectation of reinforcement

four processes required for imitation

latent learning

observational learning

role model

steps for improving self-control

30. In Skinner's view, operant conditioning did not need to invoke cognitive factors. However, psychologists have now concluded that learning involves changes in outward behavior and the _____.

31. _____ is a term used by psychologists when some skill has been learned but is not demonstrated due to the absence of a reinforcer.

32. Attention, memory, motor skills, and motivation are the _____.

33. According to cognitive psychologists, reinforcement is not essential for learning to occur, but rather the _____ is sufficient for learning to occur.

34. Make a commitment, use self-reinforcements, control stimulus, focus on delayed reinforcer, and observe good role models are _____.

35. As discussed in the video, in contrast to strict behaviorists, psychologist Edward Tolman believed that _____ played an important role operant conditioning.

36. In the video, psychologist Albert Bandura described _____ as a process whereby people acquire attitudes, values, and new ways of thinking and behaving by observing the actions of others.

37. In the video, you saw the Bobo doll experiment. This experiment is used to demonstrate that we use our _____ to help us choose which behaviors we will emulate.

38. In the video, dance instructor Barbara Noel introduced Carlos to her students. Carlos was a positive _____ for the other students in the dance class.

Answer Key

Multiple-Choice Questions

1. b	4. a	7. d	10. c
2. c	5. b	8. b	11. b
3. d	6. c	9. c	12. a

Short-Answer Questions

13. The cognitive perspective of classical conditioning states that higher mental processes, like thinking, anticipating, or deciding, are involved in classical conditioning. Using experiments with rats, Edward Tolman proved that the acquisition of knowledge is involved in operant conditioning. (pages 222–223)

14. A cognitive map is a mental representation of a familiar layout. If you are going home and your normal route is blocked, you would you use a cognitive map to come up with an alternate route. (page 222)

15. Latent learning is a term coined by Tolman to describe learning that occurs in the absence of reinforcement but is not behaviorally demonstrated until an appropriate reinforcer is introduced. (page 223)

16. Instinctive drift is the tendency of an animal to revert to instinctive behaviors. This tendency can interfere with performance of an operant conditioned response. (pages 225–226)

17. The four processes required for imitation are: you must first pay attention, then you must remember the behavior you are going to imitate, next you must transform your mental representation of the behavior into actions that you are capable of performing, and, finally, you must be motivated to imitate the behavior. (pages 227 and 230)

18. Observational learning is learning by observing the action of others. The training of pilots, nurses, electricians, and police officers routinely involves watching experienced professionals correctly perform a task, then imitating it. (page 226)

19. Modeling is another word for observational learning. The classic Bobo doll experiment demonstrated the powerful influence of modeling, especially in children. (page 227)

20. There is a definite relationship between exposure to media violence and aggressive behaviors. (pages 228–229)

Matching Exercises

21. learned helplessness

22. discovery learning

23. observational learning

24. latent learning

25. role model

26. imitation

27. cognitive map

28. self-control

29. instinctive drift

Completion Exercises

30. acquisition of knowledge

31. latent learning

32. four processes required for imitation

33. expectation of reinforcement

34. steps for improving self-control

35. cognition

36. observational learning

37. cognitive abilities

38. role model

Study Matrix
Lesson 8
Learning: Observational and Cognitive Approaches

Please Note: Use this matrix to guide your study and achieve the learning objectives of this lesson. It will also help you to view the video, which defines and demonstrates important concepts and objectives as they relate to everyday life and actual case studies.

Learning Objective	Textbook	Telecourse Student Guide
Explain the roles played by cognitive processes in classical and operant conditioning.	pp. 221–223	Key Terms and Concepts; Study Activities 13, 30, 35.
Explain the concepts of latent learning and cognitive maps.	pp. 222–223	Key Terms and Concepts; Study Activities 1, 2, 8, 9, 14, 15, 24, 27, 31.
Discuss the concept of learned helplessness.	pp. 223–225	Key Terms and Concepts; Study Activities 3, 21.
Define instinctive drift, and give an example of instinctive drift.	pp. 225–226	Key Terms and Concepts; Study Activities 4, 16, 29.
Define observational learning, and give an example of this form of learning.	pp. 226–227	Key Terms and Concepts; Study Activities 5, 6, 18, 28, 36.
Identify the four processes that must be present for imitation to occur.	pp. 227, 230	Key Terms and Concepts; Study Activities 10, 11, 17, 28, 30, 32.
Compare and contrast observational and cognitive learning to classical conditioning and operant conditioning.	pp. 221–223	Key Terms and Concepts; Study Activities 22, 23, 30, 35.
Discuss the relationship between violence and exposure to aggressive media.	pp. 228–229	Key Terms and Concepts; Study Activities 12, 19, 22, 25, 38.
Discuss how individuals could use observational and cognitive learning to improve their lives.	p. 232	Key Terms and Concepts; Study Activities 7, 33, 34, 37.

Use the Course Compass to orient yourself in the road that you are taking to explore branches and aspects of psychology. The branch and aspects that are covered in this lesson are highlighted in the compass.

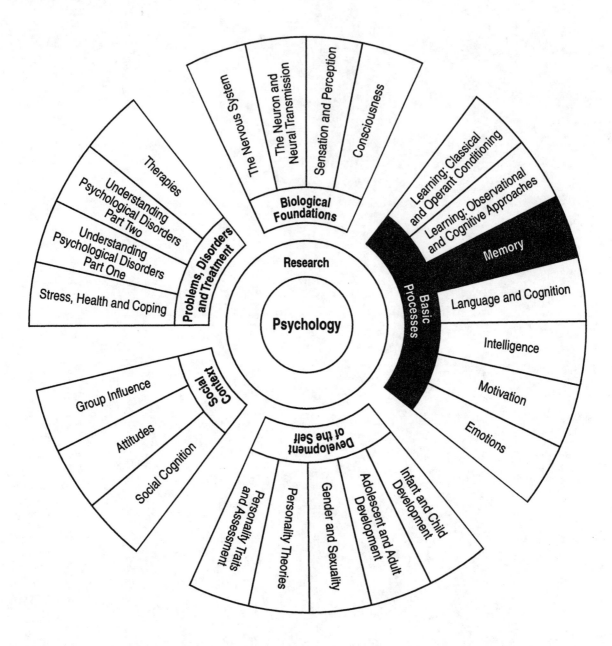

Please note: This compass does not represent the full range of topics comprising the field of psychology; it represents a map for this course only. Each of the five branches represented above has many aspects and subjects that are covered in the 26 lessons of this telecourse. You should remember that these branches and subjects all interrelate.

Lesson 9

Memory

Questions to Consider

How do psychologists define memory?

Is there more than one type of memory?

How accurate are memories?

What are the most common reasons why people forget information?

Does everyone's ability to remember information fade as they age?

What is the best method to improve memory?

Lesson Assignment

Before viewing the video program

Read the Questions to Consider, Lesson Preview, and Learning Objectives for this lesson. Use this information to guide your reading, viewing, and thinking.

Read Chapter 6, "Memory," in the textbook.

View the video program, "Memory"

After viewing the video program

Review the vocabulary listed in the Key Terms and Concepts section. (Page references are keyed to the Hockenbury textbook, *Psychology*. Remember: there is a complete Glossary at the end of the textbook.)

Review the reading assignments for this lesson.

Complete the exercises found in the Study Activities section and check your answers with the Answer Key at the end of this lesson.

Use the Study Matrix found at the end of this lesson to review and assess your knowledge of each Learning Objective.

Lesson Preview

Memory plays a critical role in our lives. Without memory you would not be able to go to work, eat, get dressed, or even recognize your own family. You would not be able to talk to other people because you would have forgotten what words mean. You would not know what you like, dislike, or even what is dangerous.

We tend to take memory for granted. However, memory is full of paradoxes. Consider the famous conductor Arturo Toscanini, who was able to memorize every single note written for every musical instrument in more than 250 symphonies and 100 operas. How can some people remember so much while other people forget such simple things, like where they parked the car? Why is it we can remember every detail of events that happened years ago but find it difficult, if not impossible, to recall something that happened only a few days ago?

This lesson explores what science knows about memory. In this video, you will follow the lives of an elderly couple named Harry and Charlotte as they demonstrate the importance of memory in everyday life. You will learn how information is encoded, stored, and retrieved. Memory experts such as Professor Duana Welch, Professor Robert Bjork, and Professor James McGaugh will introduce you to the most widely accepted model used to explain how memory functions, the stage model of memory.

Learning Objectives

When you have completed this lesson, you should be able to:

1. Define memory, and explain the processes of encoding, storage, and retrieval.

2. Describe the stage model of memory, and describe the function of each of the three stages.

3. Explain the main difference between short-term, or working memory and long-term memory.

4. Discuss the difference between maintenance rehearsal and elaborative rehearsal.

5. Describe how retrieval cues work, including the serial position effect.

6. Describe the three categories of information that can be stored in long-term memory.

7. Discuss the encoding specificity principle, and give an example of a flashbulb memory.

8. Discuss the common reasons people forget information, including encoding failure, interference theory, motivated forgetting, and decay theory.

9. List several methods a person can use to improve their memory.

Key Terms and Concepts

Page references are keyed to the Hockenbury textbook, *Psychology.*

Memory: The active mental processes that enable us to retain and use information over time. (page 239)

Encoding: The process of transforming information into a form that can be used by your memory system. (page 239)

Storage: The process of retaining information in memory. (page 239)

Retrieval: The process of recovering information stored in memory. (page 239)

Stage model of memory: A model describing memory as consisting of three distinct stages. These stages are sensory memory, short-term working memory, and long-term memory. (pages 239–240)

Sensory memory: The stage of memory that registers information from the environment and holds it for a very brief period of time. (pages 240–241)

Short-term, or working memory: The stage of memory in which information is held for about 30 seconds. (pages 240 and 242–244)

Long-term memory: The stage of memory that represents the storage of information over time. (pages 240 and 244)

Maintenance rehearsal: The process of repeating information so that remains active in your short-term working memory. (page 243)

Elaborative rehearsal: The process of adding meaning to information so that it is encoded into long-term memory. (page 245)

Recall: Refers to the recovering of information from long-term memory without the use of retrieval cues. Sometimes referred to as free recall. (page 252)

Serial position effect: The tendency to remember items at the beginning and end of a list, event, or lesson. (page 252)

Encoding specificity principle: The principle that when the conditions of retrieval are similar to the conditions in which the information was encoded, retrieval is more likely to be successful. (pages 252–253)

Mood congruence: An encoding specificity principle in which a given mood tends to evoke memories that are consistent with that mood. (page 254)

Flashbulb memory: A type of memory that is very vivid and easy to recall. This usually happens in connection with dramatic life events. (page 254)

Encoding failure: The inability to recall information because the information was not properly encoded into long-term memory. (pages 262–263)

Interference theory: The theory that one memory competing with another like memory can cause people to forget. (pages 262–263)

Decay theory: The theory that the passage of time causes people to forget information. (page 265)

Motivated forgetting: The theory that forgetting occurs because an undesired memory is held back from awareness. (page 263)

Memory trace: Refers to changes in the brain that happen when a new memory is formed. Also called an engram. (page 266)

Amnesia: Severe memory loss. (page 270)

Study Activities

These self-test questions are designed as a study exercise to aid you in understanding the most important terms and concepts in this lesson. To ensure that you have an accurate understanding of the key terms and concepts in this lesson, please check your answers with the Answer Key provided at the end of this lesson.

Multiple-Choice Questions

1. The model of memory that involves sensory memory, short-term (working) memory, and long-term memory is called

    a. the encoding retrieval mode of memory.

    b. the ascending model of memory.

    c. the stage model of memory.

    d. the box model of memory.

2. Repeating a phone number over and over to yourself is an example of

    a. elaborative rehearsal.

    b. forced recall.

    c. motivated learning.

    d. maintenance rehearsal.

3. The most effective way to transfer information from short-term working memory to long-term memory is to

    a. use procedural learning.

    b. use maintenance rehearsal.

    c. use elaborative rehearsal.

    d. use echoic sensory memory.

4. The tendency to remember the first and last items in a list is an example of

    a. the serial position effect.

    b. mood congruence.

    c. motivated encoding.

    d. retrieval cue dependency.

5. When you have a very vivid recall of some significant event, this is referred to as

    a. a flashbulb memory.

    b. a mood-driven memory.

    c. an episodic memory.

    d. an enhanced memory trace.

6. Which of these is NOT a recognized procedure for helping you enhance your memory?

    a. Use visual imagery.

    b. Focus your attention.

    c. Keep the information you are learning private.

    d. Organize the information you want to learn.

7. An encoding phenomenon in which a given mood tends to evoke memories that are consistent with that mood is called

    a. long-term memory.

    b. memory-enhanced retrieval.

    c. mood congruence.

    d. attitude-based recall.

8. Information is held in short-term, or working memory

    a. for approximately 30 seconds.

    b. until the information is encoded into long-term memory.

    c. until the sensory memory decays.

    d. a minimum of 2 minutes.

9. A person's ability to remember how to ride a bicycle is an example of

    a. episodic information.

    b. procedural information.

    c. semantic information.

    d. nothing; this is not an example of a memory.

10. The theory that we lose information because we do not use it and it fades over time is called

    a. time-generated memory loss.

    b. decay theory.

    c. amnesia.

    d. interference theory.

11. In this video, picking up something at the store, going to a doctor's office, taking medications, and taking children to a specific place were used as examples of

    a. a memory trace.

    b. prospective memory.

    c. long-term memory.

    d. performance memory.

12. In the video, Professor Robert Bjork explained that sensory memory storage refers to a kind of fleeting memory that

   a. can be visual or auditory.

   b. can only sensed by vision.

   c. requires both auditory and visual input.

   d. is usually neither visual nor auditory.

13. In the video, you learned that there are three different types of information stored in long-term memory. What was the example used to describe procedural memory?

   a. Harry talking to other veterans

   b. Charlotte working on a crossword puzzle

   c. Harry making coffee

   d. Charlotte looking up a work in a dictionary

14. In the video, Professor Duana Welch used the example of repeating the telephone number for Papa Pete's Pizza as an example of

   a. elaborative rehearsal.

   b. short-term, or working memory.

   c. maintenance rehearsal.

   d. recall by association.

15. In the video, Harry and the other veterans used old photographs to help them remember past events. The old photographs acted as

   a. memory enhancers.

   b. retrieval cues.

   c. free recall cues.

   d. mood-congruence stimulators.

16. In the video, Professor Bjork explained that significant or highly emotional events, such as the *Challenger* explosion, a wedding, or a funeral, often create a type of memory called

   a. emotional memory.

   b. episodic memory.

   c. event-driven memory.

   d. flashbulb memory.

17. In the video, you learned that we only have a very short amount of time, approximately 30 seconds, to get information transferred from short-term, or working memory to long-term memory. Professor Welch explained that two common reasons why this sometimes fails to happen are

   a. displacement and encoding interference.

   b. displacement and decay.

   c. decay and encoding confusion.

   d. displacement and lack of attention.

18. In the video, Professor McGaugh discussed how the learning of something new may sometimes distort or cause the loss of other memories. This phenomenon is called

   a. the relearning error.

   b. mood congruence.

   c. encoding overlap.

   d. retroactive interference.

Short-Answer Questions

19. Explain the difference between maintenance rehearsal and elaborative rehearsal.

   _____

   _____

   _____

20. Explain the encoding specificity principle.

   _____

   _____

   _____

21. Explain how the phenomenon of mood congruence might affect what a depressed person remembers.

   _____

   _____

   _____

22. List several things you can do to improve your memory skills.

   _____

   _____

   _____

Matching Exercises

Match the following terms and concepts with the correct definition.

memory   motivated forgetting   encoding failure

sensory memory   interference theory   memory trace

recall   retrieval cue

23. _____ The stage of memory that registers information from the environment and holds it for a very brief period of time.

24. _____ Refers to changes in the brain that happen when a new memory is formed. Also called an engram.

25. _____ The theory that forgetting occurs because an undesired memory is held back from awareness.

26. _____ The process of recovering information from memory.

27. _____ The active mental processes that enable us to retain and use information over time.

28. _____ The theory that one memory competing with another like memory can cause people to forget.

29. _____ A test of long-term memory that involves retrieving information without the use of any retrieval cues.

30. _____ The inability to recall information because the information was not properly encoded into long-term memory.

31. _____ A hint that helps the recall of information from long-term memory.

Completion Exercises

Fill in each blank with the most appropriate term or terms from the list of answers provided.

amnesia   memory traces

encoded   motivated forgetting

encoding, storage, and retrieval   passage of time

exercise   sensory memory

free recall   serial position effect

long-term memory   short-term, or working memory

32. The three basic memory processes are _____.

33. Another name for severe memory loss is _____.

34. Usually because a memory was unpleasant or disturbing, _____ refers to the idea that we consciously or unconsciously try to forget some information.

35. The tendency to retrieve the first and last information you received is explained by the _____.

36. An important function of _____ is to very briefly store information so that our perceptions of the world are not a series of disconnected images or disjointed sounds.

37. The brain changes associated with stored memory are called _____.

38. Information that is stored in memory for more than two minutes is referred to as _____.

39. Problem solving, remembering, and imagining all take place in _____.

40. In the video, Professor James McGaugh used the example of a shell going off on a battlefield to explain how information is _____ into memory.

41. In the video, you learned that remembering information in response to a retrieval cue is called cued recall and that retrieving information without using cues is termed _____.

42. In the video, Professor Bjork explained that the _____ affects all types of memory and increases the likelihood of memory distortion.

43. In the video, _____ and using the brain to keep it active were introduced as scientifically proven methods for improving long-term memory.

Answer Key

Multiple-Choice Questions

1. c	6. c	11. b	16. d
2. d	7. c	12. a	17. b
3. c	8. a	13. c	18. d
4. a	9. b	14. c	
5. a	10. b	15. b	

Short-Answer Questions

19. Your answer should include that maintenance rehearsal is repeating information to extend its duration in short-term, or working memory and elaborative rehearsal is focusing on the meaning of information as a method to transfer it to long-term memory. (pages 243 and 245)

20. Your answer should include that the encoding specificity principle states that when the conditions of retrieval are similar to the conditions of encoding, retrieval is more likely to occur. (pages 252–253)

21. Your answer should point out that mood congruence refers to the idea that a given mood tends to evoke memories of a similar mood. Therefore a depressed person is most likely to remember depressing type memories. (page 254)

22. The text points out ten memory-enhancing ideas. Your answer should have included at least three of these ideas (page 275):

    focus your attention   use visual imagery

    commit the necessary time   explain it to a friend

    space your study sessions   reduce interference within a topic

    organize the information   counteract the serial position effect

    elaborate on the material   use contextual cues to jog memories

Matching Exercises

23. sensory memory

24. memory trace

25. motivated forgetting

26. retrieval

27. memory

28. interference theory

29. recall

30. encoding failure

31. retrieval cue

Completion Exercises

32. encoding, storage, and retrieval

33. amnesia

34. motivated forgetting

35. serial position effect

36. sensory memory

37. memory trace

38. long-term memory

39. short-term, or working memory

40. encoded

41. free recall

42. passage of time

43. exercise

Study Matrix
Lesson 9
Memory

Please Note: Use this matrix to guide your study and achieve the learning objectives of this lesson. It will also help you to view the video, which defines and demonstrates important concepts and objectives as they relate to everyday life and actual case studies.

Learning Objective	Textbook	Telecourse Student Guide
Define memory, and explain the processes of encoding, storage, and retrieval.	p. 239	Key Terms and Concepts; Study Activities 26, 27, 32.
Describe the stage model of memory, and describe the function of each of the three stages.	pp. 239–240	Key Terms and Concepts; Study Activities 1, 12, 36, 40.
Explain the main difference between short-term, or working memory and long-term memory.	pp. 240, 242–244	Key Terms and Concepts; Study Activities 8, 23, 38, 39.
Discuss the difference between maintenance rehearsal and elaborative rehearsal.	pp. 243–245	Key Terms and Concepts; Study Activities 2, 3, 14, 19.
Describe how retrieval cues work, including the serial position effect.	pp. 251–252	Key Terms and Concepts; Study Activities 4, 9, 11, 15, 29, 31, 35, 41.
Describe the three categories of information that can be stored in long-term memory.	pp. 246–247	Key Terms and Concepts; Study Activities 13, 24, 33, 37.
Discuss the encoding specificity principle, and give an example of a flashbulb memory.	pp. 252–254	Key Terms and Concepts; Study Activities 5, 7, 16, 20, 21.
Discuss the common reasons people forget information, including encoding failure, interference theory, motivated forgetting, and decay theory.	pp. 260–265	Key Terms and Concepts; Study Activities 10, 17, 18, 25, 28, 30, 34, 42.
List several methods a person can use to improve their memory.	p. 275	Key Terms and Concepts; Study Activities 6, 22, 43.

Use the Course Compass to orient yourself in the road that you are taking to explore branches and aspects of psychology. The branch and aspects that are covered in this lesson are highlighted in the compass.

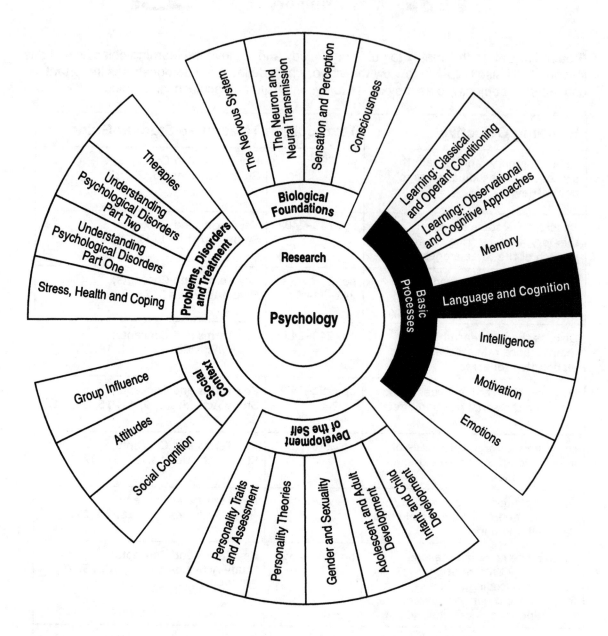

Please note: This compass does not represent the full range of topics comprising the field of psychology; it represents a map for this course only. Each of the five branches represented above has many aspects and subjects that are covered in the 26 lessons of this telecourse. You should remember that these branches and subjects all interrelate.

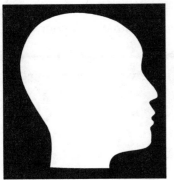

Lesson 10

Language and Cognition

Questions to Consider

How do people acquire language?

What is the nature of thought?

Do animals use language?

How does language affect thinking and perception?

Is it possible to increase one's ability to solve problems?

Do all humans share the same capacity for language and thought?

Why do some beliefs persist, even when faced with contradictory evidence?

Lesson Assignments

Before viewing the video program

Read the Questions to Consider, Lesson Preview, and Learning Objectives for this lesson. Use this information to guide your reading, viewing, and thinking.

Read Chapter 7, "Thinking, Language, and Intelligence," pages 279–296, in the textbook.

View the video program, "Language and Cognition"

After viewing the video program

Review the vocabulary listed in the Key Terms and Concepts section. (Page references are keyed to the Hockenbury textbook, *Psychology*. Remember: there is a complete Glossary at the end of the textbook.)

Review the reading assignments for this lesson.

Complete the exercises found in the Study Activities section and check your answers with the Answer Key at the end of this lesson.

Use the Study Matrix found at the end of this lesson to review and assess your knowledge of each Learning Objective.

Lesson Preview

Of all the species that roam the earth, only humans have the capacity to go beyond the moment and think of what was, what will be, what should be, or what might be. Thinking gives us meaning and purpose. Thinking allows us to create, improve, and understand the world—and possibly someday the universe. While it is now recognized that animals can also communicate, the enormous mental abilities of human beings remains as what separates us from other creatures, especially our capacity to create and use complex language.

Language is the primary means through which we communicate our thoughts to others. We use language not only to share our thoughts and ideas but also to pass on our history. In this video, we will explore the nature of language.

In this video, Dr. Elizabeth Bates, professor of psychology and cognitive science at the University of California, San Diego, will discuss how language develops. Professor Bates will also provide you with fascinating information about language usage in animals.

This video revolves around the dramatic story of Paul Sailer, who suffered three grand mal seizures. These seizures were the result of a large malignant tumor located in deep within his brain. Sailer was diagnosed as needing to undergo brain surgery—a surgery that could rob him of his ability to use language. As you watch Paul Sailer's surgery, you will see how a surgery team "mapped" his brain. You will also follow Paul as he struggles to regain his presurgical language abilities. The video concludes by discussing cognitive processes and the role of logic in problem solving.

The more you understand about language, cognition, the use of logic, and problem solving, the more you will come to appreciate and marvel at the ability of the human mind.

Learning Objectives

When you have completed this lesson, you should be able to:

1. Define cognition and thinking, and describe how mental images and concepts are involved.

2. Describe the difference between formal concepts and natural concepts, and explain the role played by prototypes in concept formation.

3. Explain how functional fixedness and mental set interferes with problem solving.

4. Compare and contrast the following cognitive strategies for problem solving: trial and error, algorithms, heuristics, and insight.

5. Define intuition and discuss the intuitive process.

6. Discuss how the belief-bias effect, confirmation bias, the fallacy of positive instances, and the overestimation effect interfere with our ability to perceive and accept contradictory information.

7. Identify the major characteristics of language.

8. Discuss some of the ways that language can influence thinking.

9. Present evidence for and against the proposition that animals can learn language.

Key Terms and Concepts

Page references are keyed to the Hockenbury textbook, *Psychology*.

Cognition: The mental activities involved in acquiring, retaining, and using knowledge. (page 280)

Thinking: The manipulation of mental representations of information in order to draw inferences and conclusions. (pages 280–281)

Mental image: A mental representation of objects or events that are not physically present. (pages 280–281)

Concept: A mental category of objects or ideas based on properties they share. (pages 282–283)

Formal concept: A mental category that is formed by learning the rules or features that define it. (pages 282–283)

Natural concept: A mental category that is formed as a result of everyday experience. (pages 282–283)

Prototype: The most typical instance of a particular concept. (page 284)

Problem solving: Thinking and behavior directed toward attaining a goal that is not readily available. (pages 284–286)

Trial and error: A problem-solving technique that involves attempting different solutions and eliminating those that do not work. (pages 284–285)

Algorithm: A problem-solving technique that involves following a specific rule, procedure, or method that inevitably produces the correct solution. (page 285)

Heuristics: A problem-solving strategy that involves following a general rule of thumb to reduce the number of possible solutions. (page 285)

Insight: The sudden realization of how a problem can be solved. (pages 286–287)

Functional fixedness: The tendency to view objects as functioning only in their usual or customary way. (pages 286–287)

Mental set: The tendency to persist in solving problems with solutions that have worked in the past. (page 287)

Intuition: Coming to a conclusion or making a judgment without conscious awareness of the thought processes involved. (pages 286–287)

Belief-bias effect: The tendency to accept only information that conforms to an existing belief. (page 290)

Confirmation bias: The tendency to search for information or evidence that confirms an existing belief, while making little or no effort to search for information that might disprove that belief. (page 290)

Fallacy of positive instances: The tendency to remember uncommon events that seem to confirm our beliefs and to forget events that disconfirm our beliefs. (page 290)

Overestimation effect: The tendency to overestimate the rarity of an event in an effort to confirm a belief. (page 290)

Language: A system for combining arbitrary symbols to produce an infinite number of meaningful statements. (pages 291–293)

Linguistic relativity hypothesis: The notion that differences among languages cause differences in thoughts. (pages 294–295)

Study Activities

These self-test questions are designed as a study exercise to aid you in understanding the most important terms and concepts in this lesson. To ensure that you have an accurate understanding of the key terms and concepts in this lesson, please check your answers with the Answer Key provided at the end of this lesson.

Multiple-Choice Questions

1. The manipulation of mental representations of information in order to draw inferences and conclusions is a good definition of

   a. thinking.

   b. cognition.

   c. problem solving.

   d. mental processes.

2. Along with mental images, thinking also involves the use of

   a. remembering.

   b. the manipulation of ideas.

   c. concepts.

   d. memories.

3. A concept that does not fit any specific rules or features is called a

   a. prototype.

   b. formal concept.

   c. mental image.

   d. natural concept.

4. Someone asked you what comes to mind when you think of an airplane, and you responded by saying a commercial passenger jet. For you, a commercial passenger jet is a

   a. mental image.

   b. prototype.

   c. formal concept.

   d. natural concept.

5. Before you begin to solve any problem, you first have to recognize that a problem exists and then

   a. select a problem-solving strategy.

   b. evaluate possible solutions.

   c. develop an accurate understanding of the problem.

   d. ask for advice.

6. The trial-and-error method of solving problems

   a. follows a step-by-step procedure.

   b. follows a general rule of thumb.

   c. creates a sudden realization when the answer is discovered.

   d. is often inefficient.

7. A major advantage of using algorithms to solve problems is that

   a. this method always produces the correct solution.

   b. it is faster than using heuristics.

   c. it is a very practical method to find answers.

   d. you will suddenly realize the solution.

8. The tendency to persist in solving problems with solutions that have worked in the past is called

   a. intuition.

   b. functional fixedness.

   c. algorithms.

   d. mental set.

9. The tendency to remember uncommon events that confirm our beliefs and forget events that disconfirm our beliefs is called

   a. belief-bias effect.

   b. fallacy of positive instances.

   c. confirmation bias.

   d. representative heuristic.

10. Language requires the use of

    a. words.

    b. concepts.

    c. shared mental sets.

    d. symbols and syntax.

11. In this video, you were told about Paul Sailer, who learned that he had a large malignant tumor that was located in an area of his brain that

    a. was inoperable.

    b. controlled his ability to use language.

    c. controlled his motor functions.

    d. might cause him to lose his ability to reason.

12. In the video, you saw Kanzi, a thirteen-year-old bonobo, communicate with researchers by using

   a. a computer.
   b. sign language.
   c. claps and yells.
   d. a symbol board.

13. In the video, Professor Bates explained that babies at birth can hear every sound used by

   a. any natural language.
   b. any animal that communicates.
   c. people who speak slowly to them.
   d. people who use their native language.

14. In the video, Professor Susan Bookheimer discussed two categories of things that Paul Sailer had a difficult time naming after his surgery. These two categories were

   a. people's names and addresses.
   b. animals and plants.
   c. places he has been and familiar faces.
   d. specific events and types of food.

15. In the video, the two types of reasoning that were introduced by Professor Jeffery Mio were

   a. analogical reasoning and digital reasoning.
   b. analogical reasoning and heuristics.
   c. heuristics and common sense reasoning.
   d. practical logic and the Gestalt insight.

16. In the video, Professor Iris Firstenberg used what example to describe the problem-solving method called algorithms?

   a. a puzzle divided into five equal shapes
   b. a flash of recognition commonly called the "aha" experience
   c. a person who believes someone smiling must be a nice person
   d. an engineer calculating the size of a beam to hold up a roof

Short-Answer Questions

17. Define cognition and thinking, and describe how mental images and concepts are involved.

_____

_____

_____

18. Describe the difference between formal concepts and natural concepts, and explain the role prototypes play in concept formation.

_____

_____

_____

19. Explain how functional fixedness and mental set interfere with problem solving.

_____

_____

_____

20. Compare and contrast the following cognitive strategies for problem solving: trial and error, algorithm, heuristic, and insight.

_____

_____

_____

21. Define intuition and discuss the intuitive process.

_____

_____

_____

22. Discuss how the belief-bias effect, confirmation bias, the fallacy of positive instances, and the overestimation effect interfere with our ability to perceive and accept contradictory information.

_____

_____

_____

23. Identify the major characteristics of language.

_____

_____

_____

24. Discuss the ways language can influence thinking.

_____

_____

_____

Matching Exercises

Match the following terms and concepts with the correct definition.

cognition   fallacy of positive instances

intuition   heuristics

language   concept

prototype   natural concept

algorithm

25. _____ Formed as a result of everyday experiences, rather than by using logic and a specific set of rules.

26. _____ The most typical instance of a particular concept.

27. _____ Involves following a specific rule, procedure, or method that inevitably produces the correct solution.

28. _____ The tendency to remember uncommon events that seem to confirm our beliefs and forget events that disconfirm our beliefs.

29. _____ Making a judgment or coming to a conclusion without awareness of the thought processes involved.

30. _____ Involves following a general rule of thumb to reduce the number of possible solutions.

31. _____ The mental activities involved in acquiring, retaining, and using knowledge.

32. _____ A system for combining arbitrary symbols to produce an infinite number of meaningful statements.

33. _____ A mental category of objects or ideas based on the properties they share.

Completion Exercises

Fill in each blank with the most appropriate term or terms from the list of answers provided.

belief-bias effect   mental images

confirmation bias   mental set

formal concepts   physically

human languages   symbolize

insight   thinking

linguistic relativity hypothesis   understand

34. Also called the aha experience, sometimes _____ will occur when you recognize how a problem is similar to a previously solved problem.

35. _____ typically involves the manipulation of mental images and concepts.

36. The _____ occurs when people accept only the evidence that conforms to their belief, rejecting or ignoring any evidence that does not.

37. If you approach a problem with a rigid _____, you may not see other ways to solve the problem.

38. Children are taught the specific rules or features that define simple _____, such as circles, squares, and boxes.

39. Thinking involves the manipulation of both _____ and concepts.

40. If you believed a certain person committed a crime, you might have the tendency to search only for evidence that supports your belief. This would be an example of the _____.

41. The _____ is the notion that differences among languages cause differences in thoughts.

42. In the video, Professor Elizabeth Bates explained that dolphins _____ and answer simple questions and follow instructions.

43. In the video, you learned that there are more than six thousand known _____.

44. In the video, Professor Elizabeth Bates explained that whenever we learn anything, it _____ changes the brain.

45. In the video, you learned that all cognition—thinking, reasoning, decision-making, and problem-solving—relies on our ability to _____.

Answer Key

Multiple-Choice Questions

1. a	5. c	9. b	13. a
2. c	6. d	10. d	14. b
3. d	7. a	11. b	15. b
4. b	8. d	12. d	16. d

Short-Answer Questions

Your answer should include the following:

17. Cognition is defined as the mental activities involved in acquiring, retaining, and using knowledge. Thinking is the manipulation of mental representation of information in order to draw inferences and conclusions. Mental images and concepts are what we think with. (pages 280–281)

18. A formal concept is a mental category that is formed by learning the rules or features that define it. A natural concept does not have clear and sharply defined rules or features, and is the result of everyday experience. The "best," or most typical, instance of a particular concept is called a prototype. (pages 282–284)

19. Functional fixedness, the tendency to view objects as functioning in only their usual ways, can prevent us from seeing the full range of ways in which an object can be used. Mental set is the tendency to persist in solving problems the "old" way, which limits our ability to recognize new alternative solutions. (pages 286–287)

20. Trial and error is an often inefficient method for solving problems that does not follow any set of rules or procedures. Heuristics and algorithm both use strategies for solving problems. Algorithm uses specific rules, procedures, or methods to solve problems. Heuristics uses a general rule of thumb to reduce the number of possible solutions. Insight, the sudden realization of a solution, is not a strategy of problem solving because it occurs without the awareness of how the problem was solved. (pages 284–286)

21. Intuition involves coming to a conclusion or making a judgment without awareness of the thought processes involved. Intuition is an orderly phenomenon probably involving the contemplation of information unconsciously prior to consciously becoming aware of the thought process used and the resultant solution. (page 286)

22. The belief-bias effect occurs when people only accept evidence that conforms to an existing belief. Confirmation bias is the tendency to search only for evidence that confirms an existing belief. The fallacy of positive instances is the tendency to remember uncommon events that confirm our beliefs and forget events that disconfirm a belief. The overestimation effect is the tendency to

overestimate the rarity of events. All of these phenomena are obstacles to logical thinking and tend to allow unwarranted beliefs to persist. (page 290)

23. The characteristics of language include the use of symbols, meanings that are that are shared by others who speak the same language, a highly organized structure of specific rules, a creative or generative quality, and displacement. (page 291)

24. Language can influence thinking by affecting our memory, perception, and gender bias. (page 293)

Matching Exercises

25. natural concept

26. prototype

27. algorithm

28. fallacy of positive instances

29. intuition

30. heuristics

31. cognition

32. language

33. concept

Completion Exercises

34. insight

35. thinking

36. belief-bias effect

37. mental set

38. formal concepts

39. mental images

40. confirmation bias

41. linguistic relativity hypothesis

42. understand

43. human languages

44. physically

45. symbolize

Lesson 10/Language and Cognition

Study Matrix
Lesson 10
Language and Cognition

Please Note: Use this matrix to guide your study and achieve the learning objectives of this lesson. It will also help you to view the video, which defines and demonstrates important concepts and objectives as they relate to everyday life and actual case studies.

Learning Objective	Textbook	Telecourse Student Guide
Define cognition and thinking, and describe how mental images and concepts are involved.	pp. 280–283	Key Terms and Concepts; Study Activities 1, 2, 17, 31, 35, 39.
Describe the difference between formal concepts and natural concepts, and explain the role played by prototypes in concept formation.	pp. 282–284	Key Terms and Concepts; Study Activities 3, 4, 18, 25, 26, 33, 38, 44.
Explain how functional fixedness and mental set interferes with problem solving.	pp. 286–287	Key Terms and Concepts; Study Activities 8, 19, 37.
Compare and contrast the following cognitive strategies for problem solving: trial and error, algorithms, heuristics, and insight.	pp. 284–286	Key Terms and Concepts; Study Activities 5, 6, 7, 15, 16, 20, 27, 30, 45.
Define intuition and discuss the intuitive process.	pp. 286–287	Key Terms and Concepts; Study Activities 21, 29, 34.
Discuss how belief-bias, confirmation bias, the fallacy of positive instances, and the overestimation effect interfere with our ability to perceive and accept contradictory information.	p. 290	Key Terms and Concepts; Study Activities 9, 22, 28, 36, 40.
Identify the major characteristics of language.	pp. 291–292	Key Terms and Concepts; Study Activities 10, 11, 23, 43.
Discuss some of the ways that language can influence thinking.	p. 293	Key Terms and Concepts; Study Activities 13, 24, 32, 41.
Present evidence for and against the proposition that animals can learn language.	pp. 295–296	Key Terms and Concepts; Study Activities 12, 42.

Use the Course Compass to orient yourself in the road that you are taking to explore branches and aspects of psychology. The branch and aspects that are covered in this lesson are highlighted in the compass.

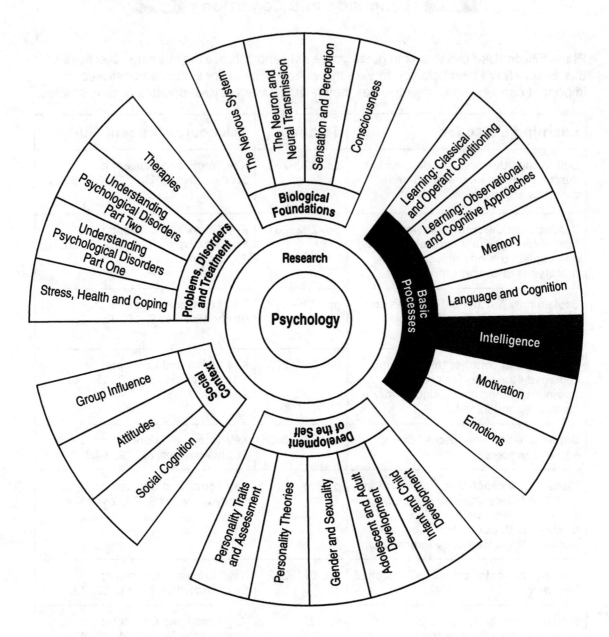

Please note: This compass does not represent the full range of topics comprising the field of psychology; it represents a map for this course only. Each of the five branches represented above has many aspects and subjects that are covered in the 26 lessons of this telecourse. You should remember that these branches and subjects all interrelate.

Lesson 11

Intelligence

Questions to Consider

What is intelligence?

Is there more than one form of intelligence?

What is the best method to measure intelligence?

How do emotions and personality affect intelligence?

Is a person's intelligence a good predictor of how successful they will become?

What has the greatest effect on intelligence—heredity or the environment?

Lesson Assignments

Before viewing the video program

Read the Questions to Consider, Lesson Preview, and Learning Objectives for this lesson. Use this information to guide your reading, viewing, and thinking.

Read Chapter 7, "Thinking, Language, and Intelligence," pages 296–314, in the textbook.

View the video program, "Intelligence"

After viewing the video program

Review the vocabulary listed in the Key Terms and Concepts section. (Page references are keyed to the Hockenbury textbook, *Psychology*. Remember: there is a complete Glossary at the end of the textbook.)

Review the reading assignments for this lesson.

Complete the exercises found in the Study Activities section and check your answers with the Answer Key at the end of this lesson.

Use the Study Matrix found at the end of this lesson to review and assess your knowledge of each Learning Objective.

Lesson Preview

It is commonly accepted that some people are smarter than others. But how can we really know who is intelligent and who is not so intelligent? Consider this. Albert Einstein was once labeled a dunce in math. Thomas Edison and Winston Churchill's teachers thought they were mentally limited.

No psychological concept has created more social, political, and scientific disagreement than the concept of intelligence. While most people have a general idea of what intelligence is, psychologists who study human intelligence do not agree on exactly what makes up intelligence. As you will learn in this lesson, exactly what intelligence is, and how best to assess intelligence, remains a hotly debated topic.

In this video, we will explore intelligence, creativity, and intelligence testing. You will learn about the nature of intelligence, the different types of intelligence, and how intelligence is measured.

This video compares the intelligence of a NASA scientist to the intelligence of a Sherpa mountain guide. As this story dramatically demonstrates, intelligence is far more than any single ability or skill. The video will describe a humble mountain guide from Nepal named Angchulodim Sherpa, who, because of his unique intelligence, saved the lives of mountain climbers on Mount Everest. Psychologist Claude Steele will discuss the history of intelligence testing and will explore the concept of multiple intelligences. Additionally in this video, noted psychologist Robert Sternberg explains his own theory, known as the triarchic theory of intelligence.

While all the answers about what intelligence is and the nature of intelligence must, for now, go partially unanswered, we do know that success is not simply a product of intelligence. In the end, success, like so many things in life, is probably more the result of determined effort than it is the result of any one trait, skill, or characteristic.

Learning Objectives

When you have completed this lesson, you should be able to:

1. Define intelligence using Wechsler's global definition.

2. Explain how and why intelligence tests (IQ) were developed.

3. Define mental age and chronological age and describe how age categories are used by the Stanford-Binet Intelligence Test.

4. Discuss the difference between an achievement test and an aptitude test.

5. Describe the importance of standardization, reliability, and validity in testing.

6. Discuss the notion that a common factor, or general mental capacity, is at the core of different mental abilities.

7. List the three forms of intelligence as defined by the triarchic theory of intelligence.

8. Describe Howard Gardner's concept of multiple intelligences.

9. Define heritability, and explain how twin studies are used in studying the heredity-environment issue.

10. Explain how culture can affect intelligence test results.

11. Define creativity and discuss how we can increase our ability to be creative.

Key Terms and Concepts

Page references are keyed to the Hockenbury textbook, *Psychology*.

Intelligence: The global capacity to think rationally, act purposefully, and deal effectively with the environment. (pages 296–297)

Mental age: A measurement of intelligence in which an individual's mental level is expressed in terms of the average abilities of a given age group. (page 297)

Chronological age: A person's actual age. (page 297)

Alfred Binet: A French psychologist who in the early 1900's developed a series of tests that became the basis for modern intelligence tests. (page 297)

Stanford-Binet IQ test: An adaptation of Binet's test by Stanford University psychologist Lewis Terman, this was for many years the standard for intelligence tests in the United States. (page 297)

David Wechsler: An American psychologist who created intelligence tests specifically for adults and expanded the range of abilities that were tested. (page 298)

Wechsler Adult Intelligence Scale (WAIS): The most common intelligence test now administered in the United States, this test assesses a variety of verbal and performance abilities. (pages 298 and 300)

Intelligence quotient (IQ): A global measure of intelligence derived by comparing an individual's score to that of others in the same age group. (page 297)

Achievement test: A test designed to measure a person's level of knowledge, skill, or accomplishment in a particular area. (page 300)

Aptitude test: A test designed to assess a person's capacity to benefit from education or training. (page 300)

Standardization: The administration of a test to a large, representative sample of people under uniform conditions for the purpose of establishing norms. (pages 300–301)

Normal curve: A bell-shaped distribution of individual differences in a normal population in which most scores cluster around the average score. Also sometimes referred to as normal distribution. (page 301)

Reliability: The ability of a test to produce consistent results when administered on repeated occasions under similar conditions. (pages 300–301)

Validity: The ability of a test to measure what it is intended to measure. (pages 300–301)

General intelligence or g factor: The notion of a general intelligence factor that is responsible for a person's overall performance on tests of mental ability. (page 302)

Triarchic theory of intelligence: The theory that there are three distinct forms of intelligence: analytic, creative, and practical. (pages 304–305)

Multiple intelligences: The theory that intelligence must be defined within the context of a particular culture and that there are several distinct, independent intelligences. (page 303)

Nature vs. nurture: A common way to refer to the controversy as to whether some trait or ability is the result of heredity or environmental factors. (pages 305–306)

Heritability: The percentage of variation within a given population that is due to heredity. (page 307)

Stereotype threat: A psychological predicament in which members of a particular group fear that they will be evaluated in terms of a negative stereotype about their group. (pages 310–311)

Creativity: A group of cognitive processes used to generate useful, original, and novel ideas or solutions to problems. (page 313)

Study Activities

These self-test questions are designed as a study exercise to aid you in understanding the most important terms and concepts in this lesson. To ensure that you have an accurate understanding of the key terms and concepts in this lesson, please check your answers with the Answer Key provided at the end of this lesson.

Multiple-Choice Questions

1. The use of mental concepts, problem solving, and decision making are all mental aspects of what we commonly call

    a. intelligence.

    b. cognition.

    c. mental sets.

    d. mental abilities and skills.

2. The observation that brighter children performed like older children led to the concept of

    a. age-dependent testing.

    b. intelligence testing.

    c. mental age.

    d. chronological age.

3. Intelligence quotient or IQ is a measure derived by comparing an individual's score to that of others in

    a. the same age group.

    b. different age groups.

    c. a bell-shaped curve.

    d. the same testing situation.

4. If a test accurately measures what it has proposed to measure, this test is

    a. standardized.

    b. reliable.

    c. accurate.

    d. valid.

5. Tests that are designed to assess a person's ability to benefit from training or education are known as

    a. aptitude tests.

    b. standardized tests.

    c. intelligence tests.

    d. achievement tests.

6. Many different personality factors are involved in achieving success, such as motivation, emotional maturity, commitment to goals, creativity, and

    a. general intelligence.

    b. socioeconomic conditions.

    c. willingness to work.

    d. specific skills and abilities.

7. The triarchic theory of intelligence involves three distinct types of mental abilities. These are analytic intelligence, creative intelligence, and

    a. linguistic intelligence.

    b. interpersonal intelligence.

    c. naturalistic intelligence.

    d. practical intelligence.

8. The percentage of variation within a given population that is due to heredity is called

    a. heritability.

    b. normal distribution.

    c. inherited variation factor.

    d. genetic makeup.

9. If a person is especially good at generating useful, original, and novel ideas, this person is highly

    a. intelligent.

    b. motivated to succeed.

    c. creative.

    d. skilled at performance tasks.

10. Cross-cultural studies have been helpful in showing the effects of

    a. genetic factors that influence intelligence.

    b. education in developing countries.

    c. social discrimination on intelligence.

    d. early intelligence testing.

11. In this video, several definitions of intelligence were presented, including defining intelligence as one's ability to solve problems and to

    a. have good verbal skills.

    b. succeed in life.

    c. do well in school.

    d. think rationally.

12. In the video, you learned that the first efforts to measure intelligence are credited to a psychologist named

    a. Lewis Terman.

    b. Claude Steele.

    c. Robert Sternberg.

    d. Alfred Binet.

13. In the video, you learned that in the early 1900's, IQ tests were used as a way of

    a. determining mental retardation.

    b. screening immigrant populations.

    c. determining entrance into colleges and universities.

    d. deciding what branch of the service a person would be assigned.

14. In the video, you learned that one of the main problems with early intelligence tests was that they were based on the notion that

    a. math was the most representative ability of intelligent people.

    b. people are born with a certain level of intelligence that rarely changes.

    c. only certain ethnic groups were intelligent.

    d. on the average men are more intelligent than women.

15. In the video, Dr. René Díaz-Lefebvre gave several examples of Howard Gardner's concept of

    a. logical-mathematical intelligence.

    b. interpersonal and intrapersonal intelligence.

    c. multiple intelligences.

    d. creativity as an intelligence.

16. In the video, Dr. Nancy Segal discussed what determines a person's intelligence. This is often referred to as the

    a. heritability question.

    b. nature or nurture question.

    c. genetic theory of intelligence.

    d. biological-societal question.

Short-Answer Questions

17. Discuss when and why intelligence tests were first developed.

_____

_____

_____

18. Explain the two major advantages the Wechsler Adult Intelligence Scale (WAIS) has over the Stanford-Binet Intelligence Test.

_____

_____

_____

19. Define standardization, reliability, and validity as they relate to testing and assessment.

_____

_____

_____

20. List the three forms of intelligence as defined by the triarchic theory of intelligence.

_____

_____

_____

21. Explain and discuss the g factor as it relates to intelligence.

_____

_____

_____

22. Describe the concept of multiple intelligences, and identify at least six of the eight forms of intelligence as defined by Howard Gardner.

_____

_____

_____

23. Describe some of the ways a person can increase the ability to be creative.

_____

_____

_____

24. Explain how culture can affect intelligence test results.

_____

_____

_____

25. In the video, Dr. Díaz-Lefebvre listed and gave examples of eight different types of intelligence. List and give examples of at least four of these different types of intelligence.

_____

_____

_____

Matching Exercises

Match the following terms and concepts with the correct definition.

aptitude test   achievement test   validity

standardization   general intelligence   multiple intelligences

intelligence quotient   intelligence

26. _____ The administration of a test to a large representative sample of people under uniform conditions for the purpose of establishing norms.

27. _____ A measurement of intelligence in which an individual's mental level is expressed in terms of the average abilities of a given age group.

28. _____ Refers to the notion that intelligence is not a single, general mental capacity, but rather consists of a variety of different mental abilities.

29. _____ The ability of a test to measure what it is intended to measure.

30. _____ A test designed to assess a person's capacity to benefit from education or training.

31. _____ The notion that a common factor is at the core of different mental abilities.

32. _____ The global capacity to think rationally, act purposefully, and deal effectively with the environment.

33. _____ A test designed to measure a person's level of knowledge, skill, or accomplishment in a particular area.

Completion Exercises

Fill in each blank with the most appropriate term or terms from the list of answers provided.

Alfred Binet	reliability
creativity	Stanford-Binet IQ Test
environment	stereotype threat
multiple intelligences	think rationally
practical intelligence	triarchic theory of intelligence

34. The _____ emphasizes both the universal aspects of intelligent behavior and the importance of adapting to a particular social and cultural environment.

35. A test is valid if it measures what it is intended to measure. A good test must also have _____, that is, it must consistently produce similar scores on different occasions.

36. Flashes of insight or inspiration can play a role in _____, but they usually occur only after a great deal of work.

37. First published in 1916, the _____ was for many years the standard in schools to measure intelligence in the United States.

38. A _____ is a concern a person might have that they will be evaluated negatively simply because of the group to which they belong.

39. The notion that intelligence is comprised of many different mental abilities that operate independently is the foundation underlying the concept of _____.

40. Deliberately not testing specific skills such as reading and mathematics, _____ focused on elementary mental abilities in an attempt to identify students who might require special help.

41. In the video, you learned that psychologist David Wechsler defined intelligence as the global capacity to _____, act purposefully, and deal effectively.

42. In the video, psychologist Robert Sternberg explains that his triarchic theory of intelligence focuses on three critical areas: analytic ability, creative intelligence, and _____.

43. In the video, you learned that psychologists now agree that both genes and the _____ play crucial roles in fashioning our intellectual ability.

Answer Key

Multiple-Choice Questions

1. a	5. a	9. c	13. b
2. c	6. c	10. c	14. b
3. a	7. d	11. b	15. c
4. d	8. a	12. d	16. b

Short-Answer Questions

Your answers should include the following:

17. The French government passed a law in the early 1900's requiring all children to attend school. Faced with the need to educate children from a wide variety of backgrounds, the government commissioned psychologist Alfred Binet to develop a procedure to identify children who might require special help. (page 297)

18. The two advantages of the WAIS are that it was specifically designed for adults and that the test provides for scores on several subtests measuring different abilities. (pages 298 and 300)

19. These three basic requirements must all be present if a test is to be considered scientifically acceptable. Standardization means that the test has established norms, or standards, against which an individual score is compared and interpreted. Reliability means the test will consistently produce similar scores regardless of circumstances. Validity simply means the test has the demonstrated ability to test what it is intended to test. (pages 300–301)

20. The triarchic theory of intelligence emphasizes both the universal aspects of intelligent behavior and the importance of adapting to social and cultural environments. The three forms of intelligence are analytic intelligence, creative intelligence, and practical intelligence. (pages 304–305)

21. The g factor stands for general intelligence. General intelligence refers to the notion held by some psychologists that there is one common factor, or general mental ability, at the core of different mental abilities. (page 302)

22. Multiple intelligences refers to the notion held by some psychologists that different mental abilities operate independently. The eight separate intelligences identified by Howard Gardner are linguistic intelligence, logical-mathematical intelligence, musical intelligence, spatial intelligence, bodily-kinesthetic intelligence, interpersonal intelligence, intrapersonal intelligence, and naturalistic intelligence. (page 303)

23. The textbook outlines six suggestions that can enhance creativity: 1) Choose the goal of creativity. 2) Reinforce creative behavior. 3) Engage in problem

finding. 4) Acquire relevant knowledge. 5) Try different approaches. 6) Exert effort and expect setbacks. (pages 313–314)

24. Culture can affect intelligence tests results in a number of ways. Home environment, socioeconomic background, educational opportunities, and social discrimination all can affect intelligence tests results. Additionally, most intelligence tests are in some ways culturally unfair inasmuch as they do not reflect the values and knowledge of all groups in any given society. (pages 310–312)

25. At least four of the following should be explained (page 303):

Naturalistic intelligence. Someone who has the ability to discern flora and fauna, such as a zoologist or biologist.

Interpersonal intelligence. Someone who understands other people, such as a teacher or nurse.

Intrapersonal intelligence. Someone who is in tune with his or her own feelings, motives, and desires.

Logical-mathematical intelligence. Someone who understands abstract thinking, such as a doctor or lawyer.

Musical intelligence. Someone who has a sense of pitch, timbre, and rhythm, such as a musician.

Spatial intelligence. Someone who can see shapes and forms in his or her mind's eye, such as an artist.

Bodily-kinesthetic intelligence. Someone who is in touch with his or her body, such as a dancer or athlete.

Linguistic intelligence. Someone who understands language, such as a poet or writer.

Matching Exercises

26. standardization

27. intelligence quotient

28. multiple intelligences

29. validity

30. aptitude test

31. general intelligence

32. intelligence

33. achievement test

Completion Exercises

34. triarchic theory of intelligence

35. reliability

36. creativity

37. Stanford-Binet IQ Test

38. stereotype threat

39. multiple intelligences

40. Alfred Binet

41. think rationally

42. practical intelligence

43. environment

Study Matrix

Lesson 11

Intelligence

Please Note: Use this matrix to guide your study and achieve the learning objectives of this lesson. It will also help you to view the video, which defines and demonstrates important concepts and objectives as they relate to everyday life and actual case studies.

Learning Objective	Textbook	Telecourse Student Guide
Define intelligence using Wechsler's global definition.	p. 296–297	Key Terms and Concepts; Study Activities 1, 11, 32, 41.
Explain how and why intelligence tests (IQ) were developed.	pp. 297–298	Key Terms and Concepts; Study Activities 3, 13, 17, 27.
Define mental age and chronological age and describe how age categories are used by the Stanford-Binet Intelligence Test.	p. 297	Key Terms and Concepts; Study Activities 2, 12, 18, 37, 40.
Discuss the difference between an achievement test and an aptitude test.	p. 300	Key Terms and Concepts; Study Activities 5, 30, 33.
Describe the importance of standardization, reliability, and validity in testing.	pp. 300–301	Key Terms and Concepts; Study Activities 4, 19, 26, 29, 35.
Discuss the notion that a common factor, or general mental capacity, is at the core of different mental abilities.	pp. 302–305	Key Terms and Concepts; Study Activities 6, 21, 31.
List the three forms of intelligence as defined by the triarchic theory of intelligence.	pp. 304–305	Key Terms and Concepts; Study Activities 7, 20, 34, 42.
Describe Howard Gardner's concept of multiple intelligences.	p. 303	Key Terms and Concepts; Study Activities 15, 22, 28, 39.
Define heritability, and explain how twin studies are used in studying the heredity-environment issue.	pp. 305–307	Key Terms and Concepts; Study Activities 8, 14, 16, 43.
Explain how culture can affect intelligence test results.	pp. 305–312	Key Terms and Concepts; Study Activities 10, 24, 38.
Define creativity and discuss how we can increase our ability to be creative.	pp. 313–314	Key Terms and Concepts; Study Activities 9, 23, 36.

Use the Course Compass to orient yourself in the road that you are taking to explore branches and aspects of psychology. The branch and aspects that are covered in this lesson are highlighted in the compass.

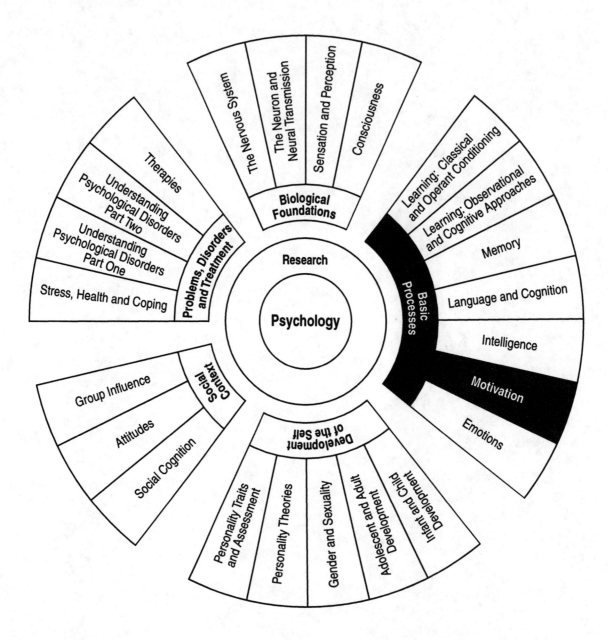

Please note: This compass does not represent the full range of topics comprising the field of psychology; it represents a map for this course only. Each of the five branches represented above has many aspects and subjects that are covered in the 26 lessons of this telecourse. You should remember that these branches and subjects all interrelate.

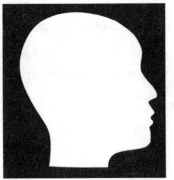

Lesson 12

Motivation

Questions to Consider

Why do people do what they do?

What is self-efficacy and how does it affect motivation?

What role does personal desire play in human motivation?

Why do so many people have problems with self-destructive behaviors, like smoking, overeating and excessive drinking or the use of drugs?

Do people vary in their needs for excitement and arousal?

Why do some people achieve so much in life while others achieve so little?

Lesson Assignments

Before viewing the video program

Read the Questions to Consider, Lesson Preview, and Learning Objectives for this lesson. Use this information to guide your reading, viewing, and thinking.

Read Chapter 8, "Motivation and Emotion," pages 319–343 and 360–362, in the textbook.

View the video program, "Motivation"

After viewing the video program

Review the vocabulary listed in the Key Terms and Concepts section. (Page references are keyed to the Hockenbury textbook, *Psychology*. Remember: there is a complete Glossary at the end of the textbook.)

Review the reading assignments for this lesson.

Complete the exercises found in the Study Activities section and check your answers with the Answer Key at the end of this lesson.

Use the Study Matrix found at the end of this lesson to review and assess your knowledge of each Learning Objective.

Lesson Preview

Understanding human motivation goes to the core of psychology. Trying to understand why we do what we do is a basic human question—the question that created the need for the field of psychology.

Before the days of Plato and Aristotle, humans were viewed as motivated by unseen forces—gods or demons. Plato and Aristotle brought forth the idea of free will. Free will is the notion that each of us can choose to control our own behavior. Free will means that each of us can make decisions by using logic and reason to control our actions. However, even in Plato's day the idea of free will was not agreed upon by everyone. Some people continued to view behavior as controlled by the gods, while others believed that all behaviors are the result of an inflexible chain of cause and effects.

Most of us want to believe that we, not a god or some rule of cause and effect, are in control of what we do. However, if we are in complete control of our behavior, then why do we humans have so many problems? Why don't we all choose to be healthy, happy, wealthy, and at peace? As we think more about it, it becomes clear that choice alone cannot completely explain human behavior.

In this lesson, we will explore the fascinating topic of motivation. You will learn about physical drives, biological needs, and all manners of psychological motives—from curiosity to competence.

In this video, you will get to know Chuck Perry, a self-avowed ice cream fanatic who became a marathon runner. Textbook author Don Hockenbury will explain the three general characteristics of motivation. Additionally, this video will give you a brief history of the different theories that psychologists have used to explain motivation.

Albert Bandura, an eminent author and professor of psychology at Stanford University, will discuss the critical role self-efficacy plays in human motivation. Possibly the most important information you will uncover in this lesson is that you can learn how to modify and control your own behavior by understanding more about motivation.

Learning Objectives

When you have completed this lesson, you should be able to:

1. Define motivation, and describe the three characteristics associated with motivation.

2. Describe the concept of drive, and explain how it is related to homeostasis.

3. Explain the incentive theory of motivation.

4. Identify the stages in Maslow's hierarchy of needs, including a definition of self-actualization.

5. Define obesity, and explain how metabolic rates work and how the set-point theory affects eating behavior.

6. Define anorexia nervosa and bulimia nervosa.

7. Explain the difference between competence motivation and achievement motivation.

8. Discuss arousal theory and sensation-seeking behavior.

9. Define self-efficacy, and discuss the role of self-efficacy in motivation.

Key Terms and Concepts

Page references are keyed to the Hockenbury textbook, *Psychology*.

Motivation: The biological, emotional, cognitive, or social forces that activate and direct behavior. (page 320)

Instinct theories: The view that some motives are innate and are the result of genetic programming. (pages 321–322)

Drive theories: The view that behavior is motivated by the desire to reduce internal tension caused by unmet biological needs. (page 322)

Homeostasis: The notion that the body monitors and maintains internal states, such as body temperature and energy level, at relatively constant levels. (pages 322–323)

Drive: An impulse that activates behavior to reduce a need and restore homeostasis. (page 323)

Incentive theories: The view that behavior is motivated by the pull of external goals, such as making another person happy. (page 323)

Hierarchy of needs: A division of motivation into levels that progress from basic physical needs to self-fulfillment needs. (pages 324 and 338–339)

Humanistic theories of motivation: The view that emphasizes the importance of psychological and cognitive factors in motivation. (page 324)

Self-actualization: The notion of a highest level of achievement in which the person makes full use of all their talents, abilities, and potential. (page 339)

Basal metabolic rate (BMR): The rate at which the body uses energy for vital bodily functions when at rest. (page 326)

Set-point weight: The particular weight that is set and maintained by increases or decreases in basal metabolic rate. (page 330)

Obese: Condition characterized by excessive body fat and a body mass index equal to or greater than 30. (pages 331–333)

Anorexia nervosa: An eating disorder in which an individual refuses to maintain normal body weight, is afraid of gaining weight or becoming fat, and has a distorted perception about his or her body. (page 336)

Bulimia nervosa: An eating disorder in which a person engages in binge eating and then purges the excessive food by self-induced vomiting, or by using laxatives or enemas. (page 336)

Arousal theory: The view that people are motivated to maintain an optimal level of arousal. (pages 323–324)

Sensation seeking: Behavior directed to experiences that produce high levels of arousal. (page 324)

Competence motivation: Motivated behavior directed toward demonstrating competence and exercising control over a situation. (pages 341–342)

Achievement motivation: Motivated behavior directed toward excelling, succeeding, or outperforming others at some task. (pages 341–343)

Self-efficacy: The degree to which a person is subjectively convinced of his or her ability to effectively meet the demands of a situation. (pages 360–362)

Study Activities

These self-test questions are designed as a study exercise to aid you in understanding the most important terms and concepts in this lesson. To ensure that you have an accurate understanding of the key terms and concepts in this lesson, please check your answers with the Answer Key provided at the end of this lesson.

Multiple-Choice Questions

1. Engaging in behaviors because of genetic programming describes

    a. evolutionary motivation.

    b. inherited drive theory of motivation.

    c. instinct theory of motivation.

    d. incentive theory of motivation.

2. Cognitive factors in learning, especially the expectation that a particular behavior will lead to a particular goal, lead to the development of

    a. instinct theories of motivation.

    b. drive theories of motivation.

    c. learning theories of motivation.

    d. incentive theories of motivation.

3. Self-actualization can be described as

    a. peak experiences.

    b. a state of realism and acceptance.

    c. prestige and a feeling of accomplishment.

    d. achieving one's full potential.

4. The rate at which your body uses energy for vital bodily functions when at rest is referred to as your

    a. set-point rate.

    b. basal metabolic rate.

    c. parasympathetic rate.

    d. energy balance rate.

5. Motivated behavior that is directed toward excelling, succeeding, or outperforming others is called

    a. achievement motivation.

    b. sensation seeking.

    c. arousal motivation.

    d. competence motivation.

6. Self-efficacy is the degree to which a person is subjectively convinced

    a. of his or her ability to effectively meet the demands of a situation.

    b. of his or her ability to outperform others.

    c. that he or she has reached his or her full potential.

    d. that he or she is self-controlled and self-motivated.

7. Anorexia nervosa is a potentially life-threatening psychological order that involves

    a. binge eating.

    b. male and females equally.

    c. near self-starvation.

    d. the lose of appetite.

8. In the video, the three general characteristics that psychologists normally associate with motivation were introduced. These characteristics are

    a. cognition, persistence, and activation.

    b. activation, persistence, and intensity.

    c. intention, persistence, and activation.

    d. activation, cognition, and intensity.

9. In the video, Professor Bernard Weiner explained that historically in the study of motivation two contexts have been used. One context is a hungry animal, and the other context is

    a. an angry or frustrated animal.

    b. a hungry person.

    c. a person working at a task.

    d. an animal that is not hungry.

10. In the video, it was explained that the basic idea in a drive theory is that we have some unmet

    a. psychological needs.

    b. instinctual needs.

    c. biological needs.

    d. personal needs.

11. In the video, Professor Weiner used the examples of body temperature and hunger to explain the concept of

    a. homeostasis.

    b. drive theory.

    c. biological motivation.

    d. instinct-driven needs.

12. In the video, Abraham Maslow's theory of motivation was introduced. This theory is called the

    a. self-actualization model.

    b. hierarchy of needs.

    c. safety to esteem ladder.

    d. human motivation chain model.

13. In the video, Professor Hockenbury explained that one of the problems with Maslow's theory of motivation is that so few people

    a. understand this theory.

    b. achieve self-actualization.

    c. get beyond their basic survival needs.

    d. have any interest in achieving their maximum potential.

14. In the video, the old adage "You can if you think you can" was used as an example of the notion of

    a. motivational thinking.

    b. cognitive processing.

    c. self-efficacy.

    d. that people can do anything they want.

15. In the video, Professor Albert Bandura explained that there are four ways to build self-efficacy and that the most powerful way is through

    a. belief in yourself.

    b. continuous effort.

    c. getting good social support.

    d. the mastering of experiences.

Short-Answer Questions

16. Define motivation, and describe the three characteristics associated with motivation.

_____

_____

_____

17. Describe the concept of drive, and explain how it is related to homeostasis.

_____

_____

_____

18. Explain the difference between instinct and incentive theories of motivation.

_____

_____

_____

19. Identify the stages in Maslow's hierarchy of needs, including a definition of self-actualization.

_____

_____

_____

20. Define obesity, and explain how metabolic rates and set-point weight affect eating behavior.

_____

_____

_____

21. Define anorexia nervosa and bulimia nervosa.

_____

_____

_____

22. Explain the difference between competence motivation and achievement motivation.

_____

_____

_____

23. Discuss arousal theory and sensation-seeking behavior.

_____

_____

_____

24. Define self-efficacy, and discuss the role of self-efficacy in motivation.

_____

_____

_____

Matching Exercises

Match the following terms and concepts with the correct definition.

obesity   competence motivation

self-actualization   self-efficacy

psychological motivation   bulimia nervosa

instinct theories   drive

arousal theory

25. _____ According to this view, people are motivated to engage in certain behaviors because of genetic programming.

26. _____ A fairly common condition in which a person weighs 20 percent or more above his or her optimal body weight.

27. _____ Motivation that is not biological or environmental in nature and results from a person's expectations, desires, and concerns.

28. _____ The notion of the highest level of achievement in which individuals make full use of their talents, abilities, and potential.

29. _____ This theory can help explain curiosity and exploratory behavior.

30. _____ An eating disorder in which a person engages in binge eating and then purges the excessive food by self-induced vomiting, or by taking laxatives or enemas.

31. _____ Produces great motivation to master situations and be persistent regardless of the obstacles encountered.

32. _____ Activates behavior to reestablish the balance of internal conditions.

33. _____ Enrolling in a course or learning a new skill in order to gain more control over your life is explained by this theory.

Completion Exercises

Fill in each blank with the most appropriate term or terms from the list of answers provided.

achievement motivation

drive theories

extrinsic

hierarchy of needs

homeostasis

incentive motivation

instinct theories

motivation

sensation-seeking behavior

set-point weight

34. A step beyond competence motivation, _____ explains behaviors such as trying to finish at the top of your class.

35. Metabolism changes that occur because your body is trying to maintain its _____ may explain many of the difficulties people encounter when trying to lose or gain weight.

36. People often use the word _____ when trying to understand or explain the behavior of others.

37. The principle of _____ states that the body monitors and maintains relatively constant levels of internal states.

38. The most popular humanistic model of motivation is the _____, which proposes that the realization of a person's full potential is our ultimate goal.

39. People who engage in _____ are highly motivated to experience the high levels of arousal associated with varied and novel activities.

40. Expanding on the theory that behavior is motivated by biological drives, _____ proposes that behavior is motivated by the "pull" of external goals.

41. In the video, it was explained that early psychologists attempted to explain motivation using _____.

42. In the video, Professor Hockenbury explained that a major drawback of _____ was at many of our behaviors do not seem to be connected to any unmet biological need.

43. In the video, it was discussed how internal rewards, such as self-satisfaction, are often more enduring than _____ rewards, such as money.

Answer Key

Multiple-Choice Questions

1. c	5. a	9. c	13. b
2. d	6. a	10. c	14. c
3. d	7. c	11. a	15. d
4. b	8. b	12. b	

Short-Answer Questions

Your answers should include the following:

16. Motivation refers to the biological, emotional, cognitive, and social forces acting on or within an organism to initiate and direct behavior. (page 320)

17. Drive theories assert that behavior is motivated by the desire to reduce internal tension caused by unmet biological needs, such as hunger or thirst. Homeostasis is the principle that states that the body monitors and maintains relatively constant levels of internal states. When an imbalance is detected in the body by homeostasis, a drive is initiated to restore the balance in the body. (pages 322–323)

18. Instinct theories of motivation are based on the notion that behavior is genetically programmed, while incentive theories of motivation propose that behavior is motivated by the "pull" of external goals, such as rewards. (pages 321–323)

19. Maslow's hierarchy of needs starts with the basic needs, physiological needs and safety needs, then goes on to psychological needs, belonging and self-esteem, and ends with the self-fulfillment need of self-actualization. Self-actualization is the realization of one's personal potential. (pages 338–339)

20. Obesity is a condition that exists when a persons has excessive body fat and a body mass index equal to or greater than 30. Set-point weight is the notion that each person has a predetermined weight that the body will continue to try to maintain by adjusting metabolic rates in order to promote weight loss or gain. (pages 330–333)

21. Anorexia is a life-threatening condition in which an individual refuses to maintain normal body weight, is extremely afraid of gaining weight or becoming fat, and has a distorted perception about the size of his or her body. Bulimia nervosa is an eating disorder in which a person engages in binge eating and then purges the excessive food by self-induced vomiting or by taking laxatives or enemas. (page 336)

22. Competence motivation is motivated behavior that is directed toward demonstrating competence and exercising control over a situation. A step beyond competence motivation, achievement motivation is motivated behavior directed toward excelling, succeeding, or outperforming others. (page 341)

23. According to arousal theory, people are motivated to maintain an optimal level of arousal. When arousal is too high, we are motivated to decrease arousal by seeking out less stimulating environments. When arousal is too low, we are motivated to increase arousal. Sensation seeking behavior increases arousal. Sensation seekers are people who are highly motivated to try risky or exciting activities. (pages 323–324)

24. Self-efficacy is the degree to which a person is subjectively convinced of his or her ability to effectively meet the demands of a situation. People with high self-efficacy will be more motivated to take on challenges and, conversely, people with low self-efficacy will not be motivated and will tend not to perform well. (video; pages 360–361)

Matching Exercises

25. instinct theories

26. obesity

27. psychological motivation

28. self-actualization

29. arousal theory

30. bulimia nervosa

31. self-efficacy

32. drive

33. competence

Completion Exercises

34. achievement motivation

35. set-point weight

36. motivation

37. homeostasis

38. hierarchy of needs

39. sensation-seeking behavior

40. incentive motivation

41. instinct theories

42. drive theories

43. extrinsic

Study Matrix

Lesson 12

Motivation

Please Note: Use this matrix to guide your study and achieve the learning objectives of this lesson. It will also help you to view the video, which defines and demonstrates important concepts and objectives as they relate to everyday life and actual case studies.

Learning Objective	Textbook	Telecourse Student Guide
Define motivation, and describe the three characteristics associated with motivation.	pp. 320–321	Key Terms and Concepts; Study Activities 8, 16, 36.
Describe the concept of drive, and explain how it is related to homeostasis.	pp. 322–323	Key Terms and Concepts; Study Activities 10, 11, 17, 32, 37, 42.
Explain the incentive theory of motivation.	p. 323	Key Terms and Concepts; Study Activities 1, 2, 9, 18, 25, 40, 41.
Identify the stages in Maslow's hierarchy of needs, including a definition of self-actualization.	pp. 338–339	Key Terms and Concepts; Study Activities 3, 12, 13, 19, 28, 38.
Define obesity, and explain how metabolic rates and set-point affect eating behavior.	pp. 330–333	Key Terms and Concepts; Study Activities 4, 20, 26, 35.
Define anorexia nervosa and bulimia nervosa.	p. 336	Key Terms and Concepts; Study Activities 7, 21, 30.
Explain the difference between competence motivation and achievement motivation.	pp. 341–343	Key Terms and Concepts; Study Activities 5, 22, 27, 33, 34, 43.
Discuss arousal theory and sensation-seeking behavior.	pp. 324–325	Key Terms and Concepts; Study Activities 23, 29, 39.
Define self-efficacy, and discuss the role of self-efficacy in motivation.	pp. 360–362	Key Terms and Concepts; Study Activities 6, 14, 15, 24, 31.

Use the Course Compass to orient yourself in the road that you are taking to explore branches and aspects of psychology. The branch and aspects that are covered in this lesson are highlighted in the compass.

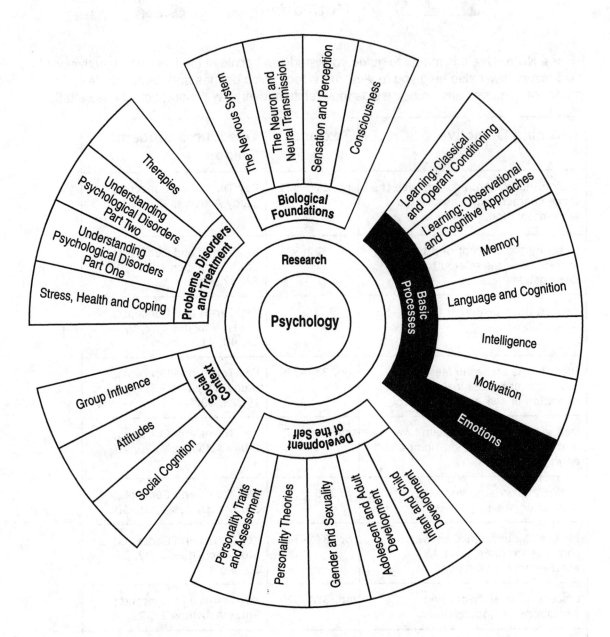

Please note: This compass does not represent the full range of topics comprising the field of psychology; it represents a map for this course only. Each of the five branches represented above has many aspects and subjects that are covered in the 26 lessons of this telecourse. You should remember that these branches and subjects all interrelate.

Lesson 13

Emotions

Questions to Consider

What exactly are emotions?

Are we born with emotions or do we learn to be emotional?

Do men and women differ in how they feel emotions?

What happens to the body during an emotion?

Why do some people develop emotional problems?

How can I become a happier person?

Lesson Assignments

Before viewing the video program

Read the Questions to Consider, Lesson Preview, and Learning Objectives for this lesson. Use this information to guide your reading, viewing, and thinking.

Read Chapter 8, "Motivation and Emotion," pages 344–362, in the textbook.

View the video program, "Emotions"

After viewing the video program

Review the vocabulary listed in the Key Terms and Concepts section. (Page references are keyed to the Hockenbury textbook, *Psychology*. Remember: there is a complete Glossary at the end of the textbook.)

Review the reading assignments for this lesson.

Complete the exercises found in the Study Activities section and check your answers with the Answer Key at the end of this lesson.

Use the Study Matrix found at the end of this lesson to review and assess your knowledge of each Learning Objective.

Lesson Preview

Emotions are an integral part of our lives. Most days we experience all manners of emotion—from pleasure to disappointment. We feel happy when things are going especially well, and frustrated or maybe angry when things don't work out as planned or anticipated. We may feel love and caring when we are with someone special. Or, we may feel estranged, anxious or even fearful if we are alone in some unfamiliar environment.

Emotions can make life worth living—or they can make life a living hell. Emotions can motivate us to do great things and can urge us closer people. But, emotions can also limit us and stop us from becoming close to others. In so many ways, it is our emotions that define us. Love, anger, happiness, fear—all emotions, and all so very important to each and every one of us.

But, what exactly are emotions? Why do we have emotions? What is the purpose of emotions? In this lesson, we will explore the nature of human emotions.

The video demonstrates emotions by observing players, parents, and coaches as they get involved in a youth soccer game. Educators and researchers—Linda Levine, Joseph Campos, and Peter Salovey—will explain what psychologists have learned about the need and purpose of human emotion. The video also explores how emotions have evolved and the role emotions play in different cultures. You will hear from Dr. Paul Ekman as he discusses the results of his extensive cross-cultural research on emotional expression.

By understanding more about human emotions, you will better equip yourself to deal with your personal emotions and the emotions of others.

Learning Objectives

When you have completed this lesson, you should be able to:

1. Define emotions and describe the function of emotions.
2. Identify the basic emotions.
3. Explain the physiological responses that accompany emotional arousal.
4. Discuss the effectiveness of polygraphs.
5. Discuss the facial feedback hypothesis.

6. Compare and contrast the James–Lange and the Cannon–Bard theories of emotion.

7. Explain the two-factor theory emotion.

8. Discuss the cognitive-mediational theory of emotions and describe how it differs from other theories of emotions.

9. Explain how cultural display rules affect how emotions are expressed.

Key Terms and Concepts

Page references are keyed to the Hockenbury textbook, *Psychology*.

Emotion: A distinct psychological state that involves subjective experience, physical arousal, and a behavioral response. (page 344)

Mood: A mild emotional state that is more general and pervasive and tends to last for an extended period of time. (page 344)

Emotional intelligence: The capacity to understand and manage your own emotional experience and perceive and understand the emotions of others. (pages 344–345)

Basic emotions: Those emotions that are universal and biologically determined. Anger, happiness, sadness, and fear are typically defined as the basic emotions. (pages 346–347)

Mixed emotions: The experience of different emotional states simultaneously or in rapid succession. (page 346)

Polygraph or lie detector: A device that measures specific indicators of physiological arousal: usually heart rate, blood pressure, respiration, and skin response. The idea behind the workings of the lie detector is that people will react emotionally and therefore physically, when lying. (page 349)

Display rules: Social and cultural rules that regulate the expression of emotions. (pages 353–354)

James–Lange theory of emotions: The theory that emotions arise from the perception and interpretation of body changes. (pages 356–357)

Facial feedback hypothesis: The view that expressing a specific emotion, especially facially, causes the subjective experience of that emotion. (page 358)

Cannon–Bard theory of emotion: The theory that emotions arise from the simultaneous activation of the nervous system, which causes physical arousal, and the cortex, which causes the subjective experience of emotion. (pages 356–357)

Two-factor theory of emotion: The theory that emotion is a result of the interaction of physiological arousal and the cognitive label that we apply to explain the arousal. (page 358)

Cognitive-mediational theory of emotion: The theory that emotions result from the cognitive appraisal of a situation's effect on personal well-being. (pages 358–359)

Study Activities

These self-test questions are designed as a study exercise to aid you in understanding the most important terms and concepts in this lesson. To ensure that you have an accurate understanding of the key terms and concepts in this lesson, please check your answers with the Answer Key provided at the end of this lesson.

Multiple-Choice Questions

1. An emotion is a distinct psychological state that involves a subjective experience, a behavioral or expressive response, and

    a. facial expressions.

    b. physical arousal.

    c. classification of the feeling as positive or negative.

    d. an adaptive response.

2. Research findings suggest men and women do not differ in their experience of emotions, but they do differ in

    a. that women cry more easily than men.

    b. that men have less emotional driven physical arousal than women.

    c. that women feel more deeply than men.

    d. expression of emotions.

3. As seen in the video, according to most psychologists, the basic emotions are happiness, sadness, anger, and

    a. surprise.

    b. guilt.

    c. frustration.

    d. fear.

4. The theory that proposes that we don't tremble and run because we are afraid, but that we are afraid because we tremble and run is the

    a. two-factor theory of emotion.

    b. James–Lange theory of emotion.

    c. Cannon–Bard theory of emotion.

    d. emotional feedback theory of emotion.

5. According to the facial feedback hypothesis,

   a. expressing a specific emotion causes us to subjectively experience that emotion.

   b. expressing basic emotions is innate.

   c. facial expressions cause all emotional experiences.

   d. facial expressions are learned and culturally determined.

6. The notion that cognition plays an important role in what emotion we experience is the basis of the

   a. Cannon–Bard theory of emotion.

   b. James–Lange theory of emotion.

   c. interactive theory of emotion.

   d. two-factor theory of emotion.

7. The two components underlying happiness are

   a. life satisfaction and a good loving relationship.

   b. health and positive emotions.

   c. life satisfaction and positive emotions.

   d. personal attitude and circumstances.

8. The theory that emotions result from the cognitive appraisal of a situation's effect on one's personal well-being is called the

   a. cognitive-mediational theory of emotion.

   b. situation driven theory of emotion.

   c. two-factor theory of emotion.

   d. subjective-interaction theory of emotion.

9. Social and cultural rules that regulate the expression of emotions, particularly facial expressions, are called

   a. social-cultural influences.

   b. display rules.

   c. expression rules.

   d. emotional normative rules.

10. In the beginning of this video, psychologists identified newborns as showing evidence of what four emotions?

   a. fear, shyness, distress, and contentment

   b. interest, surprise, shyness, and anger

   c. interest, surprise, distress, and contentment

   d. contentment, anger, fear, and distress

11. According to the video, basic emotions are common to all human beings, regardless of their

    a. age.

    b. culture or ethnic group.

    c. upbringing.

    d. intelligence levels.

12. In the video, psychologist Joseph Campos explained that emotions are absolutely essential for

    a. living a satisfying life.

    b. learning how to cope with problems.

    c. bonding with other people.

    d. survival.

13. In the video, psychologist Peter Salovey explained that the James–Lange theory of emotions was based on the belief that

    a. physiological reactions precede emotional reactions.

    b. emotional reactions precede physiological reactions.

    c. emotions and the autonomic nervous system interact to create emotions.

    d. emotions do not always require any physiological event to occur.

14. In the video, the Schachter theory of emotions was introduced. The basic claim of this theory is that the same state of physiological arousal could elicit different emotions. This theory is sometimes called the two factor or

    a. multifactor theory of emotion.

    b. emotional application theory of emotion.

    c. jukebox theory of emotion.

    d. flight-or-fight theory of emotion.

15. In the video, research psychologist Paul Ekman expressed his view that

    a. "emotions create each of us."

    b. "the face is the best window we have for knowing what someone feels."

    c. "our body language is a reflection of our feelings."

    d. "emotions are not always what they appear to be."

16. In the video, research psychologist Paul Ekman described how he needed to travel to New Guinea to find people who have had no contact with the outside world and would not have

    a. learned about psychological theories.

    b. had any opportunity to learn their emotional expressions.

    c. had the need to hide any negative emotions.

    d. had any reason to avoid showing anger, fear, or happiness.

Short-Answer Questions

17. Define emotions and describe the function of emotions.

    _____

    _____

    _____

18. Identify the basic emotions.

    _____

    _____

    _____

19. Explain the physiological responses that accompany emotional arousal.

    _____

    _____

    _____

20. Discuss the effectiveness of polygraphs.

    _____

    _____

    _____

21. Discuss the facial feedback hypothesis.

    _____

    _____

    _____

22. Compare and contrast the James–Lange and the Cannon–Bard theories of emotion.

    _____

    _____

    _____

23. Explain the two-factor theory of emotion.

_____

_____

_____

24. Discuss the cognitive-mediational theory of emotions and describe how it differs from other theories of emotions.

_____

_____

_____

25. Explain what is meant by cultural display rules.

_____

_____

_____

Matching Exercises

Match the following terms and concepts with the correct definition.

emotion

display rules

polygraph

mixed emotions

emotional intelligence

facial feedback

interactive approach to emotions

Cannon–Bard theory of emotions

two-dimensional classification

26. _____ The hypothesis that states that expressing a specific emotion causes the subjective experience of that emotion.

27. _____ The theory that the conscious experience of emotion and the physiological arousal are triggered at the same time: neither causes the other.

28. _____ Refers to the capacity to understand and manage one's own emotions and understand other people's emotions.

29. _____ The experience of different emotional states simultaneously or in rapid succession.

30. _____ The view that emotions function as a dynamic system that includes cognitive appraisal, physiological arousal, and behavioral expression.

31. _____ Viewing emotions in terms of how pleasant or unpleasant they are, and how much or how little arousal they invoke.

32. _____ Because of its high error rate, many courts will not allow this to be used in evidence.

33. _____ Societal norms of appropriate behavior that differs between cultures.

34. _____ Closely tied to motivation and involving subjective experience, physical arousal, and a behavioral or expressive response.

Completion Exercises

Fill in each blank with the most appropriate term or terms from the list of answers provided.

basic emotions	cognitive-mediational theory of emotion	managing emotion
brain		moods
Cannon–Bard theory of emotions	display rule	physiological arousal
	expression of emotion	two-factor theory of emotion
cognitive appraisal	James–Lange theory of emotion	

35. In contrast to emotions, _____ involve a milder emotional state that is more general and pervasive, lasting for a few hours or days.

36. All other components of emotion, including physiological arousal, follow after a person's subjective appraisal of a situation or event is the basis of the _____.

37. According to some psychologists, _____ are universal, and they are biologically determined products of evolution.

38. Only limited aspects of the _____, that emotions arise from the perception and interpretation of body changes, have been supported by research evidence.

39. The _____ states that emotion is the result of the interaction of physiological arousal and the cognitive label that we apply to explain the arousal.

40. According to research, men and women do not differ in the experience of emotions, but they do differ in the _____.

41. A man not crying in public is an important _____ in many cultures.

42. According to the _____, when an emotion-arousing stimulus is perceived, information is relayed simultaneously to the cortex of the brain and to the sympathetic nervous system.

43. In the video, research psychologist Peter Salovey explained that early research on emotions typically focused on the autonomic nervous system. Modern research tends to emphasize the role of the _____ in creating emotions.

44. As seen in the video, the four basic components that interact to create emotion are physical arousal, _____, subjective experience, and the expression of that experience.

45. In the video, psychologist Linda Levine pointed out that a serious problem with the James–Lange theory of emotions was that _____ and the subjective feeling of an emotion happen simultaneously.

46. In the video, the four basic skills of emotional intelligence were discussed. These four skills are perceiving and expressing emotions, understanding emotions, using emotions, and _____.

Answer Key

Multiple-Choice Questions

1. b	5. a	9. b	13. a
2. d	6. d	10. c	14. c
3. d	7. c	11. b	15. b
4. b	8. a	12. d	16. b

Short-Answer Questions

Your answers should include the following:

17. Emotion can be defined as a distinct psychological state involving three distinct components: subjective experience, physical arousal, and a behavioral or expressive response. Emotions are directly related to motivation. We are motivated to avoid experiences that produce unpleasant emotions, and we are motivated to seek out experiences that produce positive emotions. (page 344)

18. While not all psychologists agree, it is generally accepted that the basic emotions are anger, happiness, sadness, and fear. (page 346)

19. The physiological responses that accompany emotions involve the activation of the sympathetic division of the autonomic nervous system, and include reactions such as increased heart rate, increase in respiration, perspiration, and muscle tension. (pages 347–351)

20. Polygraphs, or lie detectors, have repeatedly been shown to be very inaccurate. The main problem is that lying does not create the same physiological pattern in all people. Also, some people can lie without experiencing any physiological responses. (page 349)

21. According to the facial feedback hypothesis, expressing a specific emotion, especially facially, causes us to experience that emotion subjectively. (page 358)

22. The James–Lange theory states that emotions arise from the perception and interpretation of body changes. In contrast, the Cannon–Bard theory states that emotion is a two-pronged response, including both conscious experience and psychological arousal, and that these events happen simultaneously: neither causes the other. (pages 356–337)

23. The two-factor theory of emotion states the emotion is that result of the interaction of physiological arousal and the cognitive label we attach to explain the aroused state. (pages 358–359)

24. The cognitive-mediational theory of emotion emphasizes that the most important aspect of an emotional experience is our cognitive appraisal of the emotion-causing stimulus. Some critics of this theory suggest that

physiological responses happen too rapidly for cognitive appraisal to account for all the experiences of emotion. (pages 358–359)

25. Cultural display rules give us the societal norms for what is acceptable and what is not generally acceptable for emotional expression. (pages 353–355)

Matching Exercises

26. facial feedback

27. Cannon–Bard theory of emotion

28. emotional intelligence

29. mixed emotions

30. interactive approach to emotions

31. two-dimensional classification

32. polygraph

33. display rules

34. emotion

Completion Exercises

35. moods

36. cognitive-mediational theory of emotion

37. basic emotions

38. James–Lange theory of emotion

39. two-factor theory of emotion

40. expression of emotion

41. display rule

42. Cannon–Bard theory of emotion

43. brain

44. cognitive appraisal

45. physiological arousal

46. managing emotion

Study Matrix
Lesson 13
Emotions

Please Note: Use this matrix to guide your study and achieve the learning objectives of this lesson. It will also help you to view the video, which defines and demonstrates important concepts and objectives as they relate to everyday life and actual case studies.

Learning Objective	Textbook	Telecourse Student Guide
Define emotions and describe the function of emotions.	p. 344	Key Terms and Concepts; Study Activities 1, 17, 29, 34, 35, 44.
Identify the basic emotions.	p. 346	Key Terms and Concepts; Study Activities 3, 7, 11, 18, 28, 37.
Explain the physiological responses that accompany emotional arousal.	pp. 347–351	Key Terms and Concepts; Study Activities 10, 12, 19, 30, 43.
Discuss the effectiveness of polygraphs.	p. 349	Key Terms and Concepts; Study Activities 20, 32.
Discuss the facial feedback hypothesis.	p. 358	Key Terms and Concepts; Study Activities 5, 15, 21, 26.
Compare and contrast the James–Lange and the Cannon–Bard theories of emotion.	pp. 356–358	Key Terms and Concepts; Study Activities 4, 13, 22, 27, 38, 42, 45.
Explain the two-factor theory emotion.	pp. 358–359	Key Terms and Concepts; Study Activities 6, 14, 23, 31, 39.
Discuss the cognitive-mediational theory of emotions and describe how it differs from other theories of emotions.	pp. 358–360	Key Terms and Concepts; Study Activities 8, 24, 36, 46.
Explain how cultural display rules affect how emotions are expressed.	pp. 353–355	Key Terms and Concepts; Study Activities 2, 9, 16, 25, 33, 40, 41.

Use the Course Compass to orient yourself in the road that you are taking to explore branches and aspects of psychology. The branch and aspects that are covered in this lesson are highlighted in the compass.

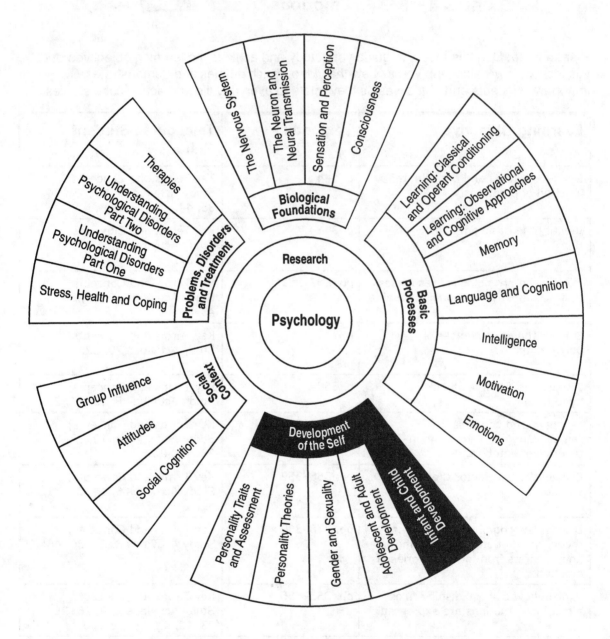

Please note: This compass does not represent the full range of topics comprising the field of psychology; it represents a map for this course only. Each of the five branches represented above has many aspects and subjects that are covered in the 26 lessons of this telecourse. You should remember that these branches and subjects all interrelate.

Lesson 14

Infant and Child Development

Questions to Consider

What is a developmental psychologist?

How are hereditary traits transmitted?

Are infants born with different abilities, or are all infants born with basically the same abilities?

How do children acquire language and learn to think?

How does a child's emotional attachment affect his or her development?

Is human development continuous, or does it occur in stages?

How different is a child's understanding of the world from that of an adult?

Lesson Assignments

Before viewing the video program

Read the Questions to Consider, Lesson Preview, and Learning Objectives for this lesson. Use this information to guide your reading, viewing, and thinking.

Read Chapter 9, "Lifespan Development," pages 367–388, in the textbook.

View the video program, "Infant and Child Development"

After viewing the video program

Review the vocabulary listed in the Key Terms and Concepts section. (Page references are keyed to the Hockenbury textbook, *Psychology*. Remember: there is a complete Glossary at the end of the textbook.)

Review the reading assignments for this lesson.

Complete the exercises found in the Study Activities section and check your answers with the Answer Key at the end of this lesson.

Use the Study Matrix found at the end of this lesson to review and assess your knowledge of each Learning Objective.

Lesson Preview

How important is heredity to human development? What happens to a child if his or her parents are neglectful, inconsistent, or insensitive? Why do some children grow up to become successful and well adjusted, and others develop severe emotional problems?

These are the kind of questions for which developmental psychologists try to find the answers.

Developmental psychology is the study of change. Developmental psychologists study how people change physically, mentally, and socially over the life span. They investigate when certain behaviors first appear and how they change with age. They explore how development in one area, for example hyperactivity, relates to behavior in other areas, for example, depression or aggression. Developmental psychologists attempt to discover universal stages of development as they look to identify the obstacles to healthy development.

In this video, we will explore infant and child development by looking into the lives of Kim, Chad, and their four children. In this video, psychologists will explain how they define infant temperament. The theories of a pioneer in the study of cognitive development, Swiss psychologist and philosopher Jean Piaget, are discussed in depth. Examples of the work of Piaget are used to help us understand child development. This video will also explore the important role attachment plays in the early development of children.

This lesson concludes with a discussion of some of the new discoveries that developmental psychologists are making about the understanding of human development. For example, Dr. Alison Gopnik, professor of psychology at the University of California, Berkeley, will explain that, contrary to what psychologists used to think, preschoolers and toddlers can demonstrate logical thought.

The more you can understand about how we develop, the better able you will be to appreciate the abilities and qualities that make each of us a unique human being.

Learning Objectives

When you have completed this lesson, you should be able to:

1. Define developmental psychology, and the interaction between heredity and environment.

2. Describe the relationship between chromosomes, DNA, and genes in creating a person's genetic makeup.

3. Identify and discuss the three phases of prenatal development.

4. Explain attachment theory, and discuss its importance in child development.

5. List the three broad categories that are used to define different infant temperaments.

6. Describe the difference between comprehension and production vocabulary.

7. List the four stages of Piaget's theory of cognitive development, and give an example of each stage.

8. Define Piaget's concepts of object permanence, symbolic thought, and egocentrism.

9. Compare and contrast the information-processing model of cognitive development to Piaget's theory of cognitive development.

Key Terms and Concepts

Page references are keyed to the Hockenbury textbook, *Psychology*.

Developmental psychology: The branch of psychology that studies how people change over the lifespan. (page 368)

Chromosome: A lone, threadlike structure composed of DNA; a person's "genetic blueprint." (pages 370–371)

Deoxyribonucleic acid (DNA): The chemical basis of heredity; carries all genetic instructions. (pages 370–371)

Gene: The basis unit of heredity that directs the development of particular characteristics; can be recessive or dominant. (pages 370–371)

Prenatal stage of development: The stage of development before birth that is divided into three stages: germinal, embryonic, and fetal periods. (page 372)

Germinal period: The first two weeks of prenatal development. (page 372)

Embryonic period: The second period of prenatal development, extending from the third week through the eighth week. (page 373)

Fetal period: The third and longest period of prenatal development, extending from the ninth week until birth. (page 373)

Teratogens: Harmful substances that can cause defects in an embryo or fetus. (page 373)

Temperament: Inborn predispositions to consistently behave and react in a certain way. (page 376)

Three categories of infant temperament: About two-thirds of infants fit into one of three broad temperamental patterns: easy, difficult, and slow-to-warm-up. The other one-third of infants are characterized as average because they do not fit neatly into one of these categories. (page 376)

Attachment: The emotional bond that forms between infant and his or her caregivers. (page 376)

Attachment theory: The theory supporting the notion that an infant's ability to thrive physically and psychologically depends in part on the quality of attachment. (pages 376–377)

Infant-directed speech: A type of speaking commonly used with infants that is characterized by very distinct pronunciation, a simplified vocabulary, and exaggerated intonation. Also called motherese. (page 378)

Comprehension vocabulary: The words that are understood by an infant or child. (page 381)

Production vocabulary: The words that an infant or child understands and can speak. (page 381)

Sensorimotor stage: In Piaget's theory, the first stage of cognitive development during which an infant explores the environment and acquires knowledge through sensing and manipulating objects. Age range: birth to age 2. (page 383)

Object permanence: The understanding that an object continues to exist even when it can no longer be seen. (page 383)

Preoperational stage: In Piaget's theory, the second stage of cognitive development characterized by increasing use of symbols and prelogical thought processes. Age range: age 2 to age 7. (page 383)

Symbolic thought: The ability to use words, images, and symbols to represent the world. (page 383)

Egocentrism: In Piaget's theory, the inability to take another person's perspective or point of view. (page 384)

Concrete operational stage: In Piaget's theory, the third stage of cognitive development characterized by the ability to think logically about concrete objects and situations. Age range: age 7 to adolescence. (page 385)

Formal operational stage: In Piaget's theory, the fourth stage of cognitive development characterized by the ability to think logically about abstract principles or hypothetical situations. Age range: adolescence to adulthood. (page 385)

Information-processing model: The model that views cognitive development as a process that is continuous over the lifespan. (page 387)

Study Activities

These self-test questions are designed as a study exercise to aid you in understanding the most important terms and concepts in this lesson. To ensure that you have an accurate understanding of the key terms and concepts in this lesson, please check your answers with the Answer Key provided at the end of this lesson.

Multiple-Choice Questions

1. The long, threadlike structure composed of DNA that contains a person's "genetic blueprint" is called a

   a. chromosome.

   b. gene.

   c. dominate gene.

   d teratogen.

2. The three phases of prenatal development are the germinal period, the embryonic period, and the

   a. organ genesis period.

   b. zygotic period.

   c. neonate period.

   d fetal period.

3. Although physically helpless, newborn infants are equipped with reflexes and sensory capabilities that enhance their

   a. motor functions.

   b. speed of maturation.

   c. chances for survival.

   d genetic endowments.

4. Infants come into the world with different temperaments. Two-thirds of all infants can be classified into one of three broad temperamental patterns:

   a. easy, average, and difficult.

   b. emotional, active, and passive.

   c. easy, difficult, and slow-to-warm-up.

   d moody, insecure, and easy-to-soothe.

5. Generally, when parents are consistently warm, responsive, and sensitive to their infant's needs, the infant develops

   a. lifelong attachments to strangers.

   b. secure attachment to his or her parents.

   c. parental bonding.

   d no need to fear strangers.

6. The words that an infant or child understands but cannot yet speak are referred to as the infant's

   a. production vocabulary.

   b. preoperational stage.

   c. symbolic thoughts.

   d comprehension vocabulary.

7. Jean Piaget's four stages of cognitive development are the sensorimotor stage, the preoperational stage, the concrete operational stage, and the

   a. postoperational stage.

   b. formal operational stage.

   c. operational behavioral stage.

   d adult operational stage.

8. In Piaget's theory, the inability to take another person's point of view is called

   a. egocentrism.

   b. irreversibility.

   c. behavioral centration.

   d me-first syndrome.

9. The information-processing model of cognitive development focuses on the development of

   a. language skills.

   b. comprehension skills.

   c. fundamental mental processes.

   d information gathering aspects of infants and children.

10. A major criticism of Piaget's theory of cognitive development is that it

   a. underestimated the impact of social and cultural influences.

   b. did not allow for differences between individual children.

   c. created hypotheses that could not be tested empirically.

   d. did not believe children took active roles in their own cognitive development.

11. In this video, you learned that developmental psychology is defined as the study of how people

    a. change mentally during their lifespan.

    b. adapt to mental, physical, and social change.

    c. change mentally, physically, and socially during their lifespan.

    d. go through changes and adapt to an ever-changing environment.

12. In the video, Connor and Ashley performed an experiment using liquid in two containers as a way of demonstrating the principle of

    a. symbolic thought.

    b. egocentrism.

    c. conservation.

    d. informal operations.

Short-Answer Questions

13. Define developmental psychology, and the interaction between heredity and environment.

14. Describe the relationship between chromosomes, DNA, and genes in creating a person's genetic makeup.

15. Identify and discuss the three phases of prenatal development.

16. Explain attachment theory, and discuss its importance in child development.

17. List the three broad categories that are used to define different infant temperaments.

_____

_____

_____

18. Describe the difference between comprehension and production vocabulary.

_____

_____

_____

19. List the four stages of Piaget's theory of cognitive development, and give an example of each stage.

_____

_____

_____

20. Define Piaget's concepts of object permanence, symbolic thought, and egocentrism.

_____

_____

_____

21. Compare and contrast the information-processing model of cognitive development to Piaget's theory of cognitive development.

_____

_____

_____

22. In the video, several examples of the difference between concrete operational stage of development and formal operational stage of development were used. Discuss the main differences between these two stages of cognitive development.

_____

_____

_____

Matching Exercises

Match the following terms and concepts with the correct definition.

DNA	germinal period	production vocabulary
symbolic thought	attachment	concrete operational stage
gene	formal operational stage	object permanence

23. _____ Beginning with adolescence, children in this stage have developed the ability to use and understand concepts such as mutual trust, loyalty, and empathy.

24. _____ Psychologists believe the quality of this is associated with a variety of long-term effects.

25. _____ Contains the chemical genetic code that directs the growth and development of many of each person's unique qualities.

26. _____ A new cognitive skill that children acquire by the end of the sensorimotor stage of development that appears to be related to the child's improved memory skills.

27. _____ During this time, the zygote undergoes rapid cell division and develops into a cluster of cells called the embryo.

28. _____ Occurring somewhere between age 2 and age 7, this is the hallmark of the preoperational stage of cognitive development.

29. _____ Psychologists use this to refer to words that infants can both understand and speak.

30. _____ The basic unit of heredity that directs the development of a particular characteristic.

31. _____ In Piaget's theory, the third stage of cognitive development that occurs between age 7 and the beginning of adolescence.

Completion Exercises

Fill in each blank with the most appropriate term or terms from the list of answers provided.

developmental psychology   preoperational stage

fetal period   sensorimotor stage

infant-directed speech   temperament

information-processing model   teratogens

32. The third month of pregnancy heralds the beginning of the _____, during which the fetus develops the ability to live outside the mother's body.

33. Alcohol, cocaine, and heroin are called _____, and can cause birth defects.

34. The _____ views cognitive development as a process of continuous change over the lifespan.

35. Virtually all psychologists agree that individual differences in _____ are the result of genetic and biological influences.

36. _____ is the study of how people change physically, mentally, and socially over the lifespan.

37. People in every culture use _____, or motherese, as a primary method to communicate with infants.

38. By the end of the _____, infants acquire a new cognitive understanding, called object permanence.

39. The _____ lasts from approximately age two to age seven, and is characterized by the child's ability to engage in symbolic thought.

Answer Key

Multiple-Choice Questions

1. a	4. c	7. b	10. a
2. d	5. b	8. a	11. c
3. c	6. d	9. c	12. c

Short-Answer Questions

Your answers should include the following:

13. Developmental psychology is the study of how people change physically, mentally, and socially over the lifespan. Most psychologists believe that we are born with a specific genetic potential that we inherit from our biological parents, and our environment influences and shapes how that potential is expressed. (pages 368–369)

14. The gene is the basic unit of heredity that directs the development of specific characteristics. Each gene is a unit of DNA—the chemical genetic code that is the basis of heredity. Each chromosome contains thousands of genes, and each gene is a unit of DNA instructions. (pages 370–371)

15. The prenatal stage has three distinct phases. The first stage is the germinal period, during which the zygote undergoes rapid cell division. The second stage is the embryonic period, during which the organs and major systems of the body form. The third stage is the fetal period in which the fetus grows and develops to a point where it can live outside the mother's body. (pages 372–373)

16. Attachment theory promotes the view that an infant's ability to thrive physically and psychologically depends in part on the quality of attachment. The quality of attachment during infancy is associated with a variety of long-term effects. (pages 376–377)

17. Approximately two-thirds of infants can be categorized as easy, difficult, or slow-to-warm up. The remaining one-third of infants can be characterized as average because they do not fit neatly into any of the three categories. (page 376)

18. Comprehension vocabulary refers to words an infant or child can understand, but not speak. Production vocabulary refers to words an infant or child can both understand and speak. (page 381)

19. The first stage of cognitive development is the sensorimotor stage in which the infant explores the environment and acquires knowledge through sensing and the manipulation of objects. The second stage is the preoperational stage, which is characterized by the increasing use of symbols and prelogical thought processes. The third stage is the concrete operational stage, which is

characterized by the ability to think logically about concrete objects and situations. The fourth stage is the formal operational stage, which is characterized by the ability to think logically about abstract principles. (pages 382–385)

20. Object permanence is the understanding that an object continues to exist even when it cannot longer be seen. Symbolic thought is the ability to use words, images, and symbols to represent the world. Egocentrism refers to the inability to take another person's perspective or point of view. (page 383)

21. Piaget believed each child goes through four distinct stages of cognitive development, each within a defined age range. The information-processing model of cognitive development focuses on the development of fundamental mental processes, and viewed cognitive development as a continuous change that occurs over the lifespan. (pages 385–387)

22. The main difference between the concrete operational stage and formal operational stage of development has to do with the ability to think logically. During the concrete operational stage, a child's ability to think logically is limited to tangible objects or events, while the formal operational stage is characterized by the ability to think logically when dealing with abstract concepts or hypothetical situations. (page 385)

Matching Exercises

23. formal operational stage

24. attachment

25. DNA

26. object permanence

27. germinal period

28. symbolic thought

29. production vocabulary

30. gene

31. concrete operational stage

Completion Exercises

32. fetal period

33. teratogens

34. information-processing model

35. temperament

36. developmental psychology

37. infant-directed speech

38. sensorimotor stage

39. preoperational stage

Study Matrix

Lesson 14

Infant and Child Development

Please Note: Use this matrix to guide your study and achieve the learning objectives of this lesson. It will also help you to view the video, which defines and demonstrates important concepts and objectives as they relate to everyday life and actual case studies.

Learning Objective	Textbook	Telecourse Student Guide
Define developmental psychology, and the interaction between heredity and environment.	pp. 368–369	Key Terms and Concepts; Study Activities 11, 13, 36.
Describe the relationship between chromosomes, DNA, and genes in creating a person's genetic makeup.	pp. 370–372	Key Terms and Concepts; Study Activities 1, 14, 25, 30.
Identify and discuss the three phases of prenatal development.	pp. 372–373	Key Terms and Concepts; Study Activities 2, 3, 15, 27, 32, 37.
Explain attachment theory, and discuss its importance in child development.	pp. 376–378	Key Terms and Concepts; Study Activities 5, 16, 24.
List the three broad categories that are used to define different infant temperaments.	p. 376	Key Terms and Concepts; Study Activities 4, 17, 35.
Describe the difference between comprehension and production vocabulary.	p. 381	Key Terms and Concepts; Study Activities 6, 12, 18, 29, 37.
List the four stages of Piaget's theory of cognitive development, and give an example of each stage.	pp. 383–385	Key Terms and Concepts; Study Activities 7, 19, 22, 23, 31.
Define Piaget's concepts of object permanence, symbolic thought, and egocentrism.	pp. 383–384	Key Terms and Concepts; Study Activities 8, 20, 36, 28, 38, 39.
Compare and contrast the information-processing model of cognitive development to Piaget's theory of cognitive development.	pp. 383–385, 387	Key Terms and Concepts; Study Activities 9, 10, 21, 34.

Use the Course Compass to orient yourself in the road that you are taking to explore branches and aspects of psychology. The branch and aspects that are covered in this lesson are highlighted in the compass.

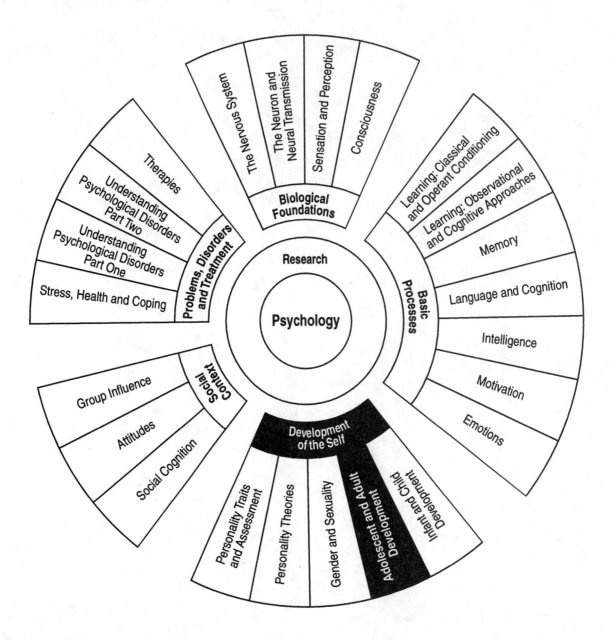

Please note: This compass does not represent the full range of topics comprising the field of psychology; it represents a map for this course only. Each of the five branches represented above has many aspects and subjects that are covered in the 26 lessons of this telecourse. You should remember that these branches and subjects all interrelate.

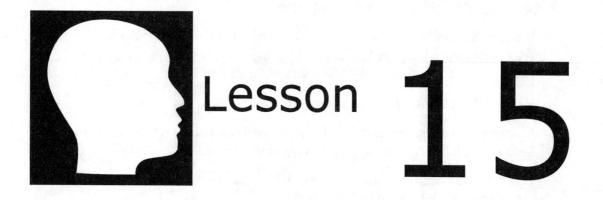

Lesson 15

Adolescent and Adult Development

Questions to Consider

Why is the stage of adolescence so difficult for so many people?

How does adult thinking differ from adolescence thinking?

What are the two key themes that dominate adult development?

How do we develop moral reasoning?

What is the best strategy for dealing with aging?

Is prejudice against elderly people commonplace?

Lesson Assignments

Before viewing the video program

Read the Questions to Consider, Lesson Preview, and Learning Objectives for this lesson. Use this information to guide your reading, viewing, and thinking.

Read Chapter 9, "Lifespan Development," pages 389–405, in the textbook.

View the video program, "Adolescent and Adult Development"

After viewing the video program

Review the vocabulary listed in the Key Terms and Concepts section. (Page references are keyed to the Hockenbury textbook, *Psychology*. Remember: there is a complete Glossary at the end of the textbook.)

Review the reading assignments for this lesson.

Complete the exercises found in the Study Activities section and check your answers with the Answer Key at the end of this lesson.

Use the Study Matrix found at the end of this lesson to review and assess your knowledge of each Learning Objective.

Lesson Preview

At the beginning of the twentieth century, only three percent of the population in the United States was over 65 years of age. By the year 2030, nearly a quarter of the American population will be over 65 years of age. We are quickly nearing the time when there will be more older aged people in the United States than young people. With such dramatic changes coming our way, psychologists are increasing their efforts to understand more about the nature of aging.

This lesson continues our study of human development. In this lesson, we will trace the human development from adolescence through adulthood to the end of life. We begin by entering the confusing and often-turbulent world of the adolescent.

Adolescence is that awkward period of life when a person is neither a child nor an adult. As you will see in this video, at the beginning of adolescence, young people are still dependent on their parents. By the end of adolescence, friends and romantic partners have come to play central roles in their lives. During adolescence, many important decisions are made—decisions that often dramatically affect the rest of their lives.

Compared to other stages of development, adult development is much less predictable—primarily because adult development is mostly a function of individual choices. Adulthood is not marked by specific age-related stages—but is more an unfolding of our biological predispositions and our past experiences, individually tailored by what each of us through the decisions we have made.

In this video, we will explore adolescence and adult development by watching a young boxer named Felipe Jamiez as trains for an upcoming match. In this video, you will learn about the significance of peer relationships during adolescence. You will also learn about how people develop their sense of morals. You will be introduced to and learn about the pros and cons of Kohlberg's theory of moral development. In this video, we will also explore aging and late adulthood. You will hear from 79-year-old boxer Willie Hardeman and from psychologists who will discuss some of the common myths associated with old age.

By understanding more about human development and the changes that each of us will experience as we transition through life, you will learn more about how you can live your life to its fullest.

Learning Objectives

When you have completed this lesson, you should be able to:

1. Define adolescence, and discuss the role peer relationships play in adolescence.

2. Discuss identity as it relates to Erikson's psychosocial theory of human development.

3. Identify and explain Kohlberg's three levels of moral reasoning.

4. Discuss some of the possible problems with Kohlberg's theory of moral development.

5. List the last three stages of Erikson's theory of human development, and identify the psychosocial conflicts associated with each stage.

6. Discuss the activity theory of aging, and identify the factors that can influence cognitive changes in late adulthood.

7. Describe the differences between authoritarian, permissive, and authoritative parenting styles.

8. List Kübler-Ross's five stages of dying.

Key Terms and Concepts

Page references are keyed to the Hockenbury textbook, *Psychology*.

Adolescence: The transitional stage between late childhood and the beginning of adulthood, during which sexual maturity is reached. (page 389)

Young adulthood: Twenties to mid-thirties; establish career and form bonds of love and friendship. (page 392)

Middle adulthood: Mid-thirties to approximately age sixty-five; concern for family and society. (page 392)

Late adulthood: Sixty-five and beyond; completion of the life cycle, hopefully with a sense of dignity and fulfillment. (page 392)

Identity: A person's definition or description of oneself including values, beliefs, and ideals that guide the individual's behavior. (pages 390–391)

Psychosocial development: A theory proposed by Erik Erikson that there are eight stages of life and that each stage is associated with a particular psychosocial conflict that can be resolved in a positive or negative direction. (pages 391–392)

Identity versus identity diffusion: In Erikson's theory, the key psychosocial conflict facing adolescence in which the adolescent must integrate various dimensions of personality into a coherent whole. (pages 390–392)

Intimacy versus isolation: In Erikson's theory, the key psychosocial conflict facing young adults in which they must establish lasting and meaningful relationships and develop a sense of connectedness and intimacy with others. (page 392)

Generativity versus stagnation: In Erikson's theory, the key psychosocial conflict facing middle age adults in which they must develop the ability to express unselfish concern for the welfare of the next generation. (page 392)

Ego integrity versus despair: In Erikson's theory, the key psychosocial conflict facing older adults in which they experience a strong sense of self-acceptance and meaningfulness based on life accomplishments. (page 392)

Moral reasoning: The aspect of cognitive development that has to do with how an individual reasons about moral decisions. (pages 392–394)

Levels of moral development: A theory proposed by Lawrence Kohlberg that moral reasoning can be categorized into three distinct levels of moral reasoning: preconventional, conventional, and postconventional. (pages 393–395)

Ethics of care and responsibility: A theory of moral development that emphasizes the importance of maintaining interpersonal relationships and responding to the needs of others, rather than focusing primarily on individual rights. (page 395)

Ethics of individual rights and justice: A theory of moral development that emphasizes the importance of each person's rights and the need for universal justice. (page 395)

Menopause: The natural cessation of menstruation and the end of reproductive capacity in women. (page 396)

Negative stereotype of aging: The tendency to associate "old age" with images of poor health, inactivity, social isolation, and mental and physical incompetence. (pages 399–401)

Activity theory of aging: The psychosocial theory that life satisfaction in late adulthood is highest when people maintain the level of activity they displayed earlier in life. (page 400)

Stages of dying: A theory by Elisabeth Kübler-Ross that states that dying consists of five distinct stages: denial, anger, bargaining, depression, and acceptance. (pages 402–403)

Authoritarian parenting style: Parenting style in which parents are demanding and unresponsive toward their children's needs or wishes. (pages 403–404)

Permissive parenting style: Parenting style in which parents are extremely tolerant and undemanding; parents may be indulgent-permissive or indifferent-permissive. (pages 403–404)

Authoritative parenting style: Parenting style in which parents set clear standards for their children, but are also responsive to their needs and wishes. (pages 403–404)

Study Activities

These self-test questions are designed as a study exercise to aid you in understanding the most important terms and concepts in this lesson. To ensure that you have an accurate understanding of the key terms and concepts in this lesson, please check your answers with the Answer Key provided at the end of this lesson.

Multiple-Choice Questions

1. Adolescence is characterized by

    a. the development of concrete thinking.

    b. negative relationships with parents.

    c. increases in the importance of friend and peer relationships.

    d. the development of generativity.

2. Psychologists refer to the values, beliefs, and ideas that guide a person's behavior as

    a. identity.

    b. ego.

    c. individualized value systems.

    d. social development.

3. According to Erikson's theory of development, the life stage that is characterized by the establishment of lasting and meaningful relationships is called

    a. adolescence.

    b. young adulthood.

    c. middle adulthood.

    d. attachment.

4. According to Erikson's theory of development, each of the eight stages of life is associated with

    a. a particular psychosocial conflict.

    b. a "letting go" of the previous stage.

    c. self-actualization.

    d. maturity.

5. According to Lawrence Kohlberg, moral reasoning unfolds in age-related distinct levels. These levels are

    a. moral reasoning, ethics, and universal moral principles.

    b. preconventional, conventional, and postconventional.

    c. premature morals, conventional morals, and universal morals.

    d. self-directed morals, other-directed morals, and social responsibility.

6. Kohlberg's theory of moral development is based on the

   a. ethics of good versus evil.

   b. ethics of care and responsibility.

   c. ethics of universal morality.

   d. ethics of individual rights and justice.

7. In his theory of psychosocial development, Erik Erikson described the two fundamental themes that dominate adulthood. These two themes are

   a. love and work.

   b. relationships and social responsibility.

   c. meaningful activities and ego development.

   d. marriage and family life.

8. During the later years of life, the majority of older adults

   a. are no longer self-sufficient or mentally competent.

   b. have poor health, become inactive, and suffer from periods of depression.

   c. enjoy relatively good health, mental alertness, and self-sufficiency.

   d. undergo cognitive changes, physical limitations, and become inactive.

9. After interviewing more than 200 terminally ill people, Elisabeth Kübler-Ross proposed that the dying go through stages. These stages are

   a. denial, anger, bargaining, depression, and acceptance.

   b. initial difficulty, anger, and passive resignation.

   c. dependence, attention to external matters, and turning inward.

   d. denial, anger, depression, and attention to others.

10. The parenting style in which parents set clear standards for their children but are also responsive to their children's needs and wishes is called

   a. authoritarian parenting.

   b. permissive parenting.

   c. authoritative parenting.

   d. responsibility and reciprocal care parenting.

11. In the video, psychologist Rita Dudley-Grant explained that one of the common ways adolescents define themselves is

   a. by learning to respect their parents.

   b. by turning away from their family of origin.

   c. by beginning to date others.

   d. by making a career choice.

12. In the video, you learned that Kohlberg's theory of moral development is based on a person's

    a. values and upbringing.

    b. ability to reason.

    c. life experiences.

    d. knowledge of right and wrong.

13. In the video, what were the two examples of the physical changes take place during middle to late adulthood?

    a. lost of memory and hearing

    b. poor sight and weight gain

    c. lack of interest in sexual activity and less stamina

    d. menopause and graying hair

Short-Answer Questions

14. Define adolescence, and discuss the role peer relationships play in adolescence.

_____

_____

_____

15. Discuss identity as it relates to Erikson's psychosocial theory of human development.

_____

_____

_____

16. List and explain Kohlberg's three levels of moral development.

_____

_____

_____

17. List the last three stages of Erikson's theory of human development and identify the psychosocial conflict associated with each stage.

_____

_____

_____

18. Discuss the activity theory of aging, and identify the factors that can influence cognitive changes in late adulthood.

_____

_____

_____

19. Describe the differences between authoritarian, permissive, and authoritative parenting styles.

_____

_____

_____

20. List Kübler-Ross's five stages of dying.

_____

_____

_____

21. In the video, you learned about the Kohlberg theory of moral development. Discuss the problem created by the fact that Kohlberg limited his research to males only.

_____

_____

_____

Matching Exercises

Match the following terms and concepts with the correct definition.

adolescence   menopause   intimacy vs. isolation
moral reasoning   activity theory of aging   ego integrity vs. despair
identity   permissive parenting   generativity vs. stagnation

22. _____ The notion that life satisfaction will be highest if you stay active and involved in life.

23. _____ A person's definition of the values, beliefs, and ideals that guide their behavior.

24. _____ Regardless of culture or ethnic background, during this period an increase in conflicts with one's parents is commonplace.

25. _____ Descriptive of parents who impose few rules or consistently fail to enforce rules.

26. _____ Negative resolution of this psychosocial conflict can result in excessive self-preoccupation and the inability to form any meaningful relationship.

27. _____ Negative resolution of this psychosocial conflict can result in self-indulgence and a lack of any meaningful accomplishments.

28. _____ Negative resolution of this psychosocial conflict can result in regret, dissatisfaction and disappointment about life.

29. _____ The cessation of menstruation and the end of reproductive capacity in women.

30. _____ An important cognitive development that typically occurs during adolescence.

Completion Exercises

Fill in each blank with the most appropriate term or terms from the list of answers provided.

authoritarian parenting style	independence
authoritative parenting style	levels of moral development
ethics of care and responsibility	negative stereotype of aging
ethics of individual rights and justice	psychosocial development
identity vs. identity diffusion	

31. A model of moral development that is based on the _____ suggested that women approach moral matters differently than men.

32. Parents who use an _____ believe that they should shape and control their child's behavior so that it corresponds to a set of standards.

33. The unfounded belief that all older adults are physically and mentally incompetent is a _____.

34. Erik Erikson's theory of _____ proposed that there are eight stages of life, each associated a particular conflict that can be resolved in a negative or positive direction.

35. According to Erikson, the key conflict facing adolescence is called _____, in which the adolescent must integrate various dimensions of his or her personality into a coherent whole.

36. According to psychologist Lawrence Kohlberg, there are three distinct _____: preconventional, conventional, and postconventional.

37. Psychologists have found a broad range of beneficial benefits associated with the _____, regardless of socioeconomic or ethnic background.

38. Kohlberg's model of moral development is based on the _____, which is a more common perspective for men.

39. In the video, psychologist Rita Dudley-Grant explained that adults raising adolescents face the difficult task of trying to support their children's _____ while still needing to protect them from some types of life experiences.

Answer Key

Multiple-Choice Questions

1. c	5. b	8. c	11. b
2. a	6. d	9. a	12. b
3. b	7. a	10. c	13. d
4. a			

Short-Answer Questions

Your answers should include the following:

14. Adolescence is the transitional stage between late childhood and the beginning of adulthood. Although parents remain influential throughout adolescence, peer relationships become increasingly important. (page 389)

15. A person's identity is the description they give themselves, which includes the values, beliefs and ideals that guide their behavior. The task of achieving an integrated identity is one important aspect of Erikson's theory of psychosocial development. (pages 390–391)

16. According to Kohlberg, moral reasoning can be divided into three levels, preconventional, conventional, and postconventional. Preconventional moral reasoning is moral reasoning that is guided by external consequences. Conventional moral reasoning is guided by conformity to social roles and rules. Postconventional moral reasoning is guided by internalized principles that protect the rights of all members of society. (pages 392–393)

17. The last three stages of human development according to Erickson are young adulthood, middle adulthood, and late adulthood. The psychosocial conflicts are intimacy vs. isolation, generativity vs. stagnation, and ego integrity vs. despair, respectively. (page 392)

18. The activity theory of aging is the psychosocial theory that life satisfaction in late adulthood is highest when people maintain the level of activity they displayed earlier in life. Research has found that it is possible to minimize declines in mental abilities in old age by staying active and engaged in a wide variety of mental activities. (page 400)

19. Authoritarian parenting style refers to parenting in which parents are demanding and unresponsive toward their child's needs or wishes. Passive parenting style is parenting in which parents are not demanding. Authoritative parenting style is parenting in which parents set standards, but are also responsive to their child's needs and wishes. (pages 403–404)

20. According to Elisabeth Kübler-Ross, the five stages of dying are denial, anger, bargaining, depression, and acceptance. (pages 402–403)

21. A major problem with Kohlberg's theory of moral development is that he researched mostly males, and his questions often put females in a subordinate role. His conclusions may not reflect the moral reasoning of both males and females. (pages 394–395)

Matching Exercises

22. activity theory of aging

23. identity

24. adolescence

25. permissive parenting

26. intimacy vs. isolation

27. generativity vs. stagnation

28. ego integrity vs. despair

29. menopause

30. moral reasoning

Completion Exercises

31. ethics of care and responsibility

32. authoritarian parenting style

33. negative stereotype of aging

34. psychosocial development

35. identity versus identity diffusion

36. levels of moral development

37. authoritative parenting style

38. ethics of individual rights and justice

39. independence

Study Matrix

Lesson 15

Adolescent and Adult Development

Please Note: Use this matrix to guide your study and achieve the learning objectives of this lesson. It will also help you to view the video, which defines and demonstrates important concepts and objectives as they relate to everyday life and actual case studies.

Learning Objective	Textbook	Telecourse Student Guide
Define adolescence, and discuss the role peer relationships play in adolescence.	pp. 389–390	Key Terms and Concepts; Study Activities 1, 14, 24.
Discuss identity as it relates to Erikson's psychosocial theory of human development.	pp. 390–392	Key Terms and Concepts; Study Activities 2, 15, 23.
Identify and explain Kohlberg's three levels of moral reasoning.	pp. 392–394	Key Terms and Concepts; Study Activities 5, 12, 16, 30, 36.
Discuss some of the possible problems with Kohlberg's theory of moral development.	pp. 394–395	Key Terms and Concepts; Study Activities 6, 21, 31, 38.
List the last three stages of Erikson's theory of human development, and identify the psychosocial conflicts associated with each stage.	pp. 392, 396–401	Key Terms and Concepts; Study Activities 3, 4, 7, 11, 17, 26, 27, 28, 34, 35.
Discuss the activity theory of aging, and identify the factors that can influence cognitive changes in late adulthood.	p. 400	Key Terms and Concepts; Study Activities 8, 11, 13, 18, 22, 29, 33.
Describe the differences between authoritarian, permissive, and authoritative parenting styles.	pp. 403–404	Key Terms and Concepts; Study Activities 10, 19, 25, 32, 37, 39.
List Kübler-Ross's five stages of dying.	p. 402	Key Terms and Concepts; Study Activities 9, 20.

Use the Course Compass to orient yourself in the road that you are taking to explore branches and aspects of psychology. The branch and aspects that are covered in this lesson are highlighted in the compass.

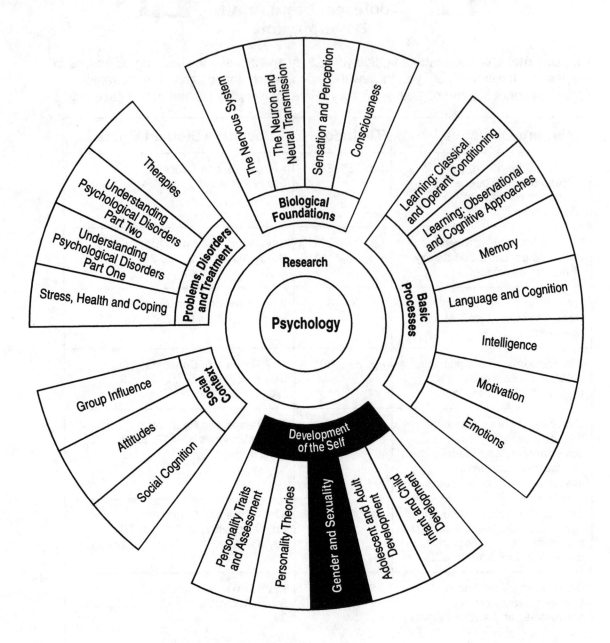

Please note: This compass does not represent the full range of topics comprising the field of psychology; it represents a map for this course only. Each of the five branches represented above has many aspects and subjects that are covered in the 26 lessons of this telecourse. You should remember that these branches and subjects all interrelate.

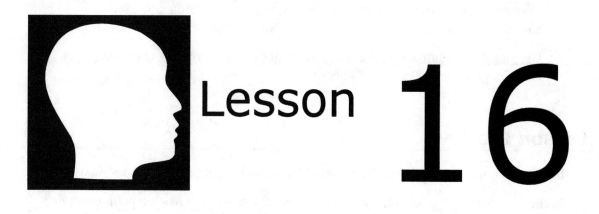

Lesson 16

Gender and Sexuality

Questions to Consider

What is the difference between gender and sex?

How are gender roles and gender identity acquired?

When does sexual behavior in humans first appear?

What causes individual differences in sex drive?

How do we develop our sexual orientation?

What are the most common sexual problems?

Lesson Assignments

Before viewing the video program

Read the Questions to Consider, Lesson Preview, and Learning Objectives for this lesson. Use this information to guide your reading, viewing, and thinking.

Read Chapter 10, "Gender and Sexuality," in the textbook.

View the video program, "Gender and Sexuality"

After viewing the video program

Review the vocabulary listed in the Key Terms and Concepts section. (Page references are keyed to the Hockenbury textbook, *Psychology*. Remember: there is a complete Glossary at the end of the textbook.)

Review the reading assignments for this lesson.

Complete the exercises found in the Study Activities section and check your answers with the Answer Key at the end of this lesson.

Use the Study Matrix found at the end of this lesson to review and assess your knowledge of each Learning Objective.

Lesson Preview

In this lesson, we will explore two fundamental issues, gender and human sexuality.

In the first part of this lesson, we will explore the question, "How do people acquire the traits, behaviors, attitudes, preferences, and interest that the culture consider appropriate for that gender?" In other words, what make a male, a male, and a female, a female? How does our culture and society influence this very personal aspect of our lives?

We will also explore human sexuality. All human beings are sexual beings. And, the fact that we are all sexual beings sometimes seems to cause various conflicts. Sex is a cloudy area where self-esteem, societal demands, individual differences, others' expectations, and the values we were raised with often collide.

While gender identity and sexual orientation are often linked to each other, in this lesson you will learn that gender identity and sexual orientation are separate entities and can be completely independent of one another. We will discuss how your gender roles are shaped by culture and how both sexual orientation and gender identity contribute to personal identity.

In this video, you will be introduced to two people who have chosen occupations that are not typical for their gender. You will discover what obstacles and opportunities lie in wait for those courageous people who violate gender stereotypes. As you will learn in this video, gender identification begins at birth and has a tremendous effect on us throughout our lives.

Professor Mark Stevens and Professor Judith Rosener will explain how our sense of personal identity is directly linked and, in many ways, controlled by our sense of being masculine or feminine. You will be introduced to the two major theories of gender development: social learning theory and gender schema theory. Additionally in this video, you will learn about what differences really exists between the sexes.

From childhood to old age, gender identity and sexuality play an important role throughout our lives. Understanding more about gender identity gender roles, and your own sexuality will provide you with an increased understanding of your role, and the role of others, in your society.

Learning Objectives

When you have completed this lesson, you should be able to:

1. Distinguish between sex and gender.

2. Discuss the meaning of the concepts of gender role and gender identity.

3. Define gender-role stereotypes, and identify the personality characteristics that differ between men and women.

4. Explain social learning theory and gender schema theory as it relates to gender-role development.

5. Describe the four stages of the human sexual response.

6. Discuss the factors that may play a role in determining sexual orientation.

7. List the common sexually transmitted diseases, and discuss effective strategies to avoid contracting these diseases.

8. Define AIDS, and describe how a person can become infected with this virus.

9. Define sexual dysfunction, and describe the most common types of sexual dysfunction for men and women.

Key Terms and Concepts

Page references are keyed to the Hockenbury textbook, *Psychology*.

Sex: The biological category of male or female as defined by physical characteristics and the behavioral expression of the sexual urge. (page 411)

Gender: The cultural, social, and psychological meanings that are associated with masculinity or femininity. (page 411)

Gender roles: The behaviors, attitudes, and personality traits that are designated as either masculine or feminine in a given culture. (page 411)

Gender identity: A person's psychological sense of being male or female. (page 411)

Sexual orientation: The direction of a person's emotional and erotic attraction. (page 411)

Gender-role stereotypes: The beliefs and expectations people hold about the typical characteristics, preferences, and behavior of men and women. (page 412)

Social learning theory: The theory that social roles, including gender roles, are acquired through the basic processes of learning, including reinforcement, punishment, and modeling. (page 420)

Schema: An organized cluster of information about a particular topic. (page 421)

Gender schema theory: The theory that gender-role development is influenced by the formation of schemas of masculinity and femininity. (pages 420–421)

Stages of human sexual response: According to Masters and Johnson, human sexual response can be described as a cycle with four stages: stage 1 excitement; stage 2 plateau; stage 3 orgasm; and stage 4 resolution. (pages 423–424)

Puberty: The stage of adolescence in which an individual reaches sexual maturity and becomes capable of sexual reproduction. (pages 432–433)

Primary sexual characteristics: Sexual organs that are directly involved in reproduction. (pages 432–433)

Secondary sexual characteristics: Sexual characteristics that develop during puberty and are not directly involved in reproduction, but differentiate between the sexes. (pages 432–433)

Sexual dysfunction: A consistent disturbance in sexual desire, arousal, or orgasm that causes psychological distress and interpersonal difficulties. (pages 439–440)

Male erectile disorder: A common male sexual dysfunction characterized by a recurring inability to achieve or maintain an erect penis. (page 440)

Premature ejaculation: A common male sexual dysfunction characterized by orgasm occurring before it is desired, often immediately or shortly after sexual stimulation or penetration. (page 440)

Female orgasmic disorder: A common female sexual dysfunction characterized by consistent delays in achieving orgasm or inability to achieve orgasm. (page 440)

Hypoactive sexual desire disorder: A sexual dysfunction characterized by little or no sexual desire. (page 440)

Vaginismus: A female sexual dysfunction characterized by persistent, involuntary contractions or spasms of the vaginal muscles, which result in uncomfortable or painful intercourse. (page 440)

Gender identity disorder: A persistent discomfort about one's assigned gender along with the desire to be a member of the opposite sex. (pages 441–442)

Sexually transmitted diseases (STDs): Any of several infectious diseases that are transmitted primarily through sexual contact. (page 442)

AIDS (acquired immune deficiency syndrome): A disease caused by contacting bodily fluids containing the human immunodeficiency virus (HIV), which attacks and weakens the immune system. (pages 442–444)

Study Activities

These self-test questions are designed as a study exercise to aid you in understanding the most important terms and concepts in this lesson. To ensure that you have an accurate understanding of the key terms and concepts in this lesson, please check your answers with the Answer Key provided at the end of this lesson.

Multiple-Choice Questions

1. The word "sex" is often used to describe sexual behavior, however the word also refers to

   a. biologically determined physical characteristics.

   b. attitudes and emotions.

   c. the direction of a person's erotic attraction.

   d. culturally designated traits.

2. Gender identity refers to

   a. behaviors, attitudes, and traits a culture designates as masculine or feminine.

   b. the direction of a person's erotic attraction.

   c. a person's psychological sense of being male or female.

   d. the biological category of male or female.

3. The direction of a person's emotional and erotic attraction toward members of the opposite sex, the same sex, or both sexes is called

   a. gender identity.

   b. sexual identity.

   c. sexual orientation.

   d. sex roles.

4. Gender-role stereotypes are the beliefs people hold about the typical characteristics, preferences, and behaviors of men and women. In general, the characteristics of males tend to be viewed as

   a. the same as females in most cultures.

   b. stronger and more active than those associated with females.

   c. less preferred by most cultures.

   d. more preferred by most cultures.

5. Psychologists who have scientifically investigated sex differences have found that

   a. females cannot have masculine traits, but males can have feminine traits.

   b. sex differences cannot be scientifically proven.

   c. in terms of emotional expression and personality characteristics, there are fundamental differences.

   d. for most cognitive abilities, there are no significant differences.

6. The theory that gender-role development is influenced by the formation of mental representation of masculinity and femininity is called

   a. gender schema theory.

   b. social learning theory.

   c. culture development theory.

   d. gender-role coding.

7. According to sexual researchers William Masters and Virginia Johnson, the human sexual response is a four-stage cycle. These stages are

   a. excitement, anticipation, orgasm, and relaxation.

   b. biological arousal, preparation, release, and relaxation.

   c. excitement, biological preparedness, orgasm, and resolution.

   d. excitement, plateau, orgasm, and resolution.

8. In terms of physical and sexual maturity, females

   a. and males are about the same.

   b. are typically about two years ahead of males.

   c. mature earlier sexually but later physically.

   d. experience menarche and males puberty.

9. AIDS is caused by the HIV virus, which is transmitted

   a. only by unprotected sex.

   b. by any physical contact with an infected person.

   c. through the exchange of infected bodily fluids.

   d. by sex with intravenous drug users.

10. For women, the most common sexual problems are low sexual desire and arousal problems. For men, the most common sexual problems are

    a. lack of availability of partners.

    b. premature ejaculation and male orgasmic disorder.

    c. problems with maintaining erections and premature ejaculation.

    d. hyperactive sexual desires.

11. In the video, the concept of gender stereotype was introduced by using the examples of

    a. male and female pilots.

    b. a male first grade teacher and a female pilot.

    c. a male pilot and a female first grade teacher.

    d. how sex discrimination creates social problems.

12. According to the video, gender-role stereotypes are prevalent in

    a. only some cultures.

    b. all collectivistic cultures.

    c. no individualistic culture.

    d. every culture.

13. In the video, Professor Mark Stevens explained that our sense of identity as male or female is one of the greatest influences on how we

    a. define ourselves.

    b. behave in public situations.

    c. select our sexual orientation.

    d. choose our occupations.

14. In the video, two major theories of how we develop our gender identification were introduced. These were the gender schema theory and the

    a. gender development theory.

    b. social learning theory.

    c. stereotype collection theory.

    d. cognitive-behavioral theory.

15. In the video, you learned that in many aspects of behavior, men and women are

    a. very different.

    b. very similar.

    c. different depending on their upbringing.

    d. exactly the same in every way.

16. In the video, Captain Paul Kirch explained that in his experience

    a. women pilots are often superior to male pilots.

    b. women pilots are treated differently than male pilots.

    c. there is no difference between male and female pilots.

    d. male pilots generally find decision making easier than do female pilots.

17. In the video, Professor Judy Rosener discussed a study conducted at Stanford University where boy babies were placed in pink blankets and girl babies were placed in blue blankets. The result of this experiment suggested that

    a. all babies are always treated the same.

    b. gender identification problem can develop early in life.

    c. babies are treated differently depending on their perceived sex.

    d. early childhood experience affects sexual orientation.

Short-Answer Questions

18. Distinguish between sex and gender.

    _____

    _____

    _____

19. Discuss the meaning of the concepts of gender role and gender identity.

    _____

    _____

    _____

20. Define gender-role stereotypes, and identify the personality characteristics that differ between men and women.

    _____

    _____

    _____

21. Explain social learning theory and gender schema theory as it relates to gender-role development.

    _____

    _____

    _____

22. Describe the four stages of the human sexual response.

    _____

    _____

    _____

23. Discuss the factors that may play a role in determining sexual orientation.

    _____

    _____

    _____

24. List the common sexually transmitted diseases, and discuss effective strategies to avoid contracting these diseases.

_____

_____

_____

25. Define AIDS, and describe how a person can become infected with this virus.

_____

_____

_____

26. Define sexual dysfunction, and describe the most common types of sexual dysfunction for men and women.

_____

_____

_____

Matching Exercises

Match the following terms and concepts with the correct definition.

social learning theory	vaginismus
puberty	gender identity disorder
male erectile disorder	gender
gender roles	female orgasmic disorder
schema	

27. _____ A sexual dysfunction characterized by consistent delays in achieving orgasm or the inability to achieve orgasm.

28. _____ The cultural, social, and psychological meanings that are associated with masculinity or femininity.

29. _____ Formally called transsexualism, when this occurs in children it is marked by an intense preoccupation with the play activities of the opposite sex.

30. _____ Generally, well-nourished and healthy children begin this stage earlier than children who have experienced serious health problems or inadequate nutrition.

31. _____ The behaviors, attitudes, and personality traits that are designated as either masculine or feminine in a given culture.

32. _____ The notion that social roles, including gender-roles, are acquired through modeling and the use of punishments and reinforcement.

33. _____ Formally called impotence, this is one of the most common sexual problems for men.

34. _____ Refers to the active process children and adults use to organize information about a particular topic, other people or appropriate behavior.

35. _____ Characterized by persistent, involuntary contractions, which result in uncomfortable or painful intercourse.

Completion Exercises

Fill in each blank with the most appropriate term or terms from the list of answers provided.

assertive	sexual dysfunction
gender identification	sexual orientation
gender-role stereotypes	spatial skills
premature ejaculation	stages of human sexual response
primary sexual characteristics	verbal fluency
sex	

36. The incidence of _____ among adults is surprisingly high, with more than thirty percent of men and women suffering from some type of sexual problem.

37. The beliefs people have about the typical characteristics and behaviors of each sex are referred to as _____.

38. Excitement, plateau, orgasm, and resolution are the four _____, according to Masters and Johnson.

39. Often confused with gender, _____ refers to both physical characteristics and behavioral expressions.

40. A man may experience considerable stress over episodes of _____, in which he reaches sexual climax too soon.

41. _____ refers to whether a person is sexually aroused by members of the same sex, the opposite sex, or both sexes.

42. Puberty involves the development of the _____, which are the sex organs that are directly involved in reproduction.

43. According to the video, _____ starts when we are toddlers and continues throughout childhood and adulthood.

44. In the video, you were shown a chart that depicted that males outscore women in some tests involving _____.

45. In the video, you were shown a chart that depicted that women consistently score much higher than men in the areas of _____.

46. In the video, you learned that research has proven that women do tend to be more nurturant than men, and men tend to be more _____ than women.

Answer Key

Multiple-Choice Questions

1. a	6. a	10. c	14. b
2. c	7. d	11. b	15. b
3. c	8. b	12. d	16. c
4. b	9. c	13. a	17. c
5. d			

Short-Answer Questions

Your answers should include the following:

18. Sex refers to the biological category of male or female and the behavioral manifestation of the sexual urge. Gender refers to the cultural and social meanings that are associated with maleness or femaleness. (page 411)

19. Gender roles consist of the behaviors, attitudes, and personality traits that a given culture designates as either masculine or feminine. Gender identity, on the other hand, refers to a person's psychological sense of being male or female. (page 411)

20. Gender-role stereotypes are the beliefs and expectations people hold about the characteristics and behaviors of each sex. While there are no significant average differences between men and women for most personality characteristics, women are consistently more nurturing than men, and men are consistently more assertive than women. (pages 412–414)

21. Social learning theory contends that gender roles are learned through reinforcement, punishment, and modeling. In contrast to the passive role played by children in social learning theory, gender schema theory contends that children actively develop mental categories for masculinity and femininity. (pages 420–421)

22. Stage one: excitement, characterized by initial physical and psychological arousal. Stage two: plateau, characterized by further increase in physical arousal, including penis erection and vaginal lubrication. Stage three: orgasm, the shortest stage of the sex cycle. Stage four: resolution, characterized by refractory period wherein body arousal subsides. (pages 423–424)

23. There is no clear scientific evidence on sexual orientation. There are some biological factors correlated with homosexual orientation, but this does not indicate causality. Research has dismissed the notion that homosexuality is caused by some childhood abnormality. However, there is clear evidence of a relation between pattern of childhood sex-typed behavior and later sexual orientation. (pages 427–429)

24. Common sexually transmitted diseases include gonorrhea, syphilis, chlamydia, lice, herpes, and AIDS. The most effective strategy is abstinence. Health experts recommend carefully selecting sexual partners and using condoms and spermicides. (pages 442–444)

25. AIDS (acquired immune deficiency syndrome) is a disease caused by the exchange of bodily fluids (semen, blood, or blood products) containing the human immunodeficiency virus (HIV), which attacks and weakens the immune system. (pages 442–444)

26. Sexual dysfunctions are consistent disturbances in sexual desire, arousal, or orgasm that cause psychological distress. For women, the most common sexual problems are low sexual desire and arousal problems. For men, the most common sexual problems are premature ejaculation and problems achieving and maintaining an erection. (pages 439–440)

Matching Exercises

27. female orgasmic disorder

28. gender

29. gender identity disorder

30. puberty

31. gender roles

32. social learning theory

33. male erectile disorder

34. schema

35. vaginismus

Completion Exercises

36. sexual dysfunction

37. gender-role stereotypes

38. stages of human sexual response

39. sex

40. premature ejaculation

41. sexual orientation

42. primary sexual characteristics

43. gender identification

44. spatial skills

45. verbal fluency

46. assertive

Study Matrix

Lesson 16

Gender and Sexuality

Please Note: Use this matrix to guide your study and achieve the learning objectives of this lesson. It will also help you to view the video, which defines and demonstrates important concepts and objectives as they relate to everyday life and actual case studies.

Learning Objective	Textbook	Telecourse Student Guide
Distinguish between sex and gender.	p. 411	Key Terms and Concepts; Study Activities 1, 5, 18, 39.
Discuss the meaning of the terms gender role and gender identity.	p. 411	Key Terms and Concepts; Study Activities 13, 19, 28, 29, 43.
Define gender-role stereotypes, and identify the personality characteristics that differ between men and women.	pp. 412–417	Key Terms and Concepts; Study Activities 2, 4, 8, 11, 15, 16, 20, 37, 42, 44, 45, 46.
Explain social learning theory and gender schema theory as it relates to gender-role development.	pp. 418–421	Key Terms and Concepts; Study Activities 6, 12, 14, 17, 21, 30, 31, 32, 34.
Describe the four stages of the human sexual response.	pp. 423–424	Key Terms and Concepts; Study Activities 7, 22, 39.
Discuss the factors that may play a role in determining sexual orientation.	pp. 427–429	Key Terms and Concepts; Study Activities 3, 23, 41.
List the common sexually transmitted diseases, and discuss effective strategies to avoid contracting these diseases.	pp. 442–443	Key Terms and Concepts; Study Activity 24.
Define AIDS, and describe how a person can become infected with this virus.	pp. 442–444	Key Terms and Concepts; Study Activities 9, 25.
Define sexual dysfunction, and describe the most common types of sexual dysfunction for men and women.	pp. 439–441	Key Terms and Concepts; Study Activities 10, 26, 27, 33, 35, 36, 40.

Use the Course Compass to orient yourself in the road that you are taking to explore branches and aspects of psychology. The branch and aspects that are covered in this lesson are highlighted in the compass.

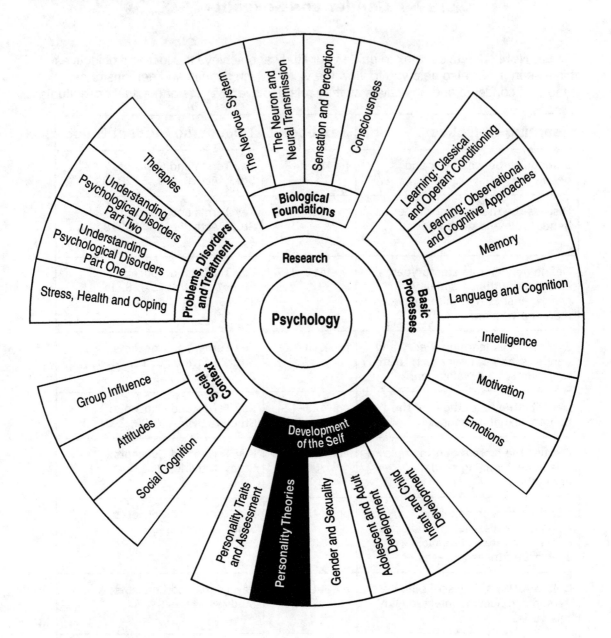

Please note: This compass does not represent the full range of topics comprising the field of psychology; it represents a map for this course only. Each of the five branches represented above has many aspects and subjects that are covered in the 26 lessons of this telecourse. You should remember that these branches and subjects all interrelate.

Lesson 17

Personality Theories

Questions to Consider

What is personality and how is it developed?

Are personalities inherited or the result of how we were raised?

Why do some people develop personalities that make it difficult for them to cope with life?

Do psychologists still believe in the ideas of Sigmund Freud?

What is the difference between humanism and social cognition?

Can we change our personality?

Lesson Assignments

Before viewing the video program

Read the Questions to Consider, Lesson Preview, and Learning Objectives for this lesson. Use this information to guide your reading, viewing, and thinking.

Read Chapter 11, "Personality," pages 451–477, in the textbook.

View the video program, "Personality Theories"

After viewing the video program

Review the vocabulary listed in the Key Terms and Concepts section. (Page references are keyed to the Hockenbury textbook, *Psychology*. Remember: there is a complete Glossary at the end of the textbook.)

Review the reading assignments for this lesson.

Complete the exercises found in the Study Activities section and check your answers with the Answer Key at the end of this lesson.

Use the Study Matrix found at the end of this lesson to review and assess your knowledge of each Learning Objective.

Lesson Preview

We all recognize that people are similar in many ways and are also different in many ways. Each of us is unique in our own way. When we learn about the differences or similarities between people, or when we are trying to describe ourselves, we are talking about personality. In this lesson, we will explore the intriguing question of personality—and the theories that explain personality.

This lesson will focus on three different theories of personality: the psychoanalytic perspective, the humanistic perspective, and the social cognitive perspective. In this video, we explore each of these theories by listening to experts analyze a famous personality, Nelson Mandela. As each of the experts describe Mandela's personality from their particular perspective, you will be learning about the strengths and weaknesses of each of the theories.

Because of the enormous effect Sigmund Freud, one of the twentieth century's most influential thinkers, has made on the field of psychology, we will explore his theory first.

After learning about the psychoanalytic perspective, we will listen to an expert analyze Nelson Mandela from a humanistic perspective. You will learn about the importance of self-concept and the role that unconditional positive regard plays in personality development.

Finally, in this video you will hear experts discuss Nelson Mandela's personality from the social cognitive perspective. You will learn about the social cognitive concepts of reciprocal determinism and self-efficacy.

By understanding how personality develops, the door to the possibility of making changes in your own personality is opened. You will discover that most psychologists agree that personality is not a rigid, fixed entity, but rather something that is ever-evolving—something you can take an active part in shaping.

Learning Objectives

When you have completed this lesson, you should be able to:

1. Define personality and personality theory.

2. Discuss Sigmund Freud's view of personality, and define the terms id, ego, and superego.

3. Explain the concept of ego defense mechanisms, and describe several common defense mechanisms.

4. Discuss criticisms of Freud's theory and the psychoanalytic perspective.

5. Describe the humanistic theory of personality, including the role of self-concept.

6. Define and discuss the humanistic concepts of conditional and unconditional positive regard.

7. Describe the social cognitive theory of personality, including the concepts of reciprocal determinism and self-efficacy.

Key Terms and Concepts

Page references are keyed to the Hockenbury textbook, *Psychology*.

Personality: An individual's unique and relatively consistent patterns of thinking, feeling, and behaving. (page 453)

Personality theory: A theory that attempts to describe and explain individual similarities and differences. (page 453)

Sigmund Freud: One of the most influential figures of the twentieth century; founder of psychoanalysis. Many of Freud's concepts became household words, including the concept of the unconscious, dream interpretation, and the role of sexual and aggressive instincts in forming personality. (pages 454–455)

Psychoanalysis: Sigmund Freud's theory of personality, which emphasizes unconscious determinants of behavior, sexual and aggressive instinctual drives, and the enduring effects of early childhood experiences on personality development. (page 454)

Unconscious: In Freud's theory, a term used to describe thoughts, feelings, wishes, and drives that are operating below the level of conscious awareness. (page 456)

Id: In Freud's theory, the completely unconscious, irrational component of personality that seeks immediate satisfaction. (pages 456–457)

Ego: In Freud's theory, the partly conscious, rational component of personality that regulates thoughts and behavior. (page 458)

Superego: In Freud's theory, the partly conscious, self-evaluative, moralistic component of personality that is formed through internalization of parental and societal norms. (page 458)

Ego defense mechanisms: In psychoanalytic theory, largely unconscious distortions of thought or perception that act to reduce anxiety. (pages 458–460)

Repression: The complete exclusion from consciousness of anxiety-provoking thoughts, feelings, and memories; the most basic defense mechanism. (pages 459–460)

Displacement: An ego defense mechanism that involves unconsciously shifting the target of an emotional urge to a substitute target that is less threatening or dangerous. (pages 459–460)

Sublimation: An ego defense mechanism that involves redirecting sexual urges toward socially acceptable, nonsexual activities. (pages 459–460)

Projection: An ego defense mechanism in which the attribution of one's unacceptable urges or qualities are attributed to something or someone else. (page 460)

Denial: An ego defense mechanism that involves the failure to recognize or acknowledge anxiety-provoking information. (page 460)

Rationalization: An ego defense mechanism that involves justifying one's actions or feelings. (page 460)

Humanism: The perspective that emphasizes the self and the fulfillment of a person's unique potential. (pages 469–470)

Actualizing tendency: According to humanists, the innate drive to maintain and enhance the human organism. (page 470)

Self-concept: The set of perceptions and beliefs that you hold about yourself. (pages 472–473)

Conditional positive regard: The sense that you will be loved and valued only if you behave in a way that is acceptable to others. (pages 472–473)

Unconditional positive regard: The sense that you will be loved and valued even if you don't conform to the expectations of others. (pages 472–473)

Social cognitive theory: The personality theory that emphasizes the importance of observational learning, conscious cognitive processes, self-efficacy, and situational influences. (page 474)

Self-efficacy: The beliefs that people have about their ability to meet the demands of a specific situation. (page 475)

Study Activities

These self-test questions are designed as a study exercise to aid you in understanding the most important terms and concepts in this lesson. To ensure that you have an accurate understanding of the key terms and concepts in this lesson, please check your answers with the Answer Key provided at the end of this lesson.

Multiple-Choice Questions

1. Personality can be defined as an individual's unique and relatively consistent patterns of

   a. thinking, feeling, and behaving.

   b. cognitive development.

   c. self-development.

   d. behaving.

2. Psychoanalytic personality theory emphasizes the importance of unconscious processes and the

   a. id, ego, and superego.

   b. role of sexual aggression.

   c. the influence of childhood experience.

   d. needs of the whole person.

3. Humanistic personality theory emphasizes the self and the

   a. need to demonstrate competence.

   b. fulfillment of a person's unique potential.

   c. basic drives that control behavior.

   d. influence of childhood experience.

4. Social cognitive theory of personality emphasizes learning and

   a. unconscious processes.

   b. conscious cognitive processes.

   c. behavior.

   d. the innate potential of each person.

5. Sigmund Freud was one of the twentieth century's most influential thinkers and the founder of

   a. the theory that emphasizes the description of personality differences.

   b. the field of psychology.

   c. psychoanalysis.

   d. the concept that behaviors are innate in origin.

6. In psychoanalytical thinking, the id is the irrational, illogical, and impulsive dimension of personality, and the ego is the

   a. moralistic, judgmental, perfectionist dimension of personality.

   b. rational, mediating dimension of personality.

   c. part of the personality that is conscious.

   d. word psychoanalysts use to describe personality.

7. Sublimation, denial, projection, and repression are examples of

   a. unconscious ego controls.

   b. ego defense mechanisms.

   c. behaviors that act to distort thought and perception.

   d. ways the id reduces anxiety.

8. According to humanistic theories of personality, all human drives are secondary to the

   a. need to achieve.

   b. need for unconditional positive regard.

   c. need to develop a self-concept.

   d. actualizing tendency.

9. The idea that a person's conscious thought processes in different situations strongly influence his or her behavior is an important characteristic of

   a. the social cognitive perspective on personality.

   b. humanistic theories of personality.

   c. self-development.

   d. fully functioning people.

10. Meeting challenges and mastering new skills are important elements in acquiring a strong sense of

    a. self-control.

    b. self-actualization.

    c. self-efficacy.

    d. ego.

11. In the video, psychologists introduced the concept of self-actualization. Self-actualization is a fundamental principle of

    a. psychoanalysis.

    b. behaviorism.

    c. humanism.

    d. social cognition.

12. In the video, you were introduced to the social cognitive perspective of personality. The social cognitive perspective emphasizes the social origins of thoughts and actions and also stresses the human capacity

    a. for destruction.

    b. to avoid being influenced by others.

    c. to need to achieve success.

    d. for self-regulation.

Short-Answer Questions

13. Define personality and personality theory.

_____

_____

_____

14. Discuss Sigmund Freud's view of personality and, define the terms id, ego, and superego.

_____

_____

_____

15. Define the concept of ego defense mechanisms, and list several of the major ego defense mechanisms.

_____

_____

_____

16. Discuss criticisms of Freud's theory and the psychoanalytic perspective.

_____

_____

_____

17. Describe the humanistic theory of personality, including the role of self-concept.

_____

_____

_____

18. Discuss the humanistic concepts of conditional and unconditional positive regard.

_____

_____

_____

19. Describe the social cognitive theory of personality, and define self-efficacy and reciprocal determinism.

_____

_____

_____

Matching Exercises

Match the following terms and concepts with the correct definition.

personality	repression	conditional regard
self-efficacy	reciprocal determinism	social cognitive theory
unconscious	humanism	rationalization

20. _____ The idea that the most important factor in personality is the individual's conscious, subjective perception of his or her self.

21. _____ Justifying one's actions or feelings with socially acceptable explanations, rather than consciously acknowledging one's true motives or desires.

22. _____ An individual's unique and relatively consistent patterns of thinking, feeling, and behaving.

23. _____ The beliefs that people have about their ability to meet the demands of a specific situation; feelings of self-confidence or self-doubt.

24. _____ A model that explains human functioning and personality as caused by the interaction of behavioral, cognitive, and social factors.

25. _____ The complete exclusion from consciousness of anxiety-producing thoughts, feelings, or impulses.

26. _____ Emphasizes the importance of observational learning, conscious cognitive processes, social experiences, and personal beliefs about one's competence.

27. _____ A term used to describe thoughts, feelings, wishes, and drives that are operating below the level of conscious awareness.

28. _____ In Carl Rogers' humanistic theory of personality, the sense that you will be valued and loved only if you behave in a way that is acceptable to others.

Completion Exercises

Fill in each blank with the most appropriate term or terms from the list of answers provided.

ego defense mechanisms

humanism

personality theory

projection

psychoanalysis

self-concept

self-efficacy

superego

unconditional positive regard

29. Sigmund Freud was the founder of _____, which stresses the influence of the unconscious, the importance of sexual and aggressive instincts, and early childhood experiences in forming personality.

30. Sometimes referred to as the "third force" in psychology, _____ promotes the view that personality is largely shaped by a person's own self-awareness and free will.

31. A _____ is an attempt to describe and explain how people are similar, how they are different, and why every individual is unique.

32. During a game, a person takes some unfair advantage and accuses other people of cheating. This behavior would be an example of _____ according to Freud's theory.

33. As the internal representation of parental and societal values, the _____ evaluates the acceptability of behavior and thoughts.

34. According to humanistic thought, people are motivated to act in accordance with their _____.

35. In Carl Rogers' theory, the sense that you will be valued and loved even if you do not conform to the expectations of others is called _____.

36. Largely unconscious, _____ distort perception and thoughts about self in an attempt to reduce anxiety.

37. In the video, you learned that _____ refers to the degree at which you are subjectively convinced of your own capabilities and effectiveness.

Answer Key

Multiple-Choice Questions

1. a	4. b	7. b	10. c
2. a	5. c	8. d	11. c
3. b	6. b	9. a	12. d

Short-Answer Questions

Your answers should include the following:

13. Personality is defined as an individual's unique and relatively consistent patterns of thinking, feeling, and behaving. Personality theory is an attempt to describe and explain how people are similar, how they are different, and why every individual is unique. (page 453)

14. Freud saw personality as the result of a constant interplay between conflicting psychological forces. The id is the completely unconscious, irrational component of personality that seeks immediate satisfaction. The ego is the partly conscious rational component of personality that regulates thoughts and behavior and is most in touch with the demands of the external world. The superego is the partly conscious self-evaluative, moralistic component of personality that is formed through the internalization of parental and societal rules. (pages 454–458)

15. Ego defense mechanisms are largely unconscious distortions of thought or perception that act to reduce anxiety. The major ego defense mechanisms include repression, displacement, sublimation, rationalization, projection, reaction formation, denial, undoing, and regression. (pages 458–460)

16. Three of the most important criticisms of Freud and the psychoanalytic perspective are inadequacy of evidence, lack of testability, and sexism. Freud's theory relies wholly on data derived from a small number of patients. Furthermore, it is impossible not to objectively assess Freud's data or test many of his concepts. Finally, many people feel that Freud's theories reflect a sexist view of women. (pages 467–469)

17. The humanistic perspective emphasizes free will, self-awareness, and psychological growth. It is fundamentally an optimistic view believing in the inherent goodness of people and the development of a healthy personality. Self-concept is defined as a set of perceptions and beliefs that a person has about him or her self. According to Carl Rogers, people are motivated to act in accordance with their self-concept. (pages 469–470)

18. Conditional positive regard refers to feeling valued and loved only if you behave in a certain way. Unconditional positive regard refers to feeling valued and loved regardless of how you behave. (pages 472–473)

19. The social cognitive theory of personality stresses conscious thought processes, self-regulation, and the importance of situational influences. Self-efficacy refers to the beliefs that people have about their ability to meet the demands of a specific situation. Reciprocal determinism is a model proposed by Albert Bandura that explains human functioning and personality as caused by the interaction of behavioral, cognitive, and social factors. (pages 474–475)

Matching Exercises

20. humanism

21. rationalization

22. personality

23. self-efficacy

24. reciprocal determinism

25. repression

26. social cognitive theory

27. unconscious

28. conditional regard

Completion Exercises

29. psychoanalysis

30. humanism

31. personality theory

32. projection

33. superego

34. self-concept

35. unconditional positive regard

36. ego defense mechanisms

37. self-efficacy

Study Matrix
Lesson 17
Personality Theories

Please Note: Use this matrix to guide your study and achieve the learning objectives of this lesson. It will also help you to view the video, which defines and demonstrates important concepts and objectives as they relate to everyday life and actual case studies.

Learning Objective	Textbook	Telecourse Student Guide
Define personality and personality theory.	p. 453	Key Terms and Concepts; Study Activities 1, 13, 22, 31.
Discuss Sigmund Freud's view of personality, define the term id, ego, and superego.	pp. 454–458	Key Terms and Concepts; Study Activities 2, 6, 27, 29, 32, 33.
Explain the concept of ego defense mechanisms, and describe several common defense mechanisms.	pp. 458–460	Key Terms and Concepts; Study Activities 7, 15, 21, 25, 36.
Discuss criticisms of Freud's theory and the psychoanalytic perspective.	pp. 467–469	Key Terms and Concepts; Study Activities 5, 16.
Describe the humanistic theory of personality, including the role of self-concept.	pp. 469–473	Key Terms and Concepts; Study Activities 3, 8, 10, 17.
Define and discuss the humanistic concepts of conditional and unconditional positive regard.	pp. 472–473	Key Terms and Concepts; Study Activities 11, 18, 20, 28, 30, 34, 35.
Describe the social cognitive theory of personality, including the concepts of reciprocal determinism and self-efficacy.	pp. 474–477	Key Terms and Concepts; Study Activities 4, 9, 12, 19, 23, 24, 16, 37.

Use the Course Compass to orient yourself in the road that you are taking to explore branches and aspects of psychology. The branch and aspects that are covered in this lesson are highlighted in the compass.

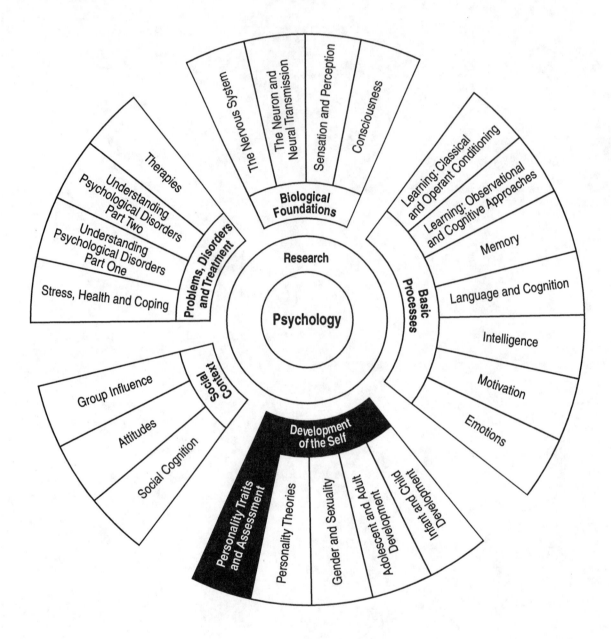

Please note: This compass does not represent the full range of topics comprising the field of psychology; it represents a map for this course only. Each of the five branches represented above has many aspects and subjects that are covered in the 26 lessons of this telecourse. You should remember that these branches and subjects all interrelate.

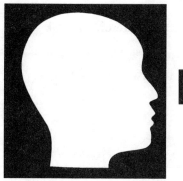

Lesson 18

Personality Traits and Assessment

Questions to Consider

What are personality traits?

How does our heredity influence personality?

What are the five broad dimensions of personality?

How do psychologists test or measure personality?

What can a personality test reveal about a person's life?

Do we have only one self-concept, or do we have many different self-concepts?

Lesson Assignments

Before viewing the video program

Read the Questions to Consider, Lesson Preview, and Learning Objectives for this lesson. Use this information to guide your reading, viewing, and thinking.

Read Chapter 11, "Personality," pages 478–492, in the textbook.

View the video program, "Personality Traits and Assessment"

After viewing the video program

Review the vocabulary listed in the Key Terms and Concepts section. (Page references are keyed to the Hockenbury textbook, *Psychology*. Remember: there is a complete Glossary at the end of the textbook.)

Review the reading assignments for this lesson.

Complete the exercises found in the Study Activities section and check your answers with the Answer Key at the end of this lesson.

Use the Study Matrix found at the end of this lesson to review and assess your knowledge of each Learning Objective.

Lesson Preview

How would you describe yourself? Are you quiet and shy, or are you talkative and outgoing? Are you friendly and cooperative, or are you serious and sad? When you describe your personality, you probably do so by listing the personal characteristics that best apply to you. These are your traits. In this lesson, we will explore how people differ, and the ways psychologists assess differences between people.

To understand personality, psychologists attempt to classify behavior into traits, and then identify ways to discover how certain traits might influence a person's life. In this lesson, we will explore the several widely accepted trait approaches to personality.

The trait approach to personality is very different from the theories you have learned about in other lessons. The theories you have studied so far have focused primarily on similarities among people. Although these theories do deal with individual differences, they do so indirectly. In contrast, the trait approach you will learn about in this video focuses primarily on describing individual differences.

In this video, we will enter the Career Counseling Center at UCLA. In the Career Counseling Center, you will meet Norm Stahl, who, after serving as a commissioned officer in the Marine Corps for 22 years, made a dramatic shift in occupations. As you will learn from Norm's story, finding the right occupation often entails getting to know yourself very well … and this might mean taking a number of different personality tests.

In this video, you will also learn about how psychologists use tests to assess personality differences. Every day, thousands of children and adults take some form of a psychological test. Virtually everyone who has attended school, gone to work, or joined the military has undergone psychological testing. In this video, we will explore psychological testing and assessment to learn more about its advantages and limitations.

This lesson concludes with a look at the impact psychological tests and assessments can have on an individual's personal and professional lives.

Learning Objectives

When you have completed this lesson, you should be able to:

1. Define traits and describe the difference between surface traits and source traits.

2. Contrast the 16 personality factors theory of personality to the three-dimensional model of personality.

3. Describe the five-factor model of personality.

4. Define behavioral genetics, and the influence of genetics and the environment of personality traits.

5. List the advantages and limitations of using the trait perspective to describe personality.

6. List the two basic types of psychological tests, and give an example of each.

7. Discuss the strengths and weaknesses of self-report inventories.

8. Explain the concept of possible selves, and discuss how it differs from the traditional view of self-concept.

Key Terms and Concepts

Page references are keyed to the Hockenbury textbook, *Psychology*.

Trait theory: A theory of personality that focuses on identifying, describing, and measuring individual differences. (pages 478 and 484)

Traits: A relatively stable, enduring predisposition to consistently behave in a certain way. (page 478)

Surface traits: Personality characteristics or attributes that can easily be inferred from observable behavior. (page 478)

Source traits: The most fundamental dimensions of personality; the broad, basic traits that are believed to be universal and few in number. (page 478)

16 personality factors: A concept by psychologist Raymond Cattell stating that personality could be described in terms of 16 basic personality factors, or traits. Each factor represents a dimension that ranges between two extremes. (page 479)

Three-dimensional model of personality: A theory of personality developed by British psychologist Hans Eysenck proposing that personality is the result of biological differences in people; includes three basic dimensions: introversion-extraversion, neuroticism, and psychoticism. (page 479)

Five-factor model of personality: A trait theory of personality that identifies five basic traits as the fundamental building blocks of personality. Those traits are extraversion, neuroticism, agreeableness, conscientiousness, and openness to experience. (pages 480–481)

Introversion: Refers to the way a person directs his or her energies. An introverted person directs energies toward the self; a person high in introversion tends to be quiet, solitary and reserved. (page 479)

Extraversion: Refers to the way a person directs his or her energies. An extraverted person directs energies outward toward the environment. A person high in extraversion tends to be outgoing, sociable, and enjoys new and stimulating environments. (page 479)

Behavioral genetics: An interdisciplinary field that studies the effects of genes and heredity on behavior. (page 482)

Psychological test: A test that assesses a person's abilities, interests, or personality. (page 486)

Projective test: A type of personality test that involves a person's interpretation of an ambiguous image. (page 486)

Rorschach Inkblot Test: A projective test using ambiguous inkblots developed by a Swiss psychiatrist named Rorschach. (page 486)

Thematic Apperception Test (TAT): A projective personality test that involves creating stories about ambiguous scenes. (page 488)

Self-report inventory: A type of psychological test in which a person's responses to standardized questions are compared to established norms. (pages 488–489)

Minnesota Multiphasic Personality Inventory (MMPI): A self-report inventory that assesses personality characteristics and psychological disorders. (pages 488–489)

Graphology: A pseudoscience that claims to assess personality and other personal attributes based on a person's handwriting and drawings. (page 487)

Possible selves: The notion that self-concept is multifaceted and includes images of the selves that you think you might become. (page 491)

Study Activities

These self-test questions are designed as a study exercise to aid you in understanding the most important terms and concepts in this lesson. To ensure that you have an accurate understanding of the key terms and concepts in this lesson, please check your answers with the Answer Key provided at the end of this lesson.

Multiple-Choice Questions

1. The trait approach to personality focuses

    a. on the similarities among people.

    b. behaviors you can observe.

    c. on describing individual differences.

    d. on only a limited number of characteristics.

2. Broad, basic traits that are hypothesized to be universal and few in number are called

    a. source traits.

    b. fundamental traits.

    c. surface traits.

    d. universal base traits.

3. According to psychologist Raymond Cattell, there are 16 basic personality factors, and each factor represents

    a. a characteristic that all people share.

    b. a dimension that ranges between two extremes.

    c. a trait that can be compared to a specific personality type.

    d. a common surface trait.

4. Hans Eysenck believed that personality included just three dimensions. These dimensions are introversion-extraversion, neuroticism-emotional stability, and

    a. submissive-dominant.

    b. relaxed-tense.

    c. conservative-liberal.

    d. psychoticism.

5. Most trait researchers now believe that there are five basic personality dimensions called the Big Five, or the five-factor model. These five factors are neuroticism, extraversion, openness to experience, agreeableness, and

    a. conscientiousness.

    b. introversion.

    c. psychoticism.

    d. emotional stability.

6. Behavioral genetics studies the effects of

    a. traits on personality.

    b. genes and heredity on behavior.

    c. behavior on genes.

    d. environmental factors.

7. The Minnesota Multiphasic Personality Inventory, the California Personality Inventory, and the Sixteen Personality Factor Questionnaire are all examples of

    a. tests used to measure mental competence.

    b. projective tests.

    c. tests that assess personal characteristics in normal populations.

    d. self-report inventories.

8. Graphology claims to assess personality attributes based on

    a. the location of planets and stars.

    b. graphs.

    c. handwriting.

    d. traits that can be observed.

9. Some psychologists believe that self-concept is not a singular mental self-image but a multifaceted system of related images. This is the basis of the notion of

    a. trait assessment.

    b. self-efficacy beliefs.

    c. personality change potential.

    d. possible selves.

10. Personality differences among siblings are primarily due to

    a. birth order.

    b. shared experiences.

    c. nonshared experiences.

    d. genetic differences.

11. In this video, you were introduced to Cindy Chernow, a career consultant who counsels and give lectures on how to find the right job for

    a. the most money.

    b. your personality and abilities.

    c. people who want to change careers.

    d. alumni of UCLA and other universities.

Short-Answer Questions

12. Define traits and describe the difference between surface traits and source traits.

_____

_____

_____

13. Contrast the 16 personality factors theory to the three-dimensional model of personality.

_____

_____

_____

14. Describe the five-factor model of personality.

_____

_____

_____

15. Define behavioral genetics, and the influence of genetics and the environment on personality traits.

_____

_____

_____

16. List the advantages and limitations of using the trait perspective to describe personality.

_____

_____

_____

17. List the two basic types of psychological tests, and give examples of each.

_____

_____

_____

18. Discuss the strengths and weaknesses of self-report inventories.

_____

_____

_____

19. Explain the concept of possible selves, and discuss how it differs from the traditional notion of self-concept.

_____

_____

_____

Matching Exercises

Match the following terms and concepts with the correct definition.

traits	behavioral genetics	self-report inventory
graphology	psychological test	possible selves
surface traits	five-factor model	Thematic Apperception Test

20. _____ Developed because many trait researchers believed that the 16 personality factors model was too complex.

21. _____ Characteristics possessed by people in different degrees and tend to be relatively stable and endure over time.

22. _____ Uses the method of comparing adopted individuals to their adoptive siblings, their adoptive parents, or their biological parents.

23. _____ Used to assess a person's abilities, interests, or personality.

24. _____ Can be easily inferred from observable behavior.

25. _____ Uses the method of creating stories about each of a series of ambiguous scenes.

26. _____ A scientifically invalid method of assessing personality using a person's handwriting and drawings.

27. _____ A type of psychological test in which a person's responses to standardized questions are compared to established norms.

28. _____ An aspect of self-concept that includes images that a person fears, hopes, or expects might occur.

Completion Exercises

Fill in each blank with the most appropriate term or terms from the list of answers provided.

astrology	Minnesota Multiphasic Personality Inventory
building blocks	projective tests
career counselor	Rorschach Inkblot Test
extraversion	16 personality factors
introversion	source traits

29. The _____ was developed by a Swiss psychiatrist and is used to help people identify unconscious conflicts and motives.

30. A person who is high on the dimension of _____ would likely be quiet, solitary, reserved, and tend not to seek out new experiences.

31. The most fundamental dimensions of personality, _____ are thought to be universal and relatively few in numbers.

32. Self-report inventories and _____ are the two most common methods psychologists use to assess personality traits.

33. Each represents a dimension that ranges between two extremes; the _____ are an attempt to identify all the essential source traits.

34. Surveys of college students have found that more than 30 percent believe in _____, even though there is absolutely no scientific basis for its claims.

35. The five-factor model of personality identifies five major source traits. They are neuroticism, _____, openness to experience, agreeableness, and conscientiousness.

36. The most widely used self-report inventory is the _____, which is used to assess both normal and disturbed populations.

37. In this video, you meet Norm Stahl, who became a _____ after serving as a commissioned officer in the Marine Corps for 22 years.

38. In the video, you learned that the five-factor model of personality describes what are essentially the key _____ of personality.

Answer Key

Multiple-Choice Questions

1. c	4. d	7. b	10. c
2. a	5. a	8. c	11. b
3. b	6. b	9. d	

Short-Answer Questions

Your answers should include the following:

12. A trait is a relatively stable, enduring predisposition to consistently behave in a certain way. Surface traits are personality characteristics that can easily be inferred by observation, such as being cheerful. Source traits are the broad, basic traits that tend to be universal and relatively few in numbers. (page 478)

13. Raymond Cattell believed that personality could be described in terms of 16 basic personality traits or factors. The three-dimensional theory reduced the 16 factors to only three dimensions. Under the three-dimensional theory, personality types can be understood as they relate to the three dimensions: introversion-extraversion, neuroticism-emotional stability, and psychoticism. (pages 479–480)

14. The five-factor model of personality was created because many psychologists thought sixteen traits were too many and three did not cover every aspect of personality. According to the five-factor model, also called the Big Five, these five dimensions represent the structural organization of personality traits. (pages 481–482)

15. Behavioral genetics is an interdisciplinary field that studies the effects of genes and heredity on behavior. Research indicates that environmental factors are at least equal to the influence of genetics on the development of personality traits. (page 482)

16. One criticism of the trait perspective is that it does not explain personality, only labels it. Another criticism is that trait theorists don't attempt to explain why or how individual differences develop, nor do they address concepts such as motivation, unconscious mental processes or how beliefs can affect personality. A major advantage of the trait perspective is that it provides several methods that are helpful in defining what differences exist between individuals. (page 484)

17. The two types of psychological tests are self-report inventory and projective tests. Examples of self-report inventories are the Minnesota Multiphasic Personality Inventory, California Personality Inventory, and the Sixteen Personality Factor Questionnaire. Examples of projective tests are the Rorschach Inkblot Test and the Thematic Apperception Test. (pages 486–489)

18. Two important strengths of self-report inventories are standardization and their use of established norms. Weaknesses of self-report inventories are that a test-taker can fake an answer, people may inadvertently answer incorrectly, and people may not always accurately judge their own behavior. (pages 488–490)

19. The concept of possible selves stems from the notion that some psychologists have that the self-concept is not one singular mental image, but a multifaceted system of related images. Possible selves is an aspect of self-concept that includes images of the selves that a person hopes, fears, or expects to become in the future. (pages 490–492)

Matching Exercises

20. five-factor model

21. traits

22. behavioral genetics

23. psychological tests

24. surface traits

25. Thematic Apperception Test

26. graphology

27. self-report inventory

28. possible selves

Completion Exercises

29. Rorschach Inkblot Test

30. introversion

31. source traits

32. projective tests

33. 16 personality factors

34. astrology

35. extraversion

36. Minnesota Multiphasic Personality Inventory

37. career counselor

38. building blocks

Study Matrix

Lesson 18

Personality Traits and Assessment

Please Note: Use this matrix to guide your study and achieve the learning objectives of this lesson. It will also help you to view the video, which defines and demonstrates important concepts and objectives as they relate to everyday life and actual case studies.

Learning Objective	Textbook	Telecourse Student Guide
Define traits and describe the difference between surface traits and source traits.	p. 478	Key Terms and Concepts; Study Activities 1, 2, 12, 21, 24, 31.
Contrast the 16 personality factors theory of personality to the three-dimensional model of personality.	pp. 479–480	Key Terms and Concepts; Study Activities 3, 4, 13, 30, 33.
Describe the five-factor model of personality.	pp. 481–482	Key Terms and Concepts; Study Activities 5, 14, 20, 35, 38.
Define behavioral genetics, and the influence of genetics and the environment of personality traits.	p. 482	Key Terms and Concepts; Study Activities 6, 10, 15, 22.
List the advantages and limitations of using the trait perspective to describe personality.	p. 484	Study Activity 16.
List the two basic types of psychological tests, and give an example of each.	pp. 486, 488	Key Terms and Concepts; Study Activities 7, 17, 23, 25, 29, 31, 36.
Discuss the strengths and weaknesses of self-report inventories.	pp. 488–490	Key Terms and Concepts; Study Activities 11, 18, 27, 32, 36.
Explain the concept of possible selves, and discuss how it differs from the traditional view of self-concept.	pp. 490–492	Key Terms and Concepts; Study Activities 9, 19, 29, 37.

Use the Course Compass to orient yourself in the road that you are taking to explore branches and aspects of psychology. The branch and aspects that are covered in this lesson are highlighted in the compass.

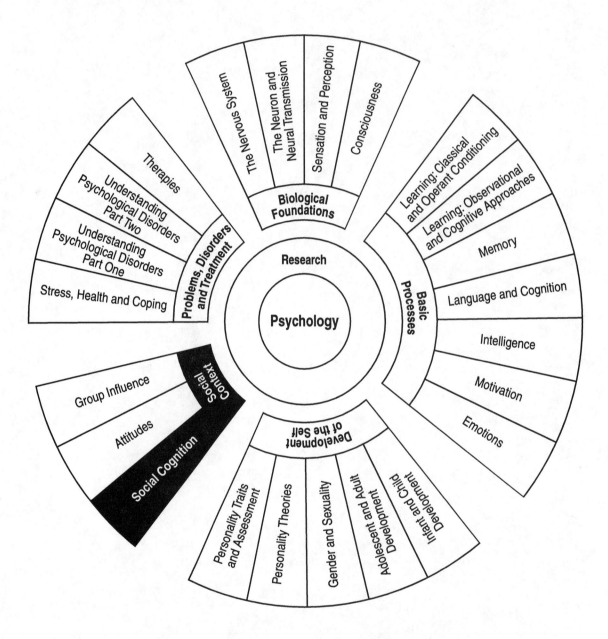

Please note: This compass does not represent the full range of topics comprising the field of psychology; it represents a map for this course only. Each of the five branches represented above has many aspects and subjects that are covered in the 26 lessons of this telecourse. You should remember that these branches and subjects all interrelate.

Lesson 19

Social Cognition

Questions to Consider

What is social psychology?

In what ways do other people affect how we think, feel, and behave?

What mental processes do we use to form perceptions of other people?

Is it true that most people believe that attractive people are more intelligent and more capable than less attractive people?

Why do people often blame the victim when something bad happens?

What role does the media play in influencing how people view themselves and others?

Lesson Assignments

Before viewing the video program

Read the Questions to Consider, Lesson Preview, and Learning Objectives for this lesson. Use this information to guide your reading, viewing, and thinking.

Read Chapter 12, "Social Psychology," pages 497–506, in the textbook.

View the video program, "Social Cognition"

After viewing the video program

Review the vocabulary listed in the Key Terms and Concepts section. (Page references are keyed to the Hockenbury textbook, *Psychology*. Remember: there is a complete Glossary at the end of the textbook.)

Review the reading assignments for this lesson.

Complete the exercises found in the Study Activities section and check your answers with the Answer Key at the end of this lesson.

Use the Study Matrix found at the end of this lesson to review and assess your knowledge of each Learning Objective.

Lesson Preview

It would be much easier to study and understand human behavior if people lived alone, isolated from the constant influences that surround each of us. But, of course, people do not live alone. We are all part of a society. In order to study and understand human behavior, we must also study how people influence, and are influenced by, other people.

In the next three lessons, we will be looking into a specialized area of psychology called social psychology. Social psychology is the branch of psychology that studies how people think, feel, and behave in social situations.

In this first lesson, we explore the mental processes people use to help make sense out of the world around them. This process, called social cognition, comes into play whenever a person comes in contact or interacts with another person. How you view others, how you explain events—and, ultimately, how you view yourself is all part of social cognition. You will learn the fundamental attribution error, a concept that explains why we often fail to understand other people's actions and motives accurately.

In the video, we will follow Julie and James as they meet for the first time on a blind date. You will learn about the importance of first impressions, and how first impressions don't always tell the whole story. Expert psychologists explain the principles of person perception, social categorization, and implicit personality theory. This video also discusses the role physical attractiveness plays in person perception.

The video concludes with a discussion of attribution—the process of inferring the cause of someone's behavior. You will also hear Julie and James discuss their impressions of one another.

As you learn more about social cognition, person perception, and attribution theory, you will increase your ability to see people objectively, and avoid some of the common mistakes that people make when observing or interacting with other people.

Learning Objectives

When you have completed this lesson, you should be able to:

1. Define social psychology, social cognition, and social influence.

2. Identity and discuss the four principles of person perception.

3. Explain the advantages and disadvantages of social categorization and implicit personality theory.

4. Discuss the role that physical attractiveness plays in person perception.

5. Define attribution theory, and explain the self-serving bias.

6. Explain what is meant by "blaming the victim" and the "just-world hypothesis."

7. Explain the difference between the fundamental attribution error and the actor-observer discrepancy.

8. Explain the concept of social norms and give an example of a social norm.

9. Compare attributional biases in collectivistic cultures and attributional biases in individualistic cultures.

Key Terms and Concepts

Page references are keyed to the Hockenbury textbook, *Psychology*.

Social psychology: The branch of psychology that studies how people think, feel, and behave in social situations. (page 498)

Social cognition: The study of the mental processes people use to make sense of their social environment. (page 498)

Social influence: The study of the effects of situational factors and other people on an individual's behavior. (page 498)

Person perception: The mental processes we use to form judgments and draw conclusions about the characteristics and motives of others. (pages 498–500)

The four principles of person perception: (pages 499–500)

- Your reactions to others are determined by your perceptions of them, not by who or what they really are.

- Your goals determine the amount and kind of information you collect about others.

- You evaluate people partly in terms of how you expect them to act.

- Your self-perception influences how you perceive others.

Social norms: The "rules," or expectations, for appropriate behavior in a particular situation. (page 498)

Social categorization: The mental process of categorizing people into groups on the basis of their shared characteristics. (page 500)

Implicit personality theory: A network of assumptions or beliefs about the relationships among various types of people, traits, and behaviors. (page 500)

Physical attractiveness stereotype: Commonly associated with a variety of desirable traits while actually not correlated with intelligence, mental health, or self-esteem. (pages 501–502)

Attribution: The mental process of inferring the causes of your own and other people's behavior. (page 503)

Fundamental attribution error: The tendency to attribute the behavior of others to internal, personal characteristics, while ignoring or underestimating the effects of external, situational factors. (pages 503 and 505)

Blaming the victim: The tendency to blame an innocent victim of misfortune for having somehow caused the problem or for not having taken steps to avoid or prevent it. (pages 503 and 505)

Just-world hypothesis: The assumption that the world is fair and that therefore people get what they deserve and deserve what they get. (pages 503 and 505)

Actor-observer discrepancy: The tendency to attribute one's own behavior to external, situational causes, while attributing the behavior of others to internal, personal causes. (pages 504–505)

Self-serving bias: The tendency to attribute successful outcomes of one's own behavior to internal causes and unsuccessful outcomes to external, situational causes. (page 505)

Collectivism: The tendency to subjugate one's own needs or desires for the good of the community or collective. (page 504)

Individualism: The tendency to value one's own needs or desires over the demands of the community or collective. (page 504)

Collectivistic cultures: Cultures that emphasize the needs and goals of the individual over the needs and goals of the group. (page 504)

Individualistic cultures: Cultures that emphasize the needs and goals of the group over the needs and goals of the individual. (page 504)

Study Activities

These self-test questions are designed as a study exercise to aid you in understanding the most important terms and concepts in this lesson. To ensure that you have an accurate understanding of the key terms and concepts in this lesson, please check your answers with the Answer Key provided at the end of this lesson.

Multiple-Choice Questions

1. Social psychology is the scientific study of how individuals think, feel, and behave

    a. in groups.

    b. in different cultures.

    c. in social situations.

    d. when they have to judge others.

2. The conclusions you reach about other people are influenced by three key components, the characteristics of the individual you are attempting to size up, the situation in which the process occurs, and

    a. your own characteristics as a perceiver.

    b. the goals you have in mind.

    c. the emotions you are feelings at the time.

    d. how the other person reacts to other people.

3. In every situation, your behavior is governed by expectations for appropriate behavior. These "rules" are called

    a. social influence.

    b. situational behaviorism.

    c. social norms.

    d. social expectations.

4. Psychologists refer to the cognitive schemas we form about the traits and behaviors of different types of people as

    a. social categorization.

    b. explicit personality theory.

    c. implicit personality theory.

    d. social schema theory.

5. Some people have a strong need to believe that we get what we deserve and deserve what we get. Psychologists refer to this as the

   a. situational attribution belief.

   b. just-world hypothesis.

   c. fundamental blaming error.

   d. actor-observer discrepancy.

6. Researchers have found that while physical attractiveness is not correlated with intelligence, self-esteem, or mental health, attractive people do tend

   a. to need other people's approval more than unattractive people.

   b. to be less lonely, more popular, and less anxious in social situations.

   c. to be less aware of their looks than their plainer counterparts.

   d. to judge less attractive people as inferior.

7. The tendency to attribute success to one's own behavior and blame failures on external circumstances is called

   a. the fundamental attribution error.

   b. blaming the victim.

   c. the success-failure hypothesis.

   d. the self-serving bias.

8. The tendency to attribute one's own behavior to external, situational causes, while attributing the behavior of others to internal, personal causes is called the

   a. actor-observer discrepancy.

   b. self-serving discrepancy.

   c. social error phenomenon.

   d. external-internal excuse hypothesis.

9. Social categorization refers to the mental process of categorizing people into groups

   a. depending on physical attractiveness.

   b. on the basis of their different qualities.

   c. depending on their assumptions about the relationships among various types of people.

   d. on the basis of their shared characteristics.

10. Social cognition is the study of the mental processes people use

    a. when interacting with others.

    b. to discover the effects of situational factors on human behavior.

    c. to make sense out of their social environment.

    d. to control how they feel, think, and behave in social situations.

11. In the video, you learned about person perception by watching

    a. several people at a party.

    b. James and Julie go on a blind date.

    c. psychologists discuss the importance of being open-minded when meeting people.

    d. a person go on a job interview.

12. In the video, expert psychologists discussed the role physical attractiveness plays in person perception and that physical attractiveness is often associated with

    a. being self-centered or conceited.

    b. having money and status.

    c. many undesirable traits.

    d. many desirable traits.

13. In the video, psychologists explained that the process of inferring the cause of someone's behavior is called

    a. the behavioral cause hypothesis.

    b. attribution.

    c. stereotyping of others.

    d. the common explanatory theory.

Short-Answer Questions

14. Define social psychology, social cognition, and social influence.

    _____

    _____

    _____

15. Identify and discuss the four principles of person perception.

    _____

    _____

    _____

16. Explain the advantages and disadvantages of social categorization and implicit personality theory.

    _____

    _____

    _____

17. Discuss the role that physical attractiveness plays in person perception.

_____

_____

_____

18. Define attribution theory, and explain the self-serving bias.

_____

_____

_____

19. Explain what is meant by the "just-world hypothesis."

_____

_____

_____

20. Explain the difference between the fundamental attribution error and the actor-observer discrepancy.

_____

_____

_____

21. Explain the concept of social norms and give an example of a social norm.

_____

_____

_____

22. Compare how attributional biases in collectivistic cultures can differ from attributional biases in individualistic cultures.

_____

_____

_____

23. Discuss the example used in the video to explain the phenomenon known as "blaming the victim."

_____

_____

_____

Matching Exercises

Match the following terms and concepts with the correct definition.

social cognition   attribution   four principles of person perception

self-serving bias   blaming the victim

social psychology   social norms   fundamental attribution error

just-world hypothesis

24. _____ Blaming the poor for their dire straits or the sick for bringing on their illness are examples of this common explanatory pattern.

25. _____ Refers to how we form impressions of other people, how we interpret the meaning of other people's behavior, and how our behavior is affected by our attitudes.

26. _____ Used to explain the tendency some people have to credit themselves for their success and blame their failures on external circumstances.

27. _____ The branch of psychology that studies how people think, feel, and behave in social situations.

28. _____ Psychologists use this word to refer to explanations people make for their behavior and the behavior of others.

29. _____ Each component influences the conclusions you reach about other people.

30. _____ Common in individualistic cultures, the tendency to attribute the behavior of others to internal, personal characteristics, while underestimating the effects of external, situational factors.

31. _____ Governs behavior in social situations and is a contributory factor to how you perceive a person.

32. _____ The assumption that the world is fair and that therefore people get what they deserve and deserve what they get.

Completion Exercises

Fill in each blank with the most appropriate term or terms from the list of answers provided.

actor-observer discrepancy

collectivistic cultures

implicit personality theory

individualistic cultures

person perception

physical attractiveness

social categorization

social influence

33. The study of _____ includes such questions as why we conform to group norms, what compels us to obey an authority figure, and under what circumstances people will help a stranger.

34. An interesting exception to the fundamental attribution error is the _____, in which we tend to use external, situational factors to explain our own behavior.

35. While most people associate _____ with a wide range of desirable traits, researchers have found very little evidence to support these assumptions.

36. Common in _____, the fundamental attribution error is the tendency to ignore or underestimate the effects of external, situational factors and attribute the behavior of others to internal, personal characteristics.

37. An active and subjective process, _____ always occurs in some interpersonal context and follows some basic principles.

38. In many _____, there is the tendency to attribute success to situational factors while blaming failure on personal factors.

39. In the video, you learned that _____ occurs when you have a limited amount of time and limited information about a person.

40. In the video, expert psychologists explained that _____ is a network of assumptions or beliefs about the relationship among various types of people, traits, and behaviors.

Answer Key

Multiple-Choice Questions

1. c	5. b	8. a	11. b
2. a	6. b	9. d	12. d
3. c	7. d	10. c	13. b
4. c			

Short-Answer Questions

Your answers should include the following:

14. Social psychology is the branch of psychology that studies how people think, feel, and behave in social situations. Social cognition is the study of the mental processes people use to make sense out of their social situations. Social influence is the study of the effects of situational factors and other people on an individual's behavior. (page 498)

15. The four principles of person perception are (1) your reactions to others are determined by your perceptions of them, (2) your goals determine the amount and kind of information you collect about others, (3) you evaluate people partly in terms of how you expect them to act, and (4) your self-perception influences how you perceive others. (pages 499–500)

16. Social categorization and implicit personality theory both are used to help us mentally organize and remember information about others more efficiently and effectively. A disadvantage is that both processes can lead to inaccurate conclusions. (pages 500–501)

17. Physical attractiveness is associated with a wide range of desirable traits. However, researchers have found that actually very few personality differences exist between attractive people and less attractive people. (pages 501–502)

18. Attribution is the process of inferring the cause of someone's behavior, including your own. The self-serving bias is the tendency to attribute successful outcomes of one's own behavior to internal causes and unsuccessful outcomes to external, situational causes. (pages 503 and 505)

19. The just-world hypothesis is the belief some people have that the world is fair and, therefore, we get what we deserve and we deserve what we get. (page 503)

20. The fundamental attribution error refers to the spontaneous tendency to attribute the behavior of others to internal, personal characteristics, while downplaying or underestimating the effects of external, situational factors. The actor-observer discrepancy is an exception to the fundamental attribution error. The actor-observer discrepancy is the tendency to attribute one's own behavior to external, situational causes, while attributing the behavior of others to internal, personal causes. (pages 503–504)

21. Social norms are the "rules" for appropriate behavior in a particular social situation. There are many examples of social norms that we encounter each day. For example, it is a social norm to avoid eye contact with strangers in a public elevator. (pages 498–500)

22. In individualistic cultures, the tendency is to attribute the behavior of others to internal, personal characteristics, while ignoring or underestimating the effects of external, situational factors. In collectivistic cultures, there is an opposite attributional bias. In collectivistic cultures, the tendency is to attribute success to external, situational factors, while ignoring or underestimating the effects of internal, personal characteristics. (page 504)

23. Blaming the victim is a common explanatory pattern wherein a victim is thought to have caused his or her misfortune. (pages 503 and 505)

Matching Exercises

24. blaming the victim

25. social cognition

26. self-serving bias

27. social psychology

28. attribution

29. four principles of person perception

30. fundamental attribution error

31. social norms

32. just-world hypothesis

Completion Exercises

33. social influence

34. actor-observer discrepancy

35. physical attractiveness

36. individualism

37. person perception

38. collectivism

39. social categorization

40. implicit personality theory

Study Matrix
Lesson 19
Social Cognition

Please Note: Use this matrix to guide your study and achieve the learning objectives of this lesson. It will also help you to view the video, which defines and demonstrates important concepts and objectives as they relate to everyday life and actual case studies.

Learning Objective	Textbook	Telecourse Student Guide
Define social psychology, social cognition, and social influence.	p. 498	Key Terms and Concepts; Study Activities 1, 10, 14, 25, 27, 33.
Identity and discuss the four principles of person perception, including the concept of social norms.	pp. 498–500	Key Terms and Concepts; Study Activities 2, 3, 11, 15, 29, 37.
Explain the advantages and disadvantages of social categorization and implicit personality theory.	pp. 500–501	Key Terms and Concepts; Study Activities 4, 9, 16, 39, 40.
Discuss the role that physical attractiveness plays in person perception.	pp. 501–502	Key Terms and Concepts; Study Activities 6, 12, 17, 35.
Define attribution theory, and explain the self-serving basis.	p. 503	Key Terms and Concepts; Study Activities 7, 13, 18, 26, 28.
Explain what is meant by "blaming the victim" and the "just-world hypothesis."	p. 503	Key Terms and Concepts; Study Activities 5, 19, 23, 24, 32.
Explain the difference between the fundamental attribution error and the actor-observer discrepancy.	pp. 503–504	Key Terms and Concepts; Study Activities 8, 20, 30, 34.
Explain social norms and give an example of how social norms affect person perception.	pp. 498–500	Key Terms and Concepts; Study Activities 3, 21, 31.
Compare attributional biases in collectivistic cultures and attributional biases in individualistic cultures.	p. 504	Key Terms and Concepts; Study Activities 22, 36, 38.

Use the Course Compass to orient yourself in the road that you are taking to explore branches and aspects of psychology. The branch and aspects that are covered in this lesson are highlighted in the compass.

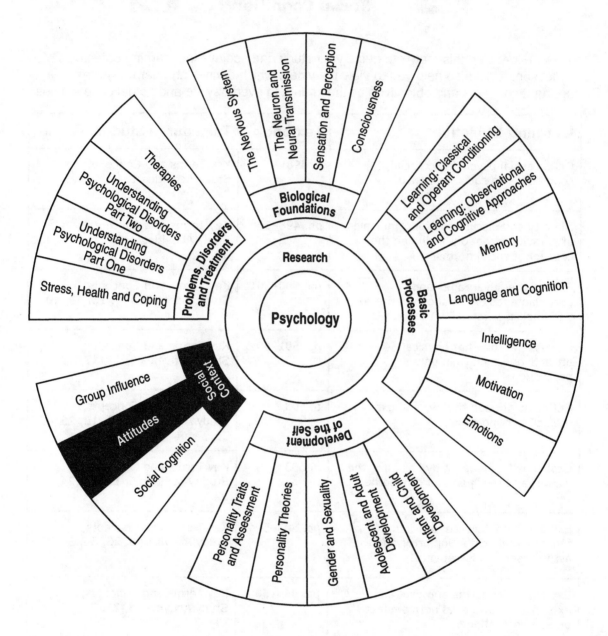

Please note: This compass does not represent the full range of topics comprising the field of psychology; it represents a map for this course only. Each of the five branches represented above has many aspects and subjects that are covered in the 26 lessons of this telecourse. You should remember that these branches and subjects all interrelate.

    Lesson 20/Attitudes

Lesson 20

Attitudes

Questions to Consider

How do people acquire their attitudes?

What is the best way to change an attitude?

Do attitudes control behavior or does behavior control attitude?

What is the difference between prejudice, discrimination, and racism?

What is the best method to get groups of people to avoid fighting and to cooperate with one another?

On a personal level, how can a person overcome a prejudice?

Lesson Assignments

Before viewing the video program

Read the Questions to Consider, Lesson Preview, and Learning Objectives for this lesson. Use this information to guide your reading, viewing, and thinking.

Read Chapter 12, "Social Psychology," pages 506–515, in the textbook.

View the video program, "Attitudes"

After viewing the video program

Review the vocabulary listed in the Key Terms and Concepts section. (Page references are keyed to the Hockenbury textbook, *Psychology*. Remember: there is a complete Glossary at the end of the textbook.)

Review the reading assignments for this lesson.

Complete the exercises found in the Study Activities section and check your answers with the Answer Key at the end of this lesson.

Use the Study Matrix found at the end of this lesson to review and assess your knowledge of each Learning Objective.

Lesson Preview

What is your attitude about gun control, television violence, or abortion? Are you prejudiced against any particular group of people? Why is there so much distrust and tension between many different ethnic and racial groups? Does you attitude control how you behave? Or, is it the other way around? Does your behavior ultimately change your attitude?

These are the questions we will investigate in this second lesson on social psychology.

It is through our attitudes that we tell the world what is important to us—what we stand for and what we stand against. This video will illustrate how negative attitudes can affect both individuals and society at large. You will learn how prejudice and stereotyping escalated into social racism that led to the oppression and unfair internment of Americans of Japanese descent during World War II. Interviews with survivors of the internment camps who discuss their ordeal and discussions among experts about psychological concepts help us understand how, in a society that prides itself on human rights, thousands of innocent American citizens were imprisoned.

Also in this video, psychologists and social scientists will explain the concepts of in-group and out-group bias. You will learn about the concept of cognitive dissonance and how it can be used to rationalize social injustices. This video concludes with a discussion of how each of us can lessen the impact of negative stereotyping and prejudice.

The more you know about how attitudes can develop into stereotyping, prejudice, discrimination, and racism, the more capable you will be of recognizing when these factors come into play in your life. You will also be better equipped to combat the tendency to group people together, rather than see people as they are—unique individuals with many similar and many different traits.

Learning Objectives

When you have completed this lesson, you should be able to:

1. Define attitude, and describe the three components of attitude.

2. Explain cognitive dissonance, and give an example of this process.

3. Discuss stereotyping, and describe how it can affect personal perception.

4. Describe the difference between in-group and out-group, and give and example of an in-group bias.

5. Define ethnocentrism, and explain the out-group homogeneity effect.

6. Discuss the Sherif Robbers Cave experiment on combating group prejudice.

7. Discuss how cooperation and competition affect group harmony.

8. Explain racism, and give an example of nonconscious racism.

9. Identify the three-step process for combating individual prejudice.

Key Terms and Concepts

Page references are keyed to the Hockenbury textbook, *Psychology*.

Attitude: A learned tendency to evaluate some object, person, or issue in a particular way that affects cognition and behavior. (page 506)

Cognitive dissonance: An unpleasant state of psychological tension or arousal (dissonance) that occurs when two thoughts or perceptions (cognitions) are inconsistent. This psychological tension can come about due to an inconsistency between a cognition and an action. (pages 508–509)

Prejudice: An evaluative attitude, which is typically negative, toward people who belong to a specific social group. (page 509)

Stereotype: A cluster of characteristics that are associated with all members of a specific social group. (pages 510–511)

In-group: A social group to which one belongs. (page 511)

Out-group: A social group to which one does not belong. (page 511)

Out-group homogeneity effect: The tendency to see members of out-groups as very similar to one another. (page 511)

In-group bias: The tendency to judge the behavior of in-group members favorably and out-group members unfavorably. (page 512)

Contact theory: The view that simply bringing members of different groups into contact with one another would inevitably reduce prejudice among groups. (page 513)

Ethnocentrism: The belief that one's own culture or ethnic group is superior to all others. (page 512)

Robbers Cave Experiment: An experiment by psychologist Muzafer Sherif that demonstrated how easily hostility and distrust could be created between two groups and, more important, how that hostility could be overcome. (pages 513–514)

Jigsaw classroom technique: An experiment by psychologist Elliot Aronson that demonstrated how cooperative efforts between members in a classroom can help promote intergroup harmony. (page 514)

Steps to combat prejudice: The three steps are as follows: (1) make a conscious decision that prejudice is wrong, (2) internalize that belief so it becomes part of your self-concept, and (3) inhibit prejudicial reactions and deliberately replace them with nonprejudicial responses. (page 514)

Discrimination: A behavior, typically negative, against an individual on the basis of that individual's membership in a particular group. (page 512)

Racism: An institutionalized form of discrimination against a particular group of people that is based on the race of those people. (page 514)

Nonconscious racism: Prejudicial reactions against a particular group of people that occur without the conscious awareness of the offender. (page 514)

Indigenous populations: People who are native to a particular area. (page 509)

Group conflict: As demonstrated by social psychologists, group tension can be increased by engaging in competitive behaviors and decreased by engaging in interdependent and cooperative behaviors. (pages 513–514)

Study Activities

These self-test questions are designed as a study exercise to aid you in understanding the most important terms and concepts in this lesson. To ensure that you have an accurate understanding of the key terms and concepts in this lesson, please check your answers with the Answer Key provided at the end of this lesson.

Multiple-Choice Questions

1. People tend to act in accordance with their attitudes when they feel strongly about an issue, anticipate a favorable outcome, and

   a. have a personal stake in the issue.

   b. know little about the subject.

   c. are told how to behave by an authority figure.

   d. are able to avoid any social conflicts.

2. Cognitive dissonance commonly occurs in situations in which you become uncomfortably aware that

   a. you made a wrong decision.

   b. your behavior and your attitude are the same.

   c. your behavior and your attitude are in conflict.

   d. you cannot change a situation or event.

3. When confronted by evidence that contradicts a stereotype, people tend to

   a. adjust their viewpoints if the evidence is strong enough.

   b. view the evidence as valuable only if it is presented by an authority figure.

   c. discount the evidence in a variety of ways.

   d. create a new stereotype based on the new information.

4. In the Robbers Cave Experiment, psychologist Muzafer Sherif demonstrated that prejudice can be overcome

   a. if rival groups meet prior to any competition.

   b. when rival groups compete for the same prize.

   c. when rival groups cooperate to achieve a common goal.

   d. if rival groups are told how to behave by an authority figure.

5. In order to combat prejudice on an individual level, it is important that

   a. we openly discuss our prejudices with others.

   b. we behave in accordance with our beliefs.

   c. we accept that prejudice is a natural phenomenon.

   d. we make a concerted effort to see each person as he or she really is—a unique individual.

6. The jigsaw classroom experiment, in which students in small, ethnically diverse groups were brought together to work on a mutual project, demonstrated

   a. that competition helps promote self-esteem.

   b. an increase in intergroup hostility when students were required to work together.

   c. a reduction in intergroup hostility when students worked together.

   d. no change in student behavior unless rewards were given.

7. Prejudice and intergroup hostility are likely to increase

   a. whenever different groups work toward a common goal.

   b. when there is competition for scarce resources.

   c. if one group sees themselves as having higher status.

   d. if the groups become dependent on each other.

8. Ethnocentric thinking contributes to the formation of negative stereotypes about

   a. people in groups to which you are not allowed to belong.

   b. other cultures whose customs differ from our own.

   c. gays and lesbians when they are competing for desired or scarce resources.

   d. people and individuals who are a threat to our self-esteem.

9. A person who believes that prejudice and racism are wrong might nevertheless react in prejudicial ways because of

   a. social pressure to be racist.

   b. nonconscious racism.

   c. in-group bias.

   d. the out-group homogeneity effect.

10. Stereotyping appears to be a fairly normal and common way of categorizing others and can

    a. easily be misused and cause numerous problems.

    b. help us see people as they really are.

    c. add to social stability by providing continuity of opinion between group members.

    d. be helpful in combating prejudice and racism.

11. In the video, psychologists explained that stereotypes

    a. are always inaccurate.

    b. can be either positive or negative.

    c. are "unnatural" phenomena that must be eliminated.

    d. only are used against minorities.

12. In the video, how did Americans of Japanese descent react to their internment?

    a. They understood that internment was necessary because of the war effort.

    b. They were all hostile and wanted to escape.

    c. They felt that being in the camps was not bad, but was sometimes even fun.

    d. Their reaction ranged from resignation to anger.

13. In the video, you learned that although society at large seemed to condone racism toward the Japanese, there were many non-Japanese who felt the internment was

    a. unjust.

    b. completely justifiable.

    c. only fair.

    d. necessary because of the Pearl Harbor attack.

14. In the video, an expert psychologist explained the three-step process for combating

    a. stereotyping.

    b. racism.

    c. prejudice.

    d. in-group conflicts.

15. In the video, you learned that attitudes

    a. cannot be changed.

    b. are genetic patterns of behavior.

    c. dependent on a person's education level.

    d. can be changed by conscious effort.

Short-Answer Questions

16. Define attitude, and describe the three components of attitude.

    _____

    _____

    _____

17. Explain cognitive dissonance, and give an example of this process.

_____

_____

_____

18. As seen in the video, discuss how stereotyping can be misused.

_____

_____

_____

19. Describe the difference between in-groups and out-groups, including what is meant by the term in-group bias.

_____

_____

_____

20. Define ethnocentrism, and explain the out-group homogeneity effect.

_____

_____

_____

21. Discuss the Sherif Robbers Cave research on combating group prejudice.

_____

_____

_____

22. Discuss the results of the jigsaw classroom technique.

_____

_____

_____

23. Explain racism, and give an example of nonconscious racism.

_____

_____

_____

24. Identify the three-step process for combating individual prejudice.

_____

_____

_____

Matching Exercises

Match the following terms and concepts with the correct definition.

attitude   racism   out-group homogeneity effect
prejudice   ethnocentrism   cognitive dissonance
group conflict   contact theory nonconscious racism

25. _____ The assumption that negative stereotypes would naturally replace negative attitudes if groups meet.

26. _____ The tendency to see people belonging to groups you are not a member of as being similar to one another.

27. _____ This concept is ultimately based on the exaggerated notion that members of other social groups are very different from members of our own social groups.

28. _____ An unpleasant state of psychological tension that occurs when there is an inconsistency between two thoughts or perceptions, this is a common cause for changes in attitude.

29. _____ You are engaging in this when you use your culture or ethnic group as the yardstick by which you judge other cultures or ethnic groups.

30. _____ While many people think that this controls behavior, social psychologists have consistently found that this is not a good predictor of future behavior.

31. _____ A more subtle form of racism that some psychologists believe has replaced blatant racism.

32. _____ This situation can be reduced by cooperating to achieve a common goal, or by substituting interdependence for competition.

33. _____ A form of prejudice that most people agree is wrong, can cause numerous serious social problems, and requires a conscious, concerted effort to overcome.

Completion Exercises

Fill in each blank with the most appropriate term or terms from the list of answers provided.

cognitive dissonance

indigenous populations

in-group and out-groups

in-group bias

jigsaw classroom technique

racism

Robbers Cave experiment

steps to combat prejudice

stereotypes

34. Like other social categories, _____ simplify social information so that we can sort out, process, and remember information about other people more easily.

35. People have a strong tendency to perceive others in terms of two very basic social categories: _____.

36. "We succeeded because we worked hard; they succeeded because they lucked out," is a statement a person with an _____ might make.

37. In the _____, psychologist Muzafer Sherif demonstrated how hostility between groups could be created and, more important, how that hostility could be overcome.

38. Historically, some groups have suffered more than others, especially_____ and people of color.

39. Attitude change due to _____ is quite common in everyday life.

40. Using the _____, social psychologist Elliot Aronson demonstrated how children brought together in ethnically diverse groups could benefit from cooperation and interdependence.

41. Making a conscious decision how to think, internalizing that belief, and learning to inhibit specific automatic responses are the _____ on a personal level.

42. In the video, you learned that _____ is often the result when one group has negative attitudes about another group.

Answer Key

Multiple-Choice Questions

1. a	5. d	9. b	13. a
2. c	6. c	10. a	14. c
3. c	7. b	11. b	15. d
4. c	8. b	12. d	

Short-Answer Questions

Your answers should include the following:

16. An attitude is a learned tendency to evaluate objects, persons, or issues. Attitudes can include three components: your thoughts and beliefs (cognitive), a predisposition to act in a particular way (behavioral), and feelings and emotions about the attitude object (emotional). (page 506)

17. Cognitive dissonance is a term psychologists use to describe an unpleasant state of psychological tension that occurs when there is an inconsistency between two thoughts. An example would be a person who had to choose between two job offers, each offer having some desirable and some not-so desirable features. This conflict creates a state of dissonance. Commonly this is resolved by changing your thoughts and attitudes to be supportive of whatever job offer you decided upon accepting. (page 508)

18. As the example of Americans of Japanese descent interned during World War II showed, stereotyping is a specific kind of social categorization. Stereotyping is the process of attributing any number of characteristics to all the people in a particular group. Stereotypes are often based on inaccurate assumptions. Stereotypes tend to lower one's ability to judge objectively and, once established, tend to resist change. (video)

19. An in-group is a social group to which one belongs. An out-group is a social group to which one does not belong. We are more likely to attribute negative traits to members of out-groups and attribute positive traits to members of groups to which we belong. This tendency is called in-group bias. (pages 511–512)

20. Ethnocentrism is the belief that one's own culture or ethnic group is superior to all others. Ethnocentrism is related to the tendency to use one's own culture as a standard by which to judge other cultures. The out-group homogeneity effect is the tendency to see members of groups that you do not belong to as being very similar to one another. (pages 511–512)

21. The Robbers Cave Experiment is a classic series of studies conducted by psychologist Muzafer Sherif to investigate methods to combat prejudice at the group level. The experiment was conducted at Robbers Cave State Park, hence

the name. In this study, boys were randomly assigned to two groups, and hostility and distrust quickly developed. To combat the prejudices that had developed, Sherif had the two groups work on several projects with a common goal. After a series of such joint efforts, the rivalry between the two groups diminished. (pages 513–514)

22. The jigsaw classroom technique replaced competition with interdependence and cooperation. The children benefited from the results. They had higher self-esteem and a greater liking for other children, had less negative stereotypes, and reduced hostility toward children from other groups. (page 514)

23. Racism is a form of prejudicial thinking that is aimed at a particular group, usually based solely on race or ethnicity. Nonconscious racism is a more subtle form of racism in which a person acts, speaks, or behaves in a racist manner without being aware of his or her actions. (page 514)

24. The three-step process to reduce prejudice includes: (1) individuals must decide that prejudiced responses are wrong and consciously reject prejudice, (2) individuals must internalize nonprejudiced beliefs so that those beliefs become an integral part of their personal self-concept, and (3) individuals must learn to inhibit automatic prejudicial reactions. (page 514)

Matching Exercises

25. contact theory

26. out-group homogeneity effect

27. prejudice

28. cognitive dissonance

29. ethnocentrism

30. attitude

31. nonconscious racism

32. group conflict

33. racism

Completion Exercises

34. stereotypes

35. in-groups and out-groups

36. in-group bias

37. Robbers Cave experiment

38. indigenous populations

39. cognitive dissonance

40. jigsaw classroom technique

41. steps to combat prejudice

42. racism

Study Matrix

Lesson 20

Attitudes

Please Note: Use this matrix to guide your study and achieve the learning objectives of this lesson. It will also help you to view the video, which defines and demonstrates important concepts and objectives as they relate to everyday life and actual case studies.

Learning Objective	Textbook	Telecourse Student Guide
Define attitude, and describe the three components of attitude.	pp. 506–507	Key Terms and Concepts; Study Activities 1, 15, 16, 30.
Explain cognitive dissonance, and give an example of this process.	pp. 508–509	Key Terms and Concepts; Study Activities 2, 17, 28, 39.
Discuss stereotyping, and describe how it can affect person perception.	pp. 510–511	Key Terms and Concepts; Study Activities 3, 10, 11, 18, 34.
Describe the difference between in-group and out-group, and give and example of an in-group bias.	pp. 511–512	Key Terms and Concepts; Study Activities 12, 19, 27, 35, 36.
Define ethnocentrism, and explain the out-group homogeneity effect.	pp. 511–512	Key Terms and Concepts; Study Activities 8, 20, 26, 29.
Recall the Sherif Robbers Cave experiment on combating group prejudice.	pp. 513–514	Key Terms and Concepts; Study Activities 4, 21, 25, 37.
Discuss how cooperation and competition affect group harmony.	pp. 513–514	Key Terms and Concepts; Study Activities 6, 22, 32, 40.
Explain racism, and give an example of nonconscious racism.	p. 514	Key Terms and Concepts; Study Activities 9, 13, 23, 31, 33, 38, 42.
Identify the three-step process for combating individual prejudice.	p. 514	Key Terms and Concepts; Study Activities 5, 7, 14, 24, 41.

Use the Course Compass to orient yourself in the road that you are taking to explore branches and aspects of psychology. The branch and aspects that are covered in this lesson are highlighted in the compass.

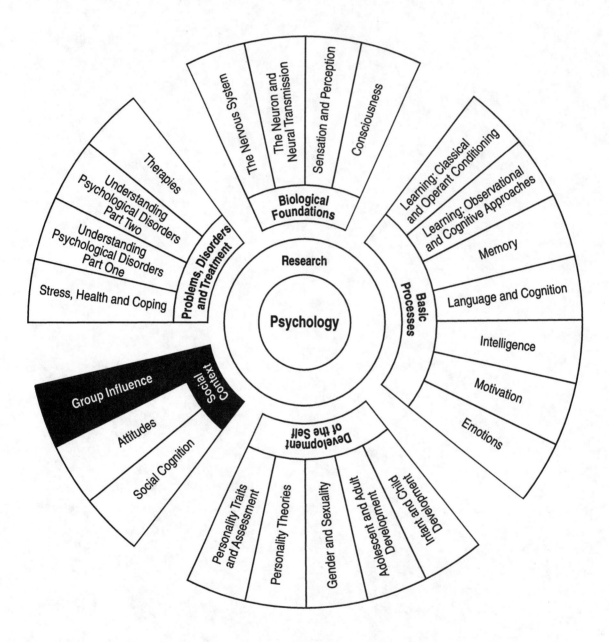

Please note: This compass does not represent the full range of topics comprising the field of psychology; it represents a map for this course only. Each of the five branches represented above has many aspects and subjects that are covered in the 26 lessons of this telecourse. You should remember that these branches and subjects all interrelate.

Lesson 21

Group Influence

Questions to Consider

Why is it difficult for most people to disobey an authority figure?

What is the "feel good, do good" effect?

Why do people tend to behave differently when they are part of a group?

What social conditions cause people to ignore someone in distress?

What is the most important factor in determining human behavior?

What is the best way to avoid being manipulated by professional persuaders?

Lesson Assignments

Before viewing the video program

Read the Questions to Consider, Lesson Preview, and Learning Objectives for this lesson. Use this information to guide your reading, viewing, and thinking.

Read Chapter 12, "Social Psychology," pages 515–533, in the textbook.

View the video program, "Group Influence"

After viewing the video program

Review the vocabulary listed in the Key Terms and Concepts section. (Page references are keyed to the Hockenbury textbook, *Psychology*. Remember: there is a complete Glossary at the end of the textbook.)

Review the reading assignments for this lesson.

Complete the exercises found in the Study Activities section and check your answers with the Answer Key at the end of this lesson.

Use the Study Matrix found at the end of this lesson to review and assess your knowledge of each Learning Objective.

Lesson Preview

What would you do if a policeman told you he needed you to throw a rock at a passing car? Would you obey or defy his instructions? How is it possible for intelligent people to get so strongly influenced by a group that they will do things they know are wrong, dangerous, or even cruel? Are you more likely to help a person in distress if you are alone, or if others are present? The importance of social and group influence is the topic in this, the last in our series of lessons in social psychology.

As psychologists have long recognized and repeatedly proven, when living in a civilized society we must, to some degree, learn conformity and obedience. However, as you will learn, blind conformity and obedience can lead to disastrous results.

In this video, we will examine how groups influence individual behavior. This video is a case study of Floyd Cochran, a former recruiter for the white supremacist group, Aryan Nation. As you will see in this lesson, group behavior can have a dramatic effect on an individual's behavior and his or her beliefs. You will hear psychologists and social science researchers discuss both the negative and positive effects of group influence.

You will also learn about the social and psychological implications of conformity and obedience by reviewing the classic experiments of psychologists Solomon Asch and Stanley Milgram. Additionally, this lesson includes discussions by psychologists of helping behavior and the role of individual responsibility.

We conclude this video by observing Floyd Cochran as he conducts a workshop on antiracism. While group influence is a powerful force, we as individuals ultimately can choose what we believe and how we behave.

Learning Objectives

When you have completed this lesson, you should be able to:

1. Describe the results of Solomon Asch's experiment on conformity.

2. Define obedience, and discuss Milgram's experiment on obedience.

3. Identify the factors that Milgram found that decrease obedience.

4. Define social influence, and give an example of normative social influence and informative social influence.

5. Describe the bystander effect, including the concept of diffusion of responsibility.

6. Define altruism and prosocial behavior, and give an example of each.

7. Define social loafing, social facilitation, and the process of deindividuation.

8. Explain persuasion rules of reciprocity and commitment, and discuss how you can defend against being manipulated by persuasion.

Key Terms and Concepts

Page references are keyed to the Hockenbury textbook, *Psychology*.

Social influence: The study of the effects of situational factors and other people on an individual's behavior. (page 515)

Normative social influence: Behavior that is motivated by the desire to gain social acceptance and approval. (pages 516–517)

Informational social influence: Behavior that is motivated by the desire to be correct. (pages 516–517)

Conformity: The tendency to adjust one's behavior, attitudes, or beliefs to group norms in response to real or imagined group pressure. (pages 516–517)

Obedience: The performance of an action in response to the direct orders of an authority or person of higher status. (page 518)

Altruism: Helping another person with no expectation of personal reward or benefit. (page 526)

Prosocial behavior: Any behavior that helps another, whether the underlying motive is self-serving or selfless. (page 526)

Feel good, do good effect: The tendency for people who feel good, successful, happy, or fortunate to help others. (page 526)

Bystander effect: The phenomenon where bystanders (those who witness an emergency situation) do not intervene. Diffusion of responsibility and other feelings are other reasons why people do not intervene. Some of these include:

feeling that intervening is too much trouble; feeling foolish by intervening when no intervention is needed (as in the boy who cried wolf); worrying about safety issues, or that intervening is too much trouble, especially if one has to wait around for hours to tell a story to the police. (page 527)

Diffusion of responsibility: The phenomenon in which the presence of other people makes it less likely that any individual will help someone in distress because the obligation to intervene is shared among all the on-lookers. (page 527)

Milgram's obedience experiment: The purpose of the experiment was to investigate obedience to authority figures. In this experiment, "teachers" were instructed to administer progressively stronger electric shocks to the "learners" whenever they gave an incorrect answer. The results were that the majority administered the maximum possible shocks, even though they believed the shocks were both very painful and dangerous. (pages 518–522)

Asch conformity studies: The purpose of these studies was to determine if people would conform to a group even if the group was clearly wrong. In this study, subjects were asked to pick a comparison line that most matched an example line. This was a simple, objective task with an obvious answer. However, when subjects were put in a room with other people, and those other people selected an obviously wrong answer, there was a tendency to conform to the group, even though this meant selecting an obviously incorrect answer. (pages 516–517)

Social loafing: The tendency to expend less effort on a task when it is a group effort. (page 529)

Social facilitation: The tendency for the presence of other people to enhance individual effort. (page 530)

Deindividuation: The reduction of self-awareness and inhibitions that can occur when a person is a part of a group whose members feel anonymous. (page 530)

Rule of reciprocity: The tendency to feel obligated if someone gives you something or does you a favor. (page 532)

Rule of commitment: The tendency to feel psychological and interpersonal pressures to behave consistently with a prior public commitment. (page 532)

Persuasion: The deliberate attempt to influence the attitudes or behavior of another person in a situation in which that person has some freedom of choice. (pages 532–533)

Study Activities

These self-test questions are designed as a study exercise to aid you in understanding the most important terms and concepts in this lesson. To ensure that you have an accurate understanding of the key terms and concepts in this lesson, please check your answers with the Answer Key provided at the end of this lesson.

Multiple-Choice Questions

1. The two basic reasons people conform to a larger group is the desire to be liked and accepted and

   a. the fear of rejection.

   b. the concern over being embarrassed.

   c. the desire to be right.

   d. the desire to be with people who behave in a like manner.

2. Stanley Milgram's classic experimental study on obedience was to determine how and why people

   a. obey the destructive dictates of an authority figure.

   b. disobey the destructive dictates of an authority figure.

   c. conform to social norms.

   d. violate social norms.

3. People are most likely to help others if they notice a situation in which help is needed, feel some sense of responsibility, and

   a. helping does not violate any social norms.

   b. anticipate that the helping behavior will be recognized and rewarded.

   c. they know how to deal with the situation.

   d. other people are present.

4. The "feel good, do good" effect refers to the phenomenon in which people

   a. who feel good help others to avoid feeling guilty.

   b. who feel good are less likely to help others.

   c. who feel good are more likely to help others.

   d. only engage in prosocial behavior that makes them feel good.

5. The bystander effect is the phenomenon where bystanders (those who witness an emergency situation) do not intervene. The reason(s) people do this are

   a. diffusion of responsibility.

   b. feeling foolish by intervening when no intervention is needed (as in the boy who cried wolf).

   c. feeling that intervening is too much trouble.

   d. all of the above.

6. The simple but powerful social norm in which you feel obligated when someone gives you something or does a favor for you is called the

   a. rule of reciprocity.

   b. rule of commitment.

   c. foot-in-the-door technique.

   d. that's-not-all technique.

7. The results of psychologist Solomon Asch's experiment on conformity revealed that implicit, unspoken group pressure

   a. has little effect.

   b. will change the majority of people's opinion.

   c. is very influential if the group members have high status.

   d. can exert a strong influence.

8. Deindividuation is the reduction of self-awareness and inhibitions that can occur when a person

   a. is part of a group whose members feel anonymous.

   b. is interacting with an out-group.

   c. has a diminished sense of self and low self-esteem.

   d. is part of a group whose rules control his or her behavior.

9. When a persuader gets you to make a commitment by deliberately understating the cost of a product, he or she is using

   a. the rule of reciprocity.

   b. a technique called that's-not-all.

   c. a technique called low-balling.

   d. playing the devil's advocate when the price is later raised.

10. Social loafing is reduced or eliminated when the group is composed of people we know, we are members of a highly valued group, and

   a. we are getting substantial rewards for our efforts.

   b. we are unable to "hide" or our work effort is seen by everyone.

   c. the task is something we normally do and is not unique.

   d. the task is meaningful and unique.

11. In this video, you learned that in many cases people behave differently when they are

   a. alone.

   b. with someone they know well.

   c. part of a group.

   d. being observed.

12. In the video, an expert psychologist defined conformity as the tendency to change one's behavior, attitudes, or beliefs to group norms in response to

   a. new learned beliefs.

   b. real group pressure.

   c. imagined group pressure.

   d. real or imagined group pressure.

13. In the video, the famous experiment by psychologist Solomon Asch demonstrated that in order to conform to others in a group, people may

   a. leave the group.

   b. not argue.

   c. give a wrong answer.

   d. rationalize their answer to a question.

14. In the video, the classic experiment by psychologist Stanley Milgram involved painful electrical shocks that were delivered to a "learner" by a "teacher" because they were ordered to do so by

   a. a policeman.

   b. a judge.

   c. a person who was going to pay them.

   d. an authority figure.

Short-Answer Questions

15. Describe the results of Solomon Asch's experiment on conformity.

_____

_____

_____

16. Define obedience, and discuss Milgram's experiment on obedience.

_____

_____

_____

17. Identify the factors that Milgram found that decrease obedience.

_____

_____

_____

18. Define social influence, and give an example of normative social influence and informational social influence.

_____

_____

_____

19. Describe the bystander effect, including the concept of diffusion of responsibility.

_____

_____

_____

20. Define social loafing and social facilitation, and give an example of each.

_____

_____

_____

21. Explain the persuasion rules of reciprocity and commitment, and discuss how you can defend against being manipulated by persuasion.

_____

_____

_____

22. Define altruism and prosocial behavior, and give an example of each.

_____

_____

_____

Matching Exercises

Match the following terms and concepts with the correct definition.

bystander effect   obedience   Milgram's obedience
prosocial behavior   social influence   experiment
social facilitation   rule of commitment   normative social influence
                                                 Asch conformity studies

23. _____ A ubiquitous and indispensable feature of social life that was studied by Stanley Milgram.

24. _____ Explains the phenomenon in which the greater the number of people present, the less likely each individual is to help someone in distress.

25. _____ One of the primary reasons why people sometimes find themselves conforming to larger groups.

26. _____ Can be motivated by altruism, guilt, or to gain recognition, rewards, or increased self-esteem.

27. _____ Explains why performance tends to increase when others are watching you do a task that you have rehearsed, and performance tends to decrease when you are attempting a task you are not proficient at performing.

28. _____ Designed to determine how and why people obey the destructive dictates of an authority figure.

29. _____ The study of the effects of situational factors and other people on an individual's behavior.

30. _____ Investigated the question, "Would people still conform to a group if the group opinion was clearly wrong?"

31. _____ The *foot-in-the-door* technique is an example of this powerful social norm that is used by people who are trying to persuade others.

Completion Exercises

Fill in each blank with the most appropriate term or terms from the list of answers provided.

acceptance

altruism

conformity

deindividuation

diffusion of responsibility

informative social influence

obedience

personal responsibility

persuasion

rule of reciprocity

social loafing

32. When other people are present, helping behavior declines partly because other people create a _____ wherein no one person feels compelled to respond.

33. _____ is not just acting as other people act, it is acting differently from the way you would act if you were alone.

34. When you are uncertain or doubt your own judgment, you may look to a group as a source of accurate information, which is called _____.

35. Everyday life is full with little acts of _____, such as opening a door for a stranger, helping a stranded driver change a tire, or taking out the trash for a sick neighbor.

36. The power of _____ can be defended against by taking your time, listing all the reasons why not to do something, and learning to trust your gut feelings.

37. Making you obligated so that you feel pressured to return a favor is an example of the _____, a simple, but powerful social norm.

38. An effective method to counter _____ is to heighten self-awareness and create an increased sense of responsibility.

39. Women are generally less likely to engage in _____ than are men.

40. In the video, it was pointed out that there are two types of compliance: conformity and _____.

41. In the video, _____ was defined as following the direct orders of an authority or person of higher status.

42. In the video, Floyd Cochran showed us that we can change if we are willing to take _____ for our behavior and our beliefs.

Answer Key

Multiple-Choice Questions

1. c	5. d	9. c	13. c
2. a	6. a	10. d	14. d
3. c	7. d	11. c	
4. c	8. a	12. d	

Short-Answer Questions

Your answers should include the following:

15. Psychologist Solomon Asch conducted several experiments to investigate if people would conform to a group even if the group opinion was clearly wrong. In his most famous study, a group of people sat at a table, looked at a series of cards, and compared the length of lines. A test subject was then brought into the room and was instructed to pick the comparison line that best matched the standard line, a very simple and easy task. However, when the group members purposely selected the wrong answer, there was a tendency for the test subject to conform to the group's opinion and select an answer that was obviously incorrect. (pages 516–518)

16. Obedience is the performance of an action in response to the direct orders of an authority or person of higher status. In the classic Milgram experiment on obedience, subjects were divided into two groups: teacher and learners. The learners were strapped to an electric chair. The teacher was taken into a different room, from which he could hear but not see the learners. The teacher was told to give an electric shock to a learner whenever a learner answered a question incorrectly. Each time a learner made an error, the teacher was told to administer a progressively stronger shock. The result was that two-thirds of Milgram's "teachers" administered what they thought were severe shocks to the learners, even though the learners screamed in agony. (pages 518–520)

17. By varying his series of experiments, Milgram identified several conditions that decreased the likelihood of destructive obedience. Willing to obey diminished sharply when the buffers that separated the "teacher" from the "learner" were lessened or removed. The proximity of the experimenter was another critical element. Finally if the "teacher" observed other teachers refusing to continue or they were free to choose the shock level, the percentage of subjects administering the maximum shock dramatically decreased. (pages 520–522)

18. Social influence is the psychological study of how our behavior is influenced by social environment and other people. Normative social influence refers to behavior that is motivated by the desire to gain social acceptance. An example would be if everyone in a concert hall rises to give a musician a standing ovation, you would feel social pressure to also stand and applaud.

Informational social influence is based on the desire to be right. An example can be found in the Asch conformity studies, in which participants were swayed to select a wrong answer in order to conform to the group opinion. (pages 515–517)

19. The bystander effect is a phenomenon in which the greater the number of people present (bystanders), the less likely each individual will be to help someone in distress. The two main reasons for the bystander effect are diffusion of responsibility and because each of is motivated to behave in a socially acceptable way (normative social influence) and to appear correct (informational social influence). Thus, we often rely on the reactions of others to help us define a situation, which may, in some cases, preclude helping behaviors. (pages 527–528)

20. Social loafing is the tendency to expend less effort on a task when it is part of a group effort. In contrast to social loafing is social facilitation, which is the tendency for the pressure of other people to enhance individual participation. Deindividuation refers to the reduction of self-awareness and inhibitions that can occur when a person is part of a group whose members feel anonymous. (pages 529–531)

21. The rule of reciprocity is a strong social norm in which an individual is made to feel an uncomfortable sense of obligation in response to being given something or in response to a favor. The rule of commitment refers to the psychological and interpersonal pressure individuals feel to be consistent with an earlier commitment they have made, especially if that commitment was made in public. Suggestions for defending against persuasion include taking time to make a decision, listing all the reason why you should not do some behavior, and learning to trust your gut feelings when something does not feel right. (pages 532–533)

22. Altruism is helping another person with no expectation of personal reward or benefit. Everyday life is full of altruistic acts, such as helping a stranded motorist simply because you feel like helping that person. Prosocial behavior refers to any behavior that helps another, regardless of the underlying motive. An example of prosocial behavior might be helping out at a fund-raiser, serving meals at a soup kitchen, or volunteering at a church event. (page 526)

Matching Exercises

23. obedience

24. bystander effect

25. normative social influence

26. prosocial behavior

27. social facilitation

28. Milgram's obedience experiment

29. social influence

30. Asch conformity studies

31. rule of commitment

Completion Exercises

32. diffusion of responsibility

33. conformity

34. informational social influence

35. altruism

36. persuasion

37. rule of reciprocity

38. deindividuation

39. social loafing

40. acceptance

41. obedience

42. personal responsibility

Study Matrix

Lesson 21

Group Influence

Please Note: Use this matrix to guide your study and achieve the learning objectives of this lesson. It will also help you to view the video, which defines and demonstrates important concepts and objectives as they relate to everyday life and actual case studies.

Learning Objective	Textbook	Telecourse Student Guide
Describe the results of Solomon Asch's experiment on conformity.	pp. 516–518	Key Terms and Concepts; Study Activities 1, 7, 13, 15, 30, 33.
Define obedience, and discuss Milgram's experiment on obedience.	pp. 518–522	Key Terms and Concepts; Study Activities 2, 14, 16, 23, 28, 41.
Identify the factors that Milgram found that decrease obedience.	pp. 521–522	Key Terms and Concepts; Study Activity 17.
Define social influence, and give an example of normative social influence and informative social influence.	pp. 515–517	Key Terms and Concepts; Study Activities 11, 18, 25, 29, 34, 40.
Describe the bystander effect, including the concept of diffusion of responsibility.	pp. 526–527	Key Terms and Concepts; Study Activities 5, 19, 24, 32, 42.
Define altruism and prosocial behavior, and give an example of each.	p. 526	Key Terms and Concepts; Study Activities 3, 4, 22, 26, 35.
Define social loafing, social facilitation, and the process of deindividuation.	pp. 529–531	Key Terms and Concepts; Study Activities 8, 10, 12, 20, 27, 38, 39.
Explain persuasion rules of reciprocity and commitment, and discuss how you can defend against being manipulated by persuasion.	pp. 532–533	Key Terms and Concepts; Study Activities 6, 9, 21, 31, 36, 37.

Use the Course Compass to orient yourself in the road that you are taking to explore branches and aspects of psychology. The branch and aspects that are covered in this lesson are highlighted in the compass.

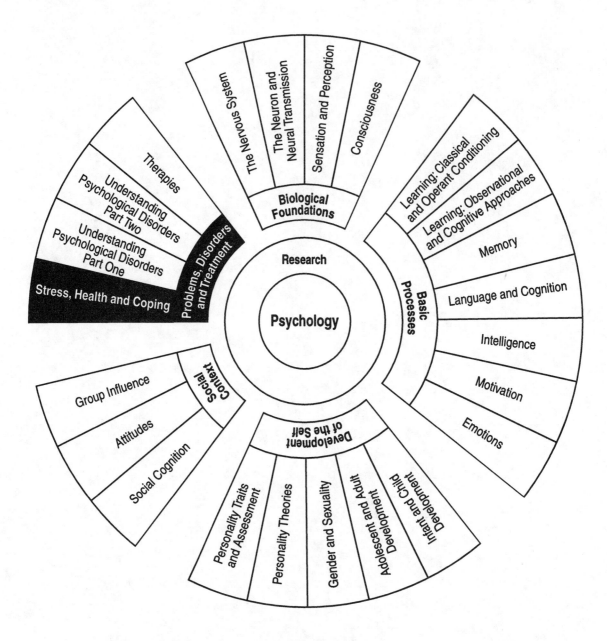

Please note: This compass does not represent the full range of topics comprising the field of psychology; it represents a map for this course only. Each of the five branches represented above has many aspects and subjects that are covered in the 26 lessons of this telecourse. You should remember that these branches and subjects all interrelate.

Lesson 22

Stress, Health, and Coping

Questions to Consider

What is health psychology?

How is stress related to health and illness?

How does stress affect how we think and behave?

What are the most effective ways to cope with stress?

Are women or men more likely to suffer the negative effects of stress?

Lesson Assignments

Before viewing the video program

Read the Questions to Consider, Lesson Preview, and Learning Objectives for this lesson. Use this information to guide your reading, viewing, and thinking.

Read Chapter 13, "Stress, Health, and Coping," in the textbook.

View the video program, "Stress, Health, and Coping"

After viewing the video program

Review the vocabulary listed in the Key Terms and Concepts section. (Page references are keyed to the Hockenbury textbook, *Psychology*. Remember: there is a complete Glossary at the end of the textbook.)

Review the reading assignments for this lesson.

Complete the exercises found in the Study Activities section and check your answers with the Answer Key at the end of this lesson.

Use the Study Matrix found at the end of this lesson to review and assess your knowledge of each Learning Objective.

Lesson Preview

At a local hospital you will see doctors, nurses, and, occasionally, a clown. At first glance, the clown seems very much out of place. Hospitals are doing very serious work, life-saving work. What is a clown doing in such a sobering place?

In this lesson, you will be introduced to the field of health psychology. As you will learn in this lesson, psychologists now have scientific evidence that stress can have both a direct and indirect effect on one's overall health, and can significantly affect one's ability to recover from serious illnesses. Researchers have been able prove that positive emotions can have a positive effect on one's health. Psychologists have also learned that for people recovering from serious illness or injury, the use of humor can both decrease their suffering and speed their recovery.

So, the clown in the hospital may not be out of place. In fact, the clown may be in the place where he is most needed.

In this video, you will meet Dora Rodriguez, who in her early fifties learned she had breast cancer. You will discover how Dora learned to cope with the tremendous stress brought on by her life-threatening illness. In this video, expert psychologists will explain the nature of stress and introduce you to the biopsychosocial model of health psychology. Author Sandy Hockenbury will explain the all-important role coping skills and explanatory style play in dealing with stress. Additionally, you will hear expert psychologists discuss the differences between coping styles and the importance of social support in dealing with stressful situations.

Health psychologists not only research the role played by stress but also take on the burden of trying to help people understand how lifestyle can affect one's overall health and longevity.

Your personal ability to recognize, understand, and effectively deal with stress can make a major difference in your life.

Learning Objectives

When you have completed this lesson, you should be able to:

1. Define stress, and describe the biopsychosocial model of health psychology.

2. Explain how life change, daily hassles, and social conditions contribute to stress.

3. Explain the conflict theory of stress, and identify the three basic types of conflict.

4. Describe the three stages of the general adaptation syndrome.

5. Explain the function of the immune system, and discuss how the immune system is affected by stress.

6. Describe the probable effects of different explanatory styles on mental and physical health.

7. Explain how social support benefits health, as well as how it can increase stress.

8. Explain the difference between problem-focused coping and emotion-focused coping.

Key Terms and Concepts

Page references are keyed to the Hockenbury textbook, *Psychology*.

Stress: A negative emotional state occurring in response to events that are perceived as taxing or exceeding a person's resources or ability to cope. (page 540)

Health psychology: The branch of psychology that studies how psychological factors influence health, medical treatment, and health-related behaviors. (pages 540–541)

Biopsychosocial model: The belief that physical health and illness are determined by the interaction of biological, psychological, and social factors. (pages 540–541)

Stressor: An event or situation that is perceived as harmful, threatening, or challenging. (pages 540–541)

Daily hassles: Everyday minor events that annoy and upset people. (page 542)

Conflict: A situation in which a person feels pulled between two or more opposing desires, motives, or goals. (page 543)

Fight-or-flight response: Rapidly occurring internal physical reactions that prepare a person to either fight or take flight from a real or perceived threat. (page 546)

General adaptation syndrome: A progress of physical changes that occur when an organism is exposed to intense and prolonged stress. The stages are alarm, resistance, and exhaustion. (page 548)

Immune system: A body system that protects the body from viruses, bacteria, and tumor cells. (page 548)

Psychoneuroimmunology: An interdisciplinary field that studies the relationships between psychological processes, the nervous system, and the immune system. (page 550)

Optimistic explanatory style: Accounting for negative events or situations with external, unstable, and specific explanations. (pages 554–555)

Pessimistic explanatory style: Accounting for negative events or situations with internal, stable, and global explanations. (pages 554–555)

Type A behavior: A behavioral and emotional style characterized by a sense of time urgency, hostility, and competitiveness. (page 556)

Social support: The resources provided by other people in time of need. (pages 558–560)

Coping: Behavioral and cognitive responses used to deal with stressors. (pages 561–563)

Problem-focused coping: Coping efforts aimed at changing or managing a stressful event or circumstance. (page 563)

Emotion-focused coping: Coping efforts aimed at relieving the emotional discomfort brought on by a stressful event or circumstance. (page 563)

Study Activities

These self-test questions are designed as a study exercise to aid you in understanding the most important terms and concepts in this lesson. To ensure that you have an accurate understanding of the key terms and concepts in this lesson, please check your answers with the Answer Key provided at the end of this lesson.

Multiple-Choice Questions

1. The study of stress is a key topic in one of the most rapidly growing specialty areas in psychology called

   a. health psychology.

   b. biological psychology.

   c. psychoneuroimmunology.

   d. social-behavioral psychology.

2. A person who is inclined to believe that no amount of personal effort will improve a situation is using

   a. a defeatist explanatory style.

   b. an optimistic explanatory style.

   c. a pessimistic explanatory style.

   d. an objective explanatory style.

3. Social support can make a stressful situation seem less threatening, promote positive moods and emotions, and

   a. can become chaotic.

   b. lower blood cholesterol levels.

   c. enhance self-esteem.

   d. adversely affect immune system functioning.

4. Researchers have found that negative life events have the greatest adverse effects on health, especially when they

   a. involve the loss of a spouse.

   b. are combined with other physical illnesses.

   c. happen just after a positive life event.

   d. are unexpected and uncontrollable.

5. The most stressful type of conflict-induced stress comes from

    a. approach-approach conflicts.

    b. approach-avoidance conflicts.

    c. avoidance-avoidance conflicts.

    d. avoidance conflicts that cannot be easily resolved.

6. People in the lowest socioeconomic levels of society tend to have

    a. fewer daily hassles.

    b. nonchronic, long-term stress.

    c. the highest levels of psychological distress, illness, and death.

    d. adequate resources to deal with negative life events.

7. Any kind of immediate threat to your well-being is a stress-producing experience that triggers multiple bodily changes. This rapidly occurring reaction is called

    a. the fight-or-flight response

    b. general adaptation syndrome

    c. a stress reaction

    d. biological stress phenomenon

8. Researchers have discovered that stress can decrease immune system functioning, which may

    a. make stress related disease inevitable.

    b. affect cognitive functioning.

    c. heighten susceptibility to health problems.

    d. make infectious agents less effective.

9. Psychological research has consistently shown that having a sense of control over a stressful situation

    a. reduces the impact of stressors.

    b. is not as important as explanatory style in controlling stress.

    c. is important for people with Type A personalities.

    d. is not as important as having a strong social support.

10. The three stages of the general adaptation syndrome are

    a. wear and tear stage, adjustment stage, and acceptance stage.

    b. alarm stage, adjustment stage, and resistance stage.

    c. alarm stage, resistance stage, and exhaustion stage.

    d. resistance stage, exhaustion stage, and acceptance stage.

11. In the video, expert psychologists explained that stress can

    a. cause people to drink alcohol and smoke cigarettes.

    b. make people unable to act in a civil manner.

    c. interfere with cognitive abilities.

    d. cause mental illnesses.

12. In the video, you learned that people who tend to use external, unstable, and specific explanations for negative events are said to have an

    a. optimistic explanatory style.

    b. pessimistic explanatory style.

    c. constantly changing explanatory style.

    d. explanatory style that depends on circumstances.

Short-Answer Questions

13. Define stress, and describe the biopsychosocial model of health psychology.

14. Explain how life change, daily hassles, and social conditions contribute to stress.

15. Explain the conflict theory of stress, and identify the three basic types of conflict.

16. Describe the three stages of the general adaptation syndrome.

17. Explain the function of the immune system, and discuss how the immune system is affected by stress.

18. Describe the probable effects of explanatory style on mental and physical health.

_____

_____

_____

19. As explained in the video, discuss the role that social support plays in helping a person cope with a stressful situation.

_____

_____

_____

20. Explain the difference between problem-focused coping and emotion-focused coping.

_____

_____

_____

Matching Exercises

Match the following terms and concepts with the correct definition.

daily hassles	biopsychosocial model	Type A behavior
stress	fight-or-flight response	general adaptation syndrome
coping	immune system	pessimistic explanatory style

21. _____ Refers to people who hate to waste time, always seem to be in a hurry, have a general sense of hostility, and often try to do two or more things at the same time.

22. _____ Produces specialized white cells called lymphocytes that protect the body from viruses, bacteria, and foreign invaders.

23. _____ Can be dangerous to your health and is usually caused by major life events, daily hassles, conflict, and social and cultural factors.

24. _____ Involves efforts to change circumstances, or your interpretation of circumstances, to make them more favorable and less threatening.

25. _____ The people who use this tend to experience more stress than people who are confident and have a generally positive outlook on life.

26. _____ A term referring to the progressive physical changes that occur in the body in response to acute or chronic stress.

27. _____ Helps ensure survival by swiftly mobilizing internal physical resources to defensively attack or flee an immediate threat.

28. _____ According to this, health and illness are determined by the complex interaction of biological, psychological, and social factors.

29. _____ Is a better predictor of physical illness and symptoms than is the number of major life changes a person experiences.

Completion Exercises

Fill in each blank with the most appropriate term or terms from the list of answers provided.

conflicts   optimistic explanatory style

coping   problem-focused coping

emotion-focused coping   psychoneuroimmunology

health psychology   social support

negative emotional state   stressor

30. People who have an _____ tend to use external, unstable, and specific explanations for negative events.

31. The _____ of friends and relatives can make a situation seem less threatening, promote positive emotions, and enhance self-esteem.

32. When individuals shift their attention away from a stressor and toward other activities, they are engaging in the _____ strategy called escape-avoidance.

33. A rapidly growing specialty area called _____ studies how psychological factors influence health and illness.

34. According to psychologists, there are three types of stress-inducing _____: approach-approach, approach-avoidance, and avoidance-avoidance.

35. The scientific study of the interconnections among psychological processes, the nervous and endocrine systems, and the immune system is called _____.

36. Virtually any event or situation can be a _____ if you question your ability to deal with it effectively.

37. Rationally analyzing a problem, trying to identify possible solutions, and then attempting to implement a solution is an example of _____.

38. In this video, textbook author Sandy Hockenbury explained that there are lots of ways to define stress, but essentially stress is a _____ that results when you perceive a threatening event as more than you can handle.

39. In the video, expert psychologists explained that _____ refers to the ways people try to change circumstances, or interpretations of circumstances, to make them less threatening.

Answer Key

Multiple-Choice Questions

1. a	4. d	7. a	10. c
2. c	5. b	8. c	11. c
3. c	6. c	9. a	12. a

Short-Answer Questions

Your answers should include the following:

13. Stress is a negative emotional state that occurs when a person is confronted with a situation or event that he or she does not feel able to cope with effectively. The biopsychosocial model of health psychology is based on the belief that biological, psychological, and social factors interact and influence health and illness. (page 540)

14. Early stress researchers believed that any change that required individuals to adjust their behavior and lifestyle caused stress. Today, most researchers agree that life changes may be stressful, but only if those changes are perceived as undesirable. Researchers have found a positive correlation between the number of daily hassles experienced and stress level. Social conditions such as crowding, crime, and unemployment can also cause stress. (pages 541–544)

15. A conflict is a situation in which a person feels pulled between two or more opposing desires, motives, or goals. Any conflict can be a source of stress. The three basic types of conflict are approach-approach, approach-avoidance, and avoidance-avoidance. (pages 543–544)

16. The general adaptation syndrome is divided into three stages: alarm, resistance, and exhaustion. During the first stage, called the alarm stage, intense arousal occurs as the body mobilizes its physical resources to meet the demands of the stress-producing event. In the next stage, the resistance stage, intensity diminishes but the body remains in a state of physical arousal in an attempt to cope with the stress. In the final stage, exhaustion, the body's energy resources become depleted, leading to physical disorders and, potentially, death. (pages 548–549)

17. The immune system is a body system that produces specialized white cells called lymphocytes that protect the body from viruses, bacteria, and tumor cells. Stress can diminish the effectiveness of the immune system, making you more susceptible to health problems. (pages 549–552)

18. According to some psychologists, how people explain failures or defeats can affect both their psychological health and their physical health. Research has shown that people who characteristically use an optimistic explanatory style were significantly healthier than those who characteristically use a pessimistic explanatory style. (pages 554–555)

19. A strong social support network is recognized as an important positive factor in helping people cope with stressful situations. The social support of friends and relatives may make threatening events seems less threatening. Also, strong social support can promote positive moods and emotions, enhance self-esteem, and increase feelings of personal control. Negative interactions with others can be a source of stress. In fact, negative interactions with other people are often more effective at creating psychological distress than positive interactions are at improving well-being. (pages 558–560)

20. Problem-focused coping is aimed at managing or changing a threatening or harmful stressor. In contrast, emotion-focused coping is aimed primarily at relieving the emotional impact of a stressful situation. In other words, problem-focused coping is used to change the stressor, and emotion-focused coping is used to change one's reaction to the stressor. (pages 561–564)

Matching Exercises

21. Type A behavior

22. immune system

23. stress

24. coping

25. pessimistic explanatory style

26. general adaptation syndrome

27. fight-or-flight response

28. biopsychosocial model

29. daily hassles

Completion Exercises

30. optimistic explanatory style

31. social support

32. emotion-focused coping

33. health psychology

34. conflicts

35. psychoneuroimmunology

36. stressor

37. problem-focused coping

38. negative emotional state

39. coping

Study Matrix

Lesson 22

Stress, Health, and Coping

Please Note: Use this matrix to guide your study and achieve the learning objectives of this lesson. It will also help you to view the video, which defines and demonstrates important concepts and objectives as they relate to everyday life and actual case studies.

Learning Objective	Textbook	Telecourse Student Guide
Define stress, and describe the biopsychosocial model of health psychology.	p. 540	Key Terms and Concepts; Study Activities 1, 13, 23, 28, 33, 38.
Explain how life change, daily hassles, and social conditions contribute to stress.	pp. 541–544	Key Terms and Concepts; Study Activities 6, 14, 29, 36.
Explain the conflict theory of stress, and identify the three basic types of conflict.	pp. 543–544	Key Terms and Concepts; Study Activities 5, 15, 34.
Describe the three stages of the general adaptation syndrome.	pp. 548–549	Key Terms and Concepts; Study Activities 7, 10, 16, 26, 27.
Explain the function of the immune system, and discuss how the immune system is affected by stress.	pp. 549–552	Key Terms and Concepts; Study Activities 4, 8, 11, 17, 22, 35.
Describe the probable effects of different explanatory styles on mental and physical health.	pp. 554–555	Key Terms and Concepts; Study Activities 2,12, 18, 25, 30.
Explain how social support benefits health, as well as how it can increase stress.	pp. 558–560	Key Terms and Concepts; Study Activities 3, 19, 31.
Explain the difference between problem-focused coping and emotion-focused coping.	pp. 561–564	Key Terms and Concepts; Study Activities 9, 20, 24, 32, 37, 39.

Use the Course Compass to orient yourself in the road that you are taking to explore branches and aspects of psychology. The branch and aspects that are covered in this lesson are highlighted in the compass.

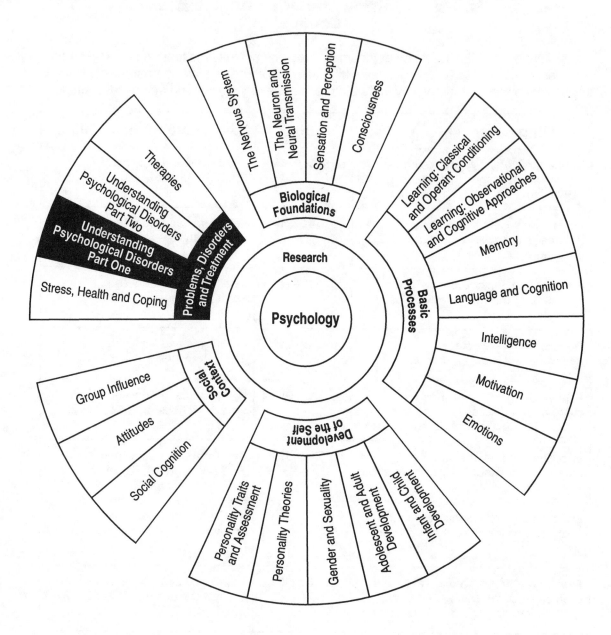

Please note: This compass does not represent the full range of topics comprising the field of psychology; it represents a map for this course only. Each of the five branches represented above has many aspects and subjects that are covered in the 26 lessons of this telecourse. You should remember that these branches and subjects all interrelate.

Lesson 23

Understanding Psychological Disorders, Part One

Questions to Consider

How prevalent are psychological disorders?

What causes people to develop psychological or mental disorders?

Is a person with a psychological disorder mentally ill?

What is the difference between normal anxiety and pathological anxiety?

What are the most common phobias, and what is a social phobia?

What is an obsessive-compulsive disorder?

Lesson Assignments

Before viewing the video program

Read the Questions to Consider, Lesson Preview, and Learning Objectives for this lesson. Use this information to guide your reading, viewing, and thinking.

Read Chapter 14, "Psychological Disorders," pages 571–586, in the textbook.

View the video program, "Understanding Psychological Disorders, Part One"

After viewing the video program

Review the vocabulary listed in the Key Terms and Concepts section. (Page references are keyed to the Hockenbury textbook, *Psychology*. Remember: there is a complete Glossary at the end of the textbook.)

Review the reading assignments for this lesson.

Complete the exercises found in the Study Activities section and check your answers with the Answer Key at the end of this lesson.

Use the Study Matrix found at the end of this lesson to review and assess your knowledge of each Learning Objective.

Lesson Preview

When a person behaves in a very abnormal manner, it can be intriguing. What could cause a person to believe he or she is from outer space? What is wrong with a person who talks to people who do not exist? How can it be that some people are so afraid that they never leave their home?

In the following two lessons we will explore the fascinating world of abnormal psychology and psychological disorders. In the first lesson, we begin by trying to define what is abnormal. This is not as easy as it may appear. Consider these examples:

- A 20-year-old student cannot make any friends. He is angry most all the time. He drinks heavily and uses drugs. He recently joined a gang and was arrested for carrying a gun at school.

- A housewife has begun to sleep 12 to 15 hours every day. She cries frequently and is afraid to be left alone. Her family cannot understand what is wrong and why she cannot "just snap out of it." She says she no longer wants to live.

- A business executive is undergoing a divorce. He has become very anxious. He is physically uncomfortable. His work is suffering. His boss tells him if he cannot get control of himself, he will be fired. He cannot sleep and fears he is losing his mind.

- A person wins the lottery and then immediately starts to give large amounts of money to strangers. The family objects and tells this person not to be so foolish. The person responds by saying that God wants him to give away all that he won to people in need.

Are these people abnormal? Do they have a mental illness? What has caused these people such distress? What is it that limits their abilities to function in a normal manner? We will begin our exploration of psychological disorders by looking at three fairly common psychological problems: anxiety disorders, phobias, and obsessive-compulsive disorder.

In this video, you will meet Lisa Firle, who suffers from obsessive-compulsive disorder and what she calls "contamination" phobias and "hoarding" rituals. Expert psychologists will explain Lisa's disorder and give you the general guidelines they use to diagnose psychological or mental disorders. They will also inform you of the prevalence of psychological disorders and discuss the stigmas that are frequently attached to these disorders. Additionally, expert psychologists discuss phobias and how they can limit a person's ability to function normally.

By understanding more about psychological disorders, you will be increasing your understanding of the human condition. And, with this understanding, you will become better able to deal effectively with the many personalities you will inevitably meet as you travel through life.

Learning Objectives

When you have completed this lesson, you should be able to:

1. Define psychopathology, and discuss the myths and misconceptions about psychological disorders.

2. Explain the DSM, and explain how mental health professionals use it.

3. Discuss the prevalence of psychological disorders in the United States.

4. Compare and contrast normal anxiety with pathological anxiety.

5. Describe the difference between generalized anxiety and panic attacks.

6. Explain what a phobia is and list several common phobias.

7. Describe posttraumatic stress disorder, and describe how it is different from other types of anxiety disorders.

8. Define obsession and compulsion, and give an example each.

9. Discuss obsessive-compulsive disorders.

Key Terms and Concepts

Page references are keyed to the Hockenbury textbook, *Psychology*.

Psychopathology: The scientific study of the origins, symptoms, and development of psychological disorders. (page 573)

Psychological disorder: A pattern of behavioral and psychological symptoms that causes significant personal distress, and impairs the ability to function in one or more important areas of daily life. Can also be called a mental disorder. (page 575)

Diagnostic and Statistical Manual of Mental Disorders **(DSM):** A book published by the American Psychiatric Association that describes the specific symptoms and diagnostic guidelines for different psychological disorders. (page 575)

Anxiety: An unpleasant emotional state characterized by physical arousal and feelings of tension, apprehension, and worry. (page 578)

Anxiety disorder: A category of psychological disorders in which extreme anxiety is the main feature and causes significant disruptions in the person's cognitive, behavioral, or interpersonal functioning. (page 578)

Generalized anxiety disorder: An anxiety disorder characterized by excessive, global, and persistent symptoms of anxiety. (pages 578–579)

Panic attack: A sudden episode of intense anxiety that rapidly escalates in intensity and is accompanied by feelings of fear. (pages 578–579)

Panic disorder: An anxiety disorder in which a person experiences frequent and unexpected panic attacks and is quick to use avoidance to lower anxiety. (pages 578–579)

Phobia: An irrational and illogical fear triggered by a specific object or situation. (pages 580–581)

Agoraphobia: Fear of having an anxiety attack and losing control in public places or unfamiliar situations; fear of leaving the house and familiar surroundings. (page 581)

Common phobias: The objects or situations that produce most common phobias tend to fall into four categories: fear of particular situations (fear of flying, known as aviaphobia; fear of closed or narrow spaces, known as claustrophobia; fear of darkness, or nyctrophobia), fear of features of the natural environment (fear of heights, known as acrophobia), fear of injury or situations arising from medical procedures (fear of blood, known as hemophobia), and fear of animals and insects (fear of spiders, known as arachnephobia; fear of snakes, known as ophidiophobia). (page 580)

Specific phobia: Fear of specific types of objects or situations and avoidance of such objects or situations; interferes with the ability to function in daily life. (pages 580–581)

Social phobia: Fear of social situations in which one can be observed, evaluated, embarrassed, or humiliated by others; avoidance of social situations, such as speaking in public. (page 581)

Posttraumatic stress disorder (PTSD): An anxiety disorder in which chronic and persistent symptoms of anxiety develop in response to an extreme physical or psychological trauma. (pages 582–583)

Obsession: Repeated, intrusive, uncontrollable thoughts or mental images. (page 583)

Compulsion: The uncontrollable urge to perform some behavior; repetitive behavior that a person feels driven to perform. (pages 584–585)

Obsessive-compulsive disorder: An anxiety disorder in which the symptoms of anxiety are triggered by intrusive, repetitive thoughts and urges to perform certain acts. (page 583)

Study Activities

These self-test questions are designed as a study exercise to aid you in understanding the most important terms and concepts in this lesson. To ensure that you have an accurate understanding of the key terms and concepts in this lesson, please check your answers with the Answer Key provided at the end of this lesson.

Multiple-Choice Questions

1. The scientific study of the origins, symptoms, and development of psychological disorders is called

    a. abnormal psychology.

    b. scientific psychology.

    c. psychopathology.

    d. psychogenesis.

2. A psychological disorder can also accurately be called

    a. a mental illness.

    b. a mental disorder.

    c. insanity.

    d. abnormal behavior.

3. The name for the book published by the American Psychiatric Association (APA) that lists the exact criteria that must be met to make a diagnosis of a mental disorder is

    a. *Diagnostic and Statistical Manual of Mental Disorders* (DSM).

    b. *American Psychiatric Association Diagnosis Manual.*

    c. *Manual of Mental Disorders for Mental-Health Professionals.*

    d. *APA Statistical Manual of Psychological Disorders.*

4. Global, persistent, chronic, and excessive apprehension is the main feature of

    a. anxiety.

    b. people who are tense.

    c. panic anxiety.

    d. generalized anxiety disorder.

5. A person who is suffering from frequent and unexpected sudden episodes of extreme anxiety is said to be suffering from

   a. panic disorder.

   b. generalized anxiety disorder.

   c. panic attacks.

   d. phobias.

6. In the general population, mild phobias are commonplace. To be diagnosed as having a psychological disorder, a person's phobia must

   a. be irrational and cause them to feel ashamed.

   b. be a fear of something unusual or typical.

   c. significantly interfere with daily life.

   d. cause panic attacks.

7. Excessive and unreasonable fear of social situations, such as eating in public or making small talk, is called

   a. a social phobia.

   b. pathological shyness.

   c. generalized social anxiety.

   d. agoraphobia.

8. A long-lasting anxiety disorder that develops in response to an extreme physical or psychological trauma is called

   a. agoraphobia.

   b. post trauma anxiety.

   c. posttraumatic stress disorder.

   d. trauma-induced panic disorder.

9. Repeated, intrusive, uncontrollable thoughts or mental images that cause anxiety and distress are called

   a. obsessive-compulsive disorders.

   b. compulsions.

   c. obsessions.

   d. cognitive-anxiety disorders.

10. A person who fears having a panic attack in a public place from which it might be difficult to escape or get help has

    a. claustrophobia–fear of closed spaces.

    b. aphephobia–fear of being touched by another person.

    c. agoraphobia–fear of the marketplace.

    d. phobophobia–fear of acquiring a phobia.

11. In the video, psychological disorders were defined as a pattern of behavioral symptoms that causes significant personal distress and/or

    a. causes interpersonal problems.

    b. impairs one's ability to function in one or more areas of life.

    c. impairs a person's ability to distinguish reality.

    d. causes a person to be unable to work.

12. In the video, you learned that Lisa Firle has many behavioral symptoms that included

    a. sleeping and eating disorders.

    b. problems with controlling her emotions.

    c. phobias and rituals.

    d. difficulty getting along with other people.

13. In the video, you learned that studies on the prevalence of psychological disorders indicate that nearly one in two people will experience symptoms of a psychological disorder

    a. during their lifetime.

    b. that will require hospitalization.

    c. that will cause them problems at work.

    d. that will cause major relationship problems.

14. In the video, you discovered that support groups can be a very effective way to provide

    a. help so that people can overcome their illnesses.

    b. support, encouragement, and education.

    c. new clients for therapists.

    d. education and medications for those in need.

Short-Answer Questions

15. Define psychopathology, and discuss the myths and misconceptions about psychological disorders.

   _____

   _____

   _____

16. Explain the DSM, and explain how mental health professionals use it.

   _____

   _____

   _____

17. Discuss the prevalence of psychological disorders in the United States.

   _____

   _____

   _____

18. Compare normal anxiety with the anxiety experienced by people with anxiety disorders.

   _____

   _____

   _____

19. Describe the difference between generalized anxiety and panic attacks.

   _____

   _____

   _____

20. Explain what a phobia is and list several common phobias.

   _____

   _____

   _____

21. Describe posttraumatic stress disorder, and describe how it is different from other types of anxiety disorders.

   _____

   _____

   _____

22. Define obsession and compulsion, and give an example of each.

   _____

   _____

   _____

23. Discuss obsessive-compulsive disorder.

_____

_____

_____

Matching Exercises

Match the following terms and concepts with the correct definition.

anxiety disorder	panic attack	psychological disorder
common phobias	obsession	compulsion
social phobia	psychopathology	generalized anxiety disorder

24. _____ Characterized by maladaptive behavior and significant disruptions in a person's activities, moods, and thought processes.

25. _____ The need to engage in certain behaviors a specific number of times or to count to a certain number before performing some action or task.

26. _____ Eating a meal in public, making small talk, and especially the need to perform in front of others causes extreme anxiety and personal distress.

27. _____ In contrast to an ongoing sense of apprehension, uneasiness, and distress, this form of anxiety occurs suddenly and rapidly escalates in intensity.

28. _____ The scientific study of the origins, symptoms, and development of mental or psychological disorders.

29. _____ People with this disorder worry excessively, are constantly tense and anxious, and their anxiety is pervasive.

30. _____ In the general population, these are extremely common and tend to affect more women than men.

31. _____ A pattern of behavioral and psychological symptoms that causes significant personal distress, impairing the ability to function in one or more important areas of daily life.

32. _____ Feeling of uncertainty about having accomplished a simple task, such as not shutting off appliances or locking a door. Typically accompanied by a strong urge to check and make sure you have accomplished the task.

Completion Exercises

Fill in each blank with the most appropriate term or terms from the list of answers provided.

agoraphobia

anxiety

fear

obsessive-compulsive disorder

panic attack

panic disorder

phobia

posttraumatic stress disorder

specific phobia

33. In all cases, people with _____ feel that something terrible will happen if what they feel they must do does not get done.

34. People with a _____ are terrified of a particular object or situation and go to great lengths to avoid that object or situation.

35. Originally _____ was primarily associated with direct experiences of military combat.

36. Classical conditioning may well be involved in the development of a specific _____ that can be traced back to some sort of traumatic event.

37. As your internal alarm, _____ puts you on physical alert, preparing you to defensively fight or flee real or imagined dangers.

38. A person with _____ fears having a panic attack in a public place from which it might be difficult to escape or get help.

39. Psychologically, people with _____ are extremely sensitive to the signs of physical arousal and changes in their bodily functions.

40. In the video, psychologists explained that a phobia is an intense, irrational _____ that is triggered by a specific object or situation.

41. In the video, you learned that a _____ is an episode of intense anxiety that rapidly escalates in intensity.

Answer Key

Multiple-Choice Questions

1. c	5. a	9. c	13. a
2. b	6. c	10. c	14. b
3. a	7. a	11. b	
4. d	8. c	12. c	

Short-Answer Questions

Your answers should include the following:

15. Psychopathology refers to the scientific study of the origins, symptoms, and development of psychological disorders. There are many myths and misconceptions about abnormal behavior and mental illness. Being labeled "crazy" carries all kinds of implications, most of which reflect negative stereotypes about people with mental problems. The entertainment industry is a major source of misinformation about mental illness. (pages 572–573)

16. The DSM stands for the *Diagnostic and Statistical Manual of Mental Disorders*. This book describes psychological disorders and includes the criteria that must be met to make a diagnosis for each disorder. (page 575)

17. Approximately 50 percent of adults have experienced the symptoms of a psychological disorder at some point in their lifetime. (page 576)

18. Normal anxiety is a familiar emotion characterized by feelings of tension, apprehension, and worry that occur during times of conflict or crisis. People with anxiety disorders have anxiety that is irrational, uncontrollable, and is disruptive to relationships and everyday activities. (page 578)

19. People with generalized anxiety experience chronic tension and a general sense of ongoing apprehension. In contrast to generalized anxiety, panic anxiety is a sudden episode of extreme anxiety that rapidly escalates in intensity. Panic attacks can come on without notice. (pages 578–580)

20. A phobia is an intense, irrational fear that is triggered by a specific object of event. Common phobias include fear of blood, snakes, closed spaces, heights, and some social occasions, like public speaking. (pages 580–582)

21. Posttraumatic stress disorder is a long-lasting anxiety disorder that develops in response to an extreme trauma. Posttraumatic stress disorder is unusual in that the source of the disorder is the traumatic event itself, rather than a cause that lies within the individual. (pages 582–583)

22. Obsessions are repeated, intrusive, uncontrollable thoughts or mental images. A compulsion is a repetitive behavior that a person feels driven to perform. Repeatedly checking windows and doors to make sure they are locked is an

example of a compulsion. Recurring worry that windows and doors are not locked is an example of an obsession. (pages 583–585)

23. Obsessive-compulsive disorder, also called OCD, is an anxiety disorder in which a person's life is dominated by repetitive thoughts and behaviors. (pages 583–585)

Matching Exercises

24. anxiety disorder

25. compulsion

26. social phobia

27. panic attack

28. psychopathology

29. generalized anxiety disorder

30. common phobias

31. psychological disorder

32. obsession

Completion Exercises

33. obsessive-compulsive disorder

34. specific phobia

35. posttraumatic stress disorder

36. phobia

37. anxiety

38. agoraphobia

39. panic disorder

40. fear

41. panic attack

Study Matrix

Lesson 23

Understanding Psychological Disorders, Part One

Please Note: Use this matrix to guide your study and achieve the learning objectives of this lesson. It will also help you to view the video, which defines and demonstrates important concepts and objectives as they relate to everyday life and actual case studies.

Learning Objective	Textbook	Telecourse Student Guide
Define psychopathology, and discuss the myths and misconceptions about psychological disorders.	pp. 572–574	Key Terms and Concepts; Study Activities 1, 2, 11, 15, 28, 31.
Explain the DSM, and explain how mental health professionals use it.	p. 575	Key Terms and Concepts; Study Activities 3, 16.
Discuss the prevalence of psychological disorders in the United States.	p. 576	Study Activities 13, 14, 17.
Compare and contrast normal anxiety with pathological anxiety.	p. 578	Key Terms and Concepts; Study Activities 18, 24, 35, 39.
Describe the difference between generalized anxiety and panic attacks.	pp. 578–580	Key Terms and Concepts; Study Activities 4, 5, 7, 19, 27, 29, 40, 42.
Explain what a phobia is and list several common phobias.	pp. 580–582	Key Terms and Concepts; Study Activities 6, 10, 12, 20, 26, 30, 35, 37, 39, 41.
Describe posttraumatic stress disorder, and describe how it is different from other types of anxiety disorders.	pp. 582–583	Key Terms and Concepts; Study Activities 7, 8, 21, 36.
Define obsession and compulsion, and give an example each.	pp. 583–585	Key Terms and Concepts; Study Activities 9, 22, 25, 32.
Discuss obsessive-compulsive disorders.	pp. 583–585	Key Terms and Concepts; Study Activities 23, 33.

Use the Course Compass to orient yourself in the road that you are taking to explore branches and aspects of psychology. The branch and aspects that are covered in this lesson are highlighted in the compass.

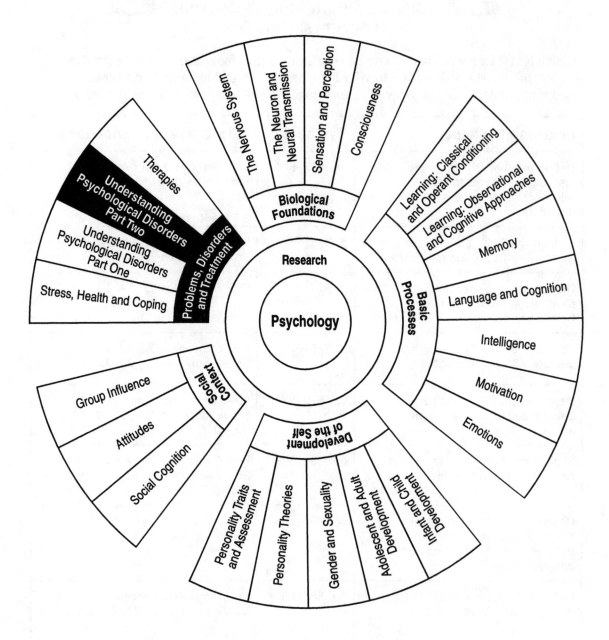

Please note: This compass does not represent the full range of topics comprising the field of psychology; it represents a map for this course only. Each of the five branches represented above has many aspects and subjects that are covered in the 26 lessons of this telecourse. You should remember that these branches and subjects all interrelate.

Lesson 24

Understanding Psychological Disorders, Part Two

Questions to Consider

What is the difference between normal behavior and "abnormal" behavior?

What is schizophrenia?

What are the most common symptoms of schizophrenia?

What is a bipolar disorder?

What causes people to become depressed?

How likely is it that a person will experience major depression sometime during his or her lifespan?

Lesson Assignments

Before viewing the video program

Read the Questions to Consider, Lesson Preview, and Learning Objectives for this lesson. Use this information to guide your reading, viewing, and thinking.

Read Chapter 14, "Psychological Disorders," pages 586–614, in the textbook.

View the video program, "Understanding Psychological Disorders, Part Two"

After viewing the video program

Review the vocabulary listed in the Key Terms and Concepts section. (Page references are keyed to the Hockenbury textbook, *Psychology*. Remember: there is a complete Glossary at the end of the textbook.)

Review the reading assignments for this lesson.

Complete the exercises found in the Study Activities section and check your answers with the Answer Key at the end of this lesson.

Use the Study Matrix found at the end of this lesson to review and assess your knowledge of each Learning Objective.

Lesson Preview

What are your reactions when you hear that someone is suffering from a mental illness? A common misconception is the belief that these people are defective, weak, or must have in some way caused their problems. As you will learn, however, this is far from the truth. People who are afflicted with serious mental disorders are not defective, nor are they weak, nor have they done anything to deserve their sufferings.

In this second lesson dealing with psychological disorders, we will focus on the serious and prevalent conditions of major depression and schizophrenia. As you will learn, in one way or another, serious psychological disorders touch the daily lives of most people. Major depression affects the lives of 1 in 4 adults, and statistics on the most distressing mental disorder, schizophrenia, are also alarming. More than 1 of every 100 people over the age of 18 will suffer from repeated episodes of schizophrenia. People diagnosed with schizophrenia comprise more than half the number of patients in mental hospitals. Even more sobering is the fact that most people with schizophrenia face a prolonged struggle, with many never fully recovering.

In this video, you will meet Robert Fernandez, a 35-year-old man who has suffered for many years from schizophrenia. You will learn how schizophrenia has affected Fernandez's life—and how he has found an effective way to deal with this potentially life-ruining illness. Additionally, the video explores mood disorders. Psychologist David Barlow will explain the all-too-common illness of depression. You will also learn about bipolar disorder and discover how these mood disorders can, if untreated, severely limit a person's ability to live a normal life.

Because mental disorders will, directly or indirectly, affect us all, we need to have an accurate understanding of these serious conditions. It is through our increased understanding that we will improve our ability to help those who are afflicted with these conditions.

Learning Objectives

When you have completed this lesson, you should be able to:

1. Describe the concepts of mood disorder and major depression.

2. Identify the cognitive, physical, emotional, and behavioral symptoms of major depression.

3. Describe seasonal affective disorder.

4. Describe bipolar disorder, and discuss the prevalence of bipolar disorder.

5. Discuss how biology, genetics, and stress may contribute to the development of mood disorders.

6. Define the concept of personality disorder, and identify common personality disorders.

7. Define the concept of dissociative disorders, and discuss the controversy surrounding dissociative identity disorder.

8. Define schizophrenia by listing the positive and negative symptoms of this disorder.

9. Describe the evidence that points to the involvement of genetic factors and brain abnormalities in the development of schizophrenia.

10. List the guidelines for helping to prevent suicide.

Key Terms and Concepts

Page references are keyed to the Hockenbury textbook, *Psychology*.

Mood disorders: A category of mental disorders in which significant and chronic disruptions in mood is the predominant symptom, causing impaired cognitive, behavioral, and physical functioning. (page 586)

Major depression: A mood disorder characterized by extreme and persistent feelings of despondency, worthlessness, and hopelessness, causing impaired emotional, cognitive, behavioral, and physical functioning. (pages 586–587)

Dysthymic disorder: A mood disorder involving chronic, low-grade feelings of depression that produce subjective discomfort, but do not seriously impair the ability to function. (page 588)

Seasonal affective disorder (SAD): A mood disorder in which episodes of depression typically recur during the fall and winter and remit during the spring and summer. (pages 588–589)

Bipolar disease: A mood disorder involving periods of incapacitating depression alternating with periods of extreme euphoria and excitement; formerly called manic depression. (pages 589–590)

Manic episode: A sudden, rapidly escalating emotional state characterized by extreme euphoria, excitement, physical energy, and rapid thoughts and speech. (pages 589–590)

Cyclothymic disorder: A mood disorder characterized by moderate but frequent mood swings that are not severe enough to qualify as bipolar disease. (page 590)

Personality disorder: Inflexible, maladaptive patterns of thoughts, emotions, behavior, and interpersonal functioning that are stable over time. (page 595)

Paranoid personality disorder: A personality disorder characterized by a pervasive distrust and suspiciousness of the motives of others. (page 596)

Antisocial personality disorder: A personality disorder characterized by a pervasive pattern of disregarding and violating the rights of others; often referred to as being a psychopath or sociopath. (page 597)

Psychopath or Sociopath: Terms used interchangeably to refer to a person who has the ability to lie, cheat, steal, and otherwise manipulate and harm other people with little or no remorse. (page 597)

Borderline personality disorder: A personality disorder characterized by instability of interpersonal relationships, self-image, and emotions. (pages 597–598)

Dissociative disorders: A category of psychological disorder in which extreme and frequent disruptions of awareness, memory, and personal identity impair the ability to function. (pages 598–599)

Dissociative amnesia: A psychological disorder involving the partial or total inability to recall important personal information. (page 600)

Dissociative identity disorder (DID): A psychological disorder involving extensive memory disruptions along with the presence of two or more personal identities; formerly called multiple personality disorder. (page 602)

Schizophrenia: A mental disorder in which the ability to function is impaired by severely distorted beliefs, perceptions, and thought processes. (page 602)

Positive symptoms of schizophrenia: Symptoms that reflect excesses or distortions of normal functioning, including delusions, hallucinations, and disorganized thoughts and behavior. (pages 602–603)

Negative symptoms of schizophrenia: Symptoms that reflect defects or deficits in normal functioning, including reduced motivation, emotional expressiveness, or speech. (pages 602–603)

Delusion: A falsely held belief that persists in spite of contradictory evidence. (pages 602–603)

Hallucination: A false or distorted perception that seems vividly real to the person experiencing it. (pages 602–603)

Study Activities

These self-test questions are designed as a study exercise to aid you in understanding the most important terms and concepts in this lesson. To ensure that you have an accurate understanding of the key terms and concepts in this lesson, please check your answers with the Answer Key provided at the end of this lesson.

Multiple-Choice Questions

1. Along with a general loss of energy and motivation, people suffering from depression also

   a. typically gain weight.

   b. have disruptions in eating and sexual interest.

   c. become impulsive.

   d. spend increased time in nondreaming sleep.

2. A mood disorder involving chronic, low-grade feelings of depression that produces personal discomfort but does not stop a person from functioning in daily life is called

   a. double depression.

   b. bipolar disorder.

   c. cyclothymic disorder.

   d. dysthymic disorder.

3. A form of depression that occurs when there is the least amount of sunlight is called

   a. seasonal affective disorder.

   b. dysthymic depression.

   c. ultraviolet or chromatic depression.

   d. agitated depression.

4. Formerly called manic depression, the disorder involving periods of incapacitating depression, alternating with periods of extreme excitement and euphoria, is called

   a. cyclothymic disorder.

   b. euphoria-depression disorder.

   c. bipolar disorder.

   d. major mood disorder.

5. In general, antidepressant medications are

   a. used for only those with recurrent episodes of depression.

   b. only helpful for depression in 50 percent of the cases.

   c. are highly effective, and eliminate symptoms in 80 percent of the cases.

   d. are not helpful for those with genetic predispositions to become depressed.

6. A person who has a pattern of inflexible, maladaptive thoughts, emotions, and behaviors that last over time has

   a. an antisocial personality.

   b. a personality disorder.

   c. a borderline personality.

   d. a paranoid personality disorder.

7. People who cannot remember who they are or wander aimlessly suffer from

   a. a dissociative disorder.

   b. dissociative amnesia.

   c. identity confusion and extensive amnesia.

   d. identity crisis with dissociative awareness.

8. People suffering from schizophrenia often have delusions, hallucinations, and

   a. disruptions in sleep and eating patterns.

   b. the presence of two or more distinct personalities.

   c. severely disorganized thought processes, speech, and behavior.

   d. greatly increased emotional expressiveness.

9. Researchers have found that about half of the people with schizophrenia

   a. were raised in a dysfunctional family environment.

   b. have a deficiency of the neurotransmitter dopamine.

   c. show some type of brain structure abnormality.

   d. had parents who had a viral infection during pregnancy.

10. The majority of people who commit suicide are

   a. women.

   b. adolescents.

   c. people over 65.

   d. young and middle-aged adults.

11. In the video, you learned that major depression and bipolar disorders are categorized as

    a. anxiety disorders.

    b. personality disorders.

    c. mood disorders.

    d. forms of abnormal behavior.

12. In the video, Robert Fernandez explained that he has suffered for many years from

    a. depression and hallucinations.

    b. schizophrenia.

    c. periods of extreme anxiety.

    d. phobias that made it difficult for him to go out in public.

13. In the video, psychologist David Barlow explained that sadness, impaired cognitive functioning, and loss of energy and motivation are characteristic of

    a. all mood disorders.

    b. bipolar disorder.

    c. schizophrenia.

    d. depression.

14. In the video, you learned that schizophrenia is a complex disorder and that the causes appear to be

    a. mostly related to a person's upbringing.

    b. function of past traumatic experiences.

    c. equally complex.

    d. a complete mystery to science.

Short-Answer Questions

15. Describe the concepts of mood disorder and major depression.

    _____

    _____

    _____

16. Identify the cognitive, physical, emotional, and behavioral symptoms of major depression.

    _____

    _____

    _____

17. Describe seasonal affective disorder.

_____

_____

_____

18. Describe bipolar disorder, and discuss the prevalence of bipolar disorder.

_____

_____

_____

19. Discuss how biology, genetics, and stress may contribute to the development of mood disorders.

_____

_____

_____

20. Define the concept of personality disorder, and identify common personality disorders.

_____

_____

_____

21. Define the concept of dissociative disorders, and discuss the controversy surrounding dissociative identity disorder.

_____

_____

_____

22. Define schizophrenia by listing positive and negative symptoms of this disorder.

_____

_____

_____

23. Describe the evidence that points to the involvement of genetic factors and brain abnormalities in the development of schizophrenia.

_____

_____

_____

24. List the guidelines for helping to prevent suicide

_____

_____

_____

25. In the video, psychologists explained that there are many factors believed to be involved in the development of mood disorders. List the three most common factors that may contribute to the development of mood disorders.

_____

_____

_____

Matching Exercises

Match the following terms and concepts with the correct definition.

mood disorders	hallucination	schizophrenia
dysthymic disorder	bipolar disease	delusion
cyclothymic disorder	seasonal affective disorder	manic episode

26. _____ A mood disorder that typically occurs during periods when there is the least amount of sunlight.

27. _____ An extremely complex disorder in which there is enormous individual variability in the onset, symptoms, duration, and length of recovery.

28. _____ These are the most disturbing experiences in schizophrenia and can involve any of the senses.

29. _____ Formerly called manic depression, this psychological disorder is characterized by periods of extreme depression alternating with periods of extreme excitement.

30. _____ In this category of mental disorders, the predominant symptoms cause impaired cognitive, behavioral, and physical functioning.

31. _____ People with this disorder are often perceived as being extremely moody, unpredictable, and inconsistent.

32. _____ Characterized by rapid thoughts, speech, and feelings of euphoria and excitement.

33. _____ This disorder is characterized by many of the symptoms of depression, does not significantly impair daily functions, and lasts for a long period of time.

34. _____ A falsely held belief that persists in spite of contradictory evidence.

Completion Exercises

Fill in each blank with the most appropriate term or terms from the list of answers provided.

bipolar disorder

borderline personality

dissociative amnesia

dissociative identity disorder

major depression

paranoid personality

personality disorder

positive symptoms of schizophrenia

psychopath

35. Pervasive mistrust and suspiciousness of others are the defining features of the _____.

36. Formerly known as multiple personality disorder, _____ is not considered a genuine psychological disorder by all mental health professionals.

37. Of all the personality disorders, the chaotic disorder called _____ is the most commonly diagnosed.

38. Feelings of sadness, hopelessness, helplessness, guilt, emptiness, or worthlessness are typical of the emotional symptoms of _____.

39. Usually becoming evident in adolescence or early adulthood, someone with a _____ has personality traits that are inflexible and maladaptive.

40. Delusions, hallucinations, and severely disorganized thought processes, speech, and behavior are _____.

41. _____ refers to the partial or total inability to recall important information that is not due to a medical condition.

42. Often referred to as a _____, the individual with antisocial personality disorder has the ability to lie, cheat, and steal without feeling any remorse or regret.

43. In the video, you learned that _____ differs from major depression in that it involves abnormal moods on both ends of the emotional spectrum.

Answer Key

Multiple-Choice Questions

1. b	5. c	9. c	13. d
2. d	6. b	10. c	14. c
3. a	7. a	11. c	
4. c	8. c	12. b	

Short-Answer Questions

Your answers should include the following:

15. A mood disorder is a serious, persistent disturbance in a person's emotions that causes psychological discomfort, and impairs the ability to function. Major depression is the most common form of mood disorder and is characterized by extreme and persistent feelings of despondency and worthlessness. (pages 586–587)

16. Cognitive symptoms of major depression include difficulty in thinking, concentrating, and remembering. Physical symptoms include changes in appetite, sleep patterns and energy level. Emotional symptoms include feelings of sadness, hopelessness, and guilt. Behavioral symptoms include episodes of crying, loss of interest in usual activities, and withdrawal from other people and social situations. (pages 587–588)

17. Seasonal affective disorder refers to a depression that typically occurs during the fall and winter months when there is the least amount of sunlight. (page 589)

18. Bipolar disorder is a mood disorder involving periods of extreme depression is alternating with periods of extreme excitement and euphoria. Bipolar disorder is not nearly as common as major depression. Bipolar disorder affects about one percent of the adult population. (pages 589–591)

19. There is strong evidence that people inherit a genetic predisposition to develop a mood disorder. There is also ample evidence of the involvement of the neurotransmitters serotonin and norepinephrine in major depression. Researchers have found that stress plays an important part in the triggering of mood disorders. Exposure to recent stressful events is one of the best predictors of episodes of major depression. (pages 591–593)

20. A personality disorder is an inflexible, maladaptive pattern of thinking, feeling, and behaving that is stable over time and deviates from the social expectations of the culture. Common personality disorders are paranoid personality, schizoid personality, antisocial personality, borderline personality, histrionic personality, narcissistic personality, obsessive-compulsive personality, and dependent personality. (pages 595–598)

21. Dissociative disorders are psychological disorders in which extreme and frequent disruptions of awareness, memory, and personal identity impair the ability to function. Dissociative identity disorder, formerly known as multiple personality disorder, is not considered by all mental health professionals as a genuine psychological disorder. (pages 598–602)

22. Schizophrenia is a mental disorder in which the ability to function is impaired by severely distorted beliefs, perceptions, and thought processes. The positive symptoms include delusions, hallucinations, and severely disorganized thinking, speech and behavior. The negative symptoms include deficits in behavior, emotion, and motivation. The most common negative symptoms are flat affect, alogia, and avolition. (pages 602–606)

23. Studies of families, twins, and adopted individuals have firmly established that genetic factors play a significant role in many cases of schizophrenia. Researchers have found that about half of the people with schizophrenia show some type of brain structure abnormality. (pages 607–612)

24. The guidelines for helping prevent suicide: if you are uncomfortable talking to a suicidal person say so in a way that encourages the person to seek help somewhere, don't minimize the person's suicidal intentions, let the person talk about his/her feelings, help identify solutions, ask the person to delay taking any action, and encourage the person to seek professional help. (pages 612–614)

25. The most common factors contributing to the development of mood disorders are genetic predisposition, biochemical factors, and traumatic or stressful events. (pages 591–593)

Matching Exercises

26. seasonal affective disorder

27. schizophrenia

28. hallucination

29. bipolar disease

30. mood disorders

31. cyclothymic disorder

32. manic episode

33. dysthymic disorder

34. delusion

Completion Exercises

35. paranoid personality

36. dissociative identity disorder

37. borderline personality

38. major depression

39. personality disorder

40. positive symptoms of schizophrenia

41. dissociative amnesia

42. psychopath

43. bipolar disorder

Study Matrix

Lesson 24

Understanding Psychological Disorders, Part Two

Please Note: Use this matrix to guide your study and achieve the learning objectives of this lesson. It will also help you to view the video, which defines and demonstrates important concepts and objectives as they relate to everyday life and actual case studies.

Learning Objective	Textbook	Telecourse Student Guide
Describe the concepts of mood disorder and major depression.	pp. 586–589	Key Terms and Concepts; Study Activities 11, 15, 38.
Identify the cognitive, physical, emotional, and behavioral symptoms of major depression.	pp. 587–588	Key Terms and Concepts; Study Activities 1, 2, 13, 16, 30, 35, 41.
Describe seasonal affective disorder.	p. 589	Key Terms and Concepts; Study Activities 3, 17, 26.
Describe bipolar disorder, and discuss the prevalence of bipolar disorder.	pp. 589–591	Key Terms and Concepts; Study Activities 4, 18, 29, 32, 34, 43.
Discuss how biology, genetics, and stress may contribute to the development of mood disorders.	pp. 591–593	Study Activities 19, 25, 31.
Define the concept of personality disorder, and identify common personality disorders.	pp. 595–598	Key Terms and Concepts; Study Activities 6, 20, 33, 36, 37, 39, 42.
Define the concept of dissociative disorders, and discuss the controversy surrounding dissociative identity disorder.	pp. 598–602	Key Terms and Concepts; Study Activities 7, 21.
Define schizophrenia by listing the positive and negative symptoms of this disorder.	pp. 602–607	Key Terms and Concepts; Study Activities 8, 12, 22, 27, 28, 40.
Describe the evidence that points to the involvement of genetic factors and brain abnormalities in the development of schizophrenia.	pp. 607–612	Key Terms and Concepts; Study Activities 9, 14, 23.
List the guidelines for helping to prevent suicide.	pp. 613–614	Study Activities 10, 24.

Use the Course Compass to orient yourself in the road that you are taking to explore branches and aspects of psychology. The branch and aspects that are covered in this lesson are highlighted in the compass.

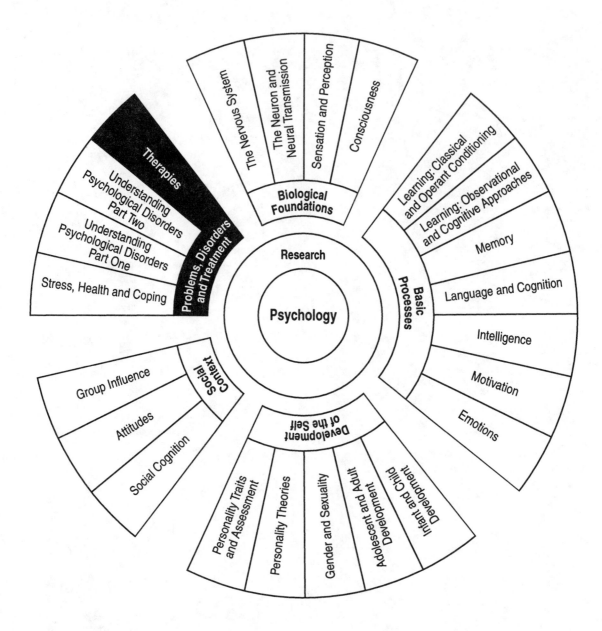

Please note: This compass does not represent the full range of topics comprising the field of psychology; it represents a map for this course only. Each of the five branches represented above has many aspects and subjects that are covered in the 26 lessons of this telecourse. You should remember that these branches and subjects all interrelate.

Lesson 25

Therapies

Questions to Consider

What is psychotherapy?

How effective is therapy? Is there scientific proof that therapy is effective?

What is the most common reason people go to see a psychotherapist?

Is it true that electric shock treatment is still used to treat mental disorders?

How do psychoactive medications help people with psychological problems?

What is the cornerstone of all good psychotherapy?

Lesson Assignments

Before viewing the video program

Read the Questions to Consider, Lesson Preview, and Learning Objectives for this lesson. Use this information to guide your reading, viewing, and thinking.

Read Chapter 15, "Therapies," in the textbook.

View the video program, "Therapies"

After viewing the video program

Review the vocabulary listed in the Key Terms and Concepts section. (Page references are keyed to the Hockenbury textbook, *Psychology*. Remember: there is a complete Glossary at the end of the textbook.)

Review the reading assignments for this lesson.

Complete the exercises found in the Study Activities section and check your answers with the Answer Key at the end of this lesson.

Use the Study Matrix found at the end of this lesson to review and assess your knowledge of each Learning Objective.

Lesson Preview

What do you think of when you hear the word psychotherapy? Do you think of some lonely, confused person telling his or her innermost secrets to some bearded old man sitting in a large leather chair? Well, if you do, you are not alone. Who goes to therapy and what happens in psychotherapy is largely misunderstood.

This is surprising when you consider that the likelihood of someone experiencing a symptom of a psychological disorder during his or her lifespan is 50 percent. Psychotherapy has been repeatedly proven to be effective in helping people with various problems and symptoms.

Some people see a therapist to overcome a specific problem, such as an irrational fear. Others seek professional help because they are going through a difficult time—maybe the death of a loved one or a divorce. Some people seek out a therapist because they are not fully satisfied with their lives. Other cases involve people struggling with drugs, problems getting along with other people, episodes of depression, insomnia, angry children, headaches, and so forth.

In a nutshell, psychotherapy exists because people have problems and, sometimes, life becomes too difficult to manage on their own.

In this video, you will meet Lynda Minkoff, age 52. Like so many people, Lynda is having life adjustment problems. We will follow Lynda as she visits several different therapists in hopes of finding someone whom she believes can help her better understand and deal with her problems.

From this video, you will gain the ability to compare and contrast several different approaches to psychotherapy. Expert psychologists and therapists discuss their particular approach to therapy in this video. While most therapy is conducted confidentially between a licensed therapist and his or her client, there are other forms of psychotherapy, such as group therapy and family therapy.

You will also discover that psychotherapy often includes the use of psychoactive medications. You will hear expert psychologists discuss the many ways in which medications can be used to help relieve suffering and aid the therapeutic process.

With a better understanding of psychotherapy, you will be better able to help yourself and others when, and if, you or they ever need the help of a psychotherapist.

Learning Objectives

When you have completed this lesson, you should be able to:

1. Discuss the process of psychotherapy.

2. Discuss the history of psychoanalysis, including the techniques of free association and dream interpretations, and the concepts of resistance and transference.

3. Describe the therapeutic techniques that are used in client-centered therapy.

4. Define behavioral therapy and discuss how basic learning principles are applied to modify behavior.

5. Compare and contrast cognitive therapy, developed by psychiatrist Aaron T. Beck, to rational-emotive therapy, developed by psychologist Albert Ellis.

6. Discuss the general effectiveness of psychotherapy.

7. List the four factors that are common to all effective therapies.

8. Identify the categories of psychoactive medications and discuss their effectiveness.

9. List some of the common misconceptions about psychotherapy.

Key Terms and Concepts

Page references are keyed to the Hockenbury textbook, *Psychology*.

Psychotherapy: The treatment of emotional, behavioral, and interpersonal problems through the use of psychological techniques designed to encourage understanding and elicit change. (page 621)

Biomedical therapies: The use of medications, and other medical treatments, to treat the symptoms associated with psychological disorders. (page 621)

Psychoanalysis: A type of psychotherapy originated by Sigmund Freud and used to explore repressed or unconscious impulses, anxieties, and internal conflicts. (pages 622–623)

Free association: A technique used in psychoanalysis in which the patient spontaneously reports all thoughts, feelings, and mental images as they come to mind. (page 623)

Resistance: In psychoanalysis, the patient's unconscious attempts to block the revelation of repressed memories and conflicts. (page 623)

Dream interpretation: A technique used in psychoanalysis in which the content of dreams is analyzed for disguised or symbolic wishes, meanings, and motivations. (page 623)

Transference: The process by which emotions and desires originally associated with a significant person in the patient's life are unconsciously transferred to the psychoanalyst. (page 624)

Client-centered therapy: A type of humanistic psychotherapy, developed by Carl Rogers, in which the therapist is nondirective and reflective and the client directs the focus of the therapy. (page 626)

Behavior therapy: A type of psychotherapy aimed at changing behavior by using basic learning principles and techniques. (pages 628–629)

Counterconditioning: A behavior therapy technique that involves changing behavior by conditioning a new response that is incompatible with a previously learned response. (page 629)

Systemic desensitization: A type of behavior therapy in which phobic responses are reduced by pairing relaxation with images or situations that a person finds fear-producing. (page 630)

Cognitive therapies: Psychotherapies that are based on the assumption that psychological problems are due to maladaptive patterns of thinking; treatment focuses on changing unhealthy thinking patterns. (page 636)

Rational-emotive therapy (RET): A type of cognitive therapy, developed by Albert Ellis, that focuses on changing irrational beliefs. (page 636)

Cognitive therapy (CT): A type of cognitive therapy, developed by Aaron T. Beck, which focuses on changing unrealistic beliefs. (pages 638–639)

Group therapy: A form of psychotherapy that involves one or more therapists working simultaneously with a small group of clients. (page 641)

Family therapy: A form of psychotherapy that is based on the assumption that the family is a system and treats the family as a unit. (page 643)

Eclecticism: The pragmatic and integrated use of techniques from different psychotherapies. (page 648)

Antipsychotic medications: Prescription drugs that are used to reduce psychotic symptoms; frequently used in the treatment of schizophrenia. (pages 650–651)

Antianxiety medications: Prescription drugs that are used to alleviate the symptoms of anxiety. (page 653)

Antidepressant medications: Prescription drugs that are used to reduce the symptoms associated with depression. (page 655)

Electroconvulsive therapy: A biomedical therapy used primarily in the treatment of depression that involves electrically inducing a brief brain seizure; also called shock therapy or electric shock therapy. (page 657)

Effectiveness of therapy: Research shows that psychotherapy is significantly more effective than no treatment is in relieving symptoms of psychological distress. (page 644)

Therapeutic relationship: Characterized by mutual respect, trust, and hope, the relationship between the therapist and client is the most important factor associated with effective therapy. (page 648)

Study Activities

These self-test questions are designed as a study exercise to aid you in understanding the most important terms and concepts in this lesson. To ensure that you have an accurate understanding of the key terms and concepts in this lesson, please check your answers with the Answer Key provided at the end of this lesson.

Multiple-Choice Questions

1. In the video, psychotherapy is described as

    a. the process used to treat mentally ill people.

    b. more of an art than a science.

    c. techniques used to treat emotional, behavioral, and interpersonal problems.

    d. a field that is being replaced by physicians prescribing drugs.

2. According to Freudian psychoanalysis, early unresolved childhood experiences

    a. can influence a person's thoughts and behavior later in life.

    b. are unimportant.

    c. can be easily uncovered using the technique of free association.

    d. can be discovered in the manifest content of dreams.

3. When a patient unconsciously responds to the therapist as though the therapist is a significant person in the patient's life, in psychoanalysis this is called

    a. interpretation.

    b. manifest or latent content.

    c. transference.

    d. a Freudian slip.

4. In client-centered therapy, the therapist must accept, value, and care for the client regardless of what his or her problems are. Carl Rogers called this quality

    a. conditional acceptance.

    b. unconditional positive regard.

    c. humanism.

    d. empathic understanding.

5. In contrast to insight-oriented therapies, behavior therapists focus on

    a. uncovering resistance by using operant and classical conditioning.

    b. current behaviors rather than past experiences.

    c. using learning techniques to resolve conflicts.

    d. problems that can be resolved by nondirective techniques.

6. The key premise of rational-emotive therapy is that people's difficulties are caused by

    a. unresolved early childhood experiences.

    b. many reasons, so it is best to concentrate on changing behaviors.

    c. unexpressed emotions and thoughts.

    d. faulty expectations and irrational thinking.

7. Most people with psychological symptoms

    a. are helped by a professional therapist.

    b. experience one or more periods of spontaneous remission.

    c. do not seek help from mental health professionals.

    d. do not need to seek help unless they become hospitalized.

8. While there are many factors that contribute to effective psychotherapy, the most important are the factors associated with the

    a. therapeutic relationship.

    b. therapist characteristics.

    c. client characteristics.

    d. external circumstances.

9. The therapeutic effect of antipsychotic medications has

    a. dramatically decreased the number of people hospitalized for mental disorders.

    b. reduced the negative and positive symptoms of schizophrenia.

    c. the common side effect of tardive dyskinesia (facial tics and grimaces).

    d. been proven effective in treating the symptoms of both depression and anxiety.

10. Electroconvulsive therapy is

    a. a time-consuming and complex treatment for depression.

    b. a very effective treatment for severe depression.

    c. much less effective than antidepressant drugs.

    d. a well-understood treatment for severe depression.

11. In the video, Lynda explained that one of the main reasons she wanted to see a therapist was that

    a. she suffers from panic attacks.

    b. she has many phobias.

    c. she is going through a difficult time in her life.

    d. she needs medications to help her sleep.

12. In the video, psychologists explained that exploring childhood issues and discussing dreams is a common technique used in the

 a. behavioral approach to therapy.

 b. humanistic approach to therapy.

 c. psychodynamic approach to therapy.

 d. cognitive approach to therapy.

Short-Answer Questions

13. Discuss the process of psychotherapy.

_____

_____

_____

14. Discuss the history of psychoanalysis, including the techniques of free association and dream interpretation, and the concepts of resistance and transference.

_____

_____

_____

15. Describe the therapeutic techniques that are used in client-centered therapy.

_____

_____

_____

16. Define behavioral therapy and describe how basic learning principles are applied to modify behavior.

_____

_____

_____

17. Compare and contrast cognitive therapy, developed by psychiatrist Aaron T. Beck, to rational-emotive therapy, developed by psychologist Albert Ellis.

_____

_____

_____

18. Discuss the general effectiveness of psychotherapy.

_____

_____

_____

19. List the four factors that are common to all effective therapies.

    _____

    _____

    _____

20. Identify the categories of psychoactive medications and discuss their effectiveness.

    _____

    _____

    _____

21. List some of the common misconceptions about what psychotherapy is and what it can accomplish.

    _____

    _____

    _____

22. In the video, you were introduced to several different approaches to therapy. Discuss the main differences between the psychoanalytic approach and the behavioral approach.

    _____

    _____

    _____

Matching Exercises

Match the following terms and concepts with the correct definition.

counterconditioning	psychotherapy	antidepressant medications
biomedical therapy	cognitive therapy	systemic desensitization
therapeutic relationship	free association	rational-emotive therapy

23. _____ Used to counteract the symptoms of guilt, dejection, hopelessness, difficulty concentrating, and disruptions in sleep, energy, appetite, and sexuality.

24. _____ The use of various psychoactive medications is the most common form of this therapy.

25. _____ A therapy developed by psychiatrist Aaron T. Beck that focuses on unrealistic beliefs and distorted thinking.

26. _____ The learning of a new response that is incompatible with a previously learned response.

27. _____ Freud's famous technique in which the patient spontaneously reports all thoughts, mental images, and feelings as they come to mind.

28. _____ The treatment of emotional, behavioral, and interpersonal problems through the use of psychological techniques designed to encourage understanding and elicit change.

29. _____ Regardless of the type of therapy, researchers have identified this as the first and most important factor associated with a positive therapy outcome.

30. _____ A behavioral therapy that uses the procedures of progressive relaxation and control scenes to reach its goal.

31. _____ Based on the assumption that "people are not disturbed by things but rather by their view of things."

Completion Exercises

Fill in each blank with the most appropriate term or terms from the list of answers provided.

antianxiety medications	eclecticism
behavior therapy	family therapy
behavioral	psychoanalysis
cognitive therapies	resistance
dream interpretation	self-awareness

32. Whereas behavior therapy assumes faulty learning is at the core of problem behaviors and emotions, the _____ assume the culprit is faulty thinking.

33. The major goal of _____ is to alter and improve the ongoing interactions among its members.

34. A therapist who uses _____ might integrate insight-oriented techniques with specific behavioral techniques to help someone overcome a psychological problem.

35. The basic strategy in _____ involves unlearning maladaptive behaviors and learning more adaptive behaviors.

36. Because he believed that psychological defenses are reduced during sleep, Sigmund Freud developed the technique of _____.

37. To a psychoanalyst, _____ is a signal that the patient is uncomfortably close to uncovering psychologically threatening material.

38. The best known _____ are in a class called benzodiazepines, which include the trade name drugs Valium and Xanax.

39. As a therapy, traditional _____ is closely interwoven with Sigmund Freud's theory of personality.

40. In the video, you learned that psychotherapy is the use of psychological techniques to treat emotional, _____, and interpersonal problems.

41. In the video, you learned that a humanistic approach emphasizes _____ and each person's unique potential as a human.

Answer Key

Multiple-Choice Questions

1. c	4. b	7. c	10. b
2. a	5. b	8. a	11. c
3. c	6. d	9. a	12. c

Short-Answer Questions

Your answers should include the following:

13. Psychotherapy is use of a wide variety of psychological techniques to treat emotional, behavioral, and interpersonal problems. There are hundreds of types of psychotherapy. Psychotherapy can be conducted individually or in a group setting. (pages 620–623)

14. Psychoanalysis was developed by Sigmund Freud in the early 1900's and is based on the idea that early childhood experiences provide the foundation for later personality development. Free association and dream interpretations are techniques used to uncover unconscious conflicts. Resistance is the unconscious attempt to block the revealing of repressed memories and conflicts. Transference is the process by which emotions and desires originally associated with a significant person in the patient's life are unconsciously transferred to the psychoanalyst. (pages 623–624)

15. In client-centered therapy, the therapist is nondirective and promotes self-awareness, psychological growth, and self-directed change. The three critical qualities in client-centered therapy are genuineness, unconditional positive regard, and empathic understanding. In client-centered therapy, the emphasis is on the client's subjective perception of himself or herself and their environments. (pages 626–628)

16. Behavior therapy is a type of psychotherapy that focuses on directly changing maladaptive behavior. Counterconditioning is a behavior technique based on classical conditioning that involves modifying behavior by conditioning a new response that is incompatible with a previously learned response. Token economy is an example of the use of operant conditioning to modify behavior. (pages 628–635)

17. Both cognitive therapy (Beck) and rational-emotive therapy (Ellis) are based on the belief that psychological problems are caused by maladaptive thinking patterns. The cognitive therapy developed by Beck is based on the assumption that psychological problems are caused by distorted thinking and unrealistic beliefs. In contrast, Ellis' rational-emotive therapy focuses on the client's irrational beliefs. (pages 636–640)

18. When meta-analysis is used to summarize studies that compare people who receive psychotherapy treatment to no-treatment controls, researchers consistently arrive at the same conclusion: psychotherapy is significantly more effective than no treatment. (pages 644–646)

19. The following four factors are common to all effective therapy: (1) the therapeutic relationship, (2) the characteristics of the therapist, (3) the characteristics of the client, and (4) external circumstances of the client. In other words, therapy is likely to be effective if (1) the therapist-client relationship is based on mutual respect and trust; (2) the therapist is sensitive, warm, and responsive; (3) the client is motivated and actively involved in the process; and (4) the client has a stable living situation and strong social support. (pages 648–649)

20. The three broad categories of psychoactive medications are antipsychotic medications, antianxiety medications, and antidepressant medications. Antipsychotic medications are effective at reducing many of the positive symptoms of schizophrenia, but are not very effective at relieving the negative symptoms of schizophrenia. Another major disadvantage of antipsychotic medications is that they have significant side effects. Antianxiety medications are effective at reducing anxiety levels. However, antianxiety medications can be easily abused and may lead to addiction. Antidepressant medications are highly effective at reducing the classic symptoms of depression. A disadvantage of antidepressants is they need to be taken a month or so before they become effective. Some negative side effects may require clients to try several different medications until they find one with minimal side effects. (page 651–657)

21. Common misconceptions occur when people expect certain things to occur in psychotherapy. In psychotherapy, the client is required to work at the process of change. Change does not occur simply because of an insight or catharsis. Change takes time and effort. The psychotherapist does not make decisions for the client, but rather helps him or her better understand their choices. Finally, a psychotherapist will often challenge a client's thinking and actions. Such challenges may be upsetting and unflattering. (pages 659–660)

22. The psychodynamic approach explores repressed or unconscious impulses, anxieties, and internal conflicts. In contract, the behavioral approach is more specific and focuses on modifying specific problem behaviors. (pages 624–625 and 628–635)

Matching Exercises

23. antidepressant medications

24. biomedical therapy

25. cognitive therapy

26. counterconditioning

27. free association

28. psychotherapy

29. therapeutic relationship

30. systemic desensitization

31. rational-emotive therapy

Completion Exercises

32. cognitive therapies

33. family therapy

34. eclecticism

35. behavior therapy

36. dream interpretation

37. resistance

38. antianxiety medications

39. psychoanalysis

40. behavioral

41. self-awareness

Study Matrix

Lesson 25

Therapies

Please Note: Use this matrix to guide your study and achieve the learning objectives of this lesson. It will also help you to view the video, which defines and demonstrates important concepts and objectives as they relate to everyday life and actual case studies.

Learning Objective	Textbook	Telecourse Student Guide
Discuss the process of psychotherapy.	pp. 620–622	Key Terms and Concepts; Study Activities 1, 13, 34, 28.
Discuss the history of psychoanalysis, including the techniques of free association and dream interpretations, and the concepts of resistance and transference.	pp. 622–624	Key Terms and Concepts; Study Activities 2, 3, 14, 27, 36, 37, 39.
Describe the therapeutic techniques that are used in client-centered therapy.	pp. 626–628	Key Terms and Concepts; Study Activities 4, 11, 15, 29, 41.
Define behavioral therapy and discuss how basic learning principles are applied to modify behavior.	pp. 628–635	Key Terms and Concepts; Study Activities 5, 16, 22, 26, 30, 35, 40.
Compare and contrast cognitive therapy developed by psychiatrist Aaron T. Beck to rational-emotive therapy developed by psychologist Albert Ellis.	pp. 636–640	Key Terms and Concepts; Study Activities 6, 17, 25, 31, 32.
Discuss the general effectiveness of psychotherapy.	pp. 644–647	Key Terms and Concepts; Study Activity 18.
List the four factors that are common to all effective therapies.	p. 648	Key Terms and Concepts; Study Activities 8, 12, 19, 29, 33, 34.
Identify the categories of psychoactive medications and discuss their effectiveness.	pp. 651–657	Key Terms and Concepts; Study Activities 9, 20, 23, 38.
List some of the common misconceptions about psychotherapy.	pp. 659–660	Study Activities 10, 21.

Use the Course Compass to orient yourself in the road that you are taking to explore branches and aspects of psychology. The branch and aspects that are covered in this lesson are highlighted in the compass.

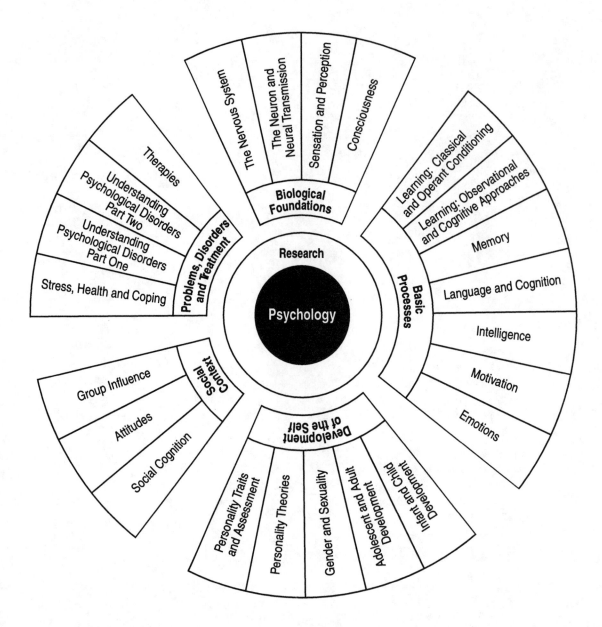

Please note: This compass does not represent the full range of topics comprising the field of psychology; it represents a map for this course only. Each of the five branches represented above has many aspects and subjects that are covered in the 26 lessons of this telecourse. You should remember that these branches and subjects all interrelate.

Lesson 26

Making Psychology
Part of Your Life

Questions to Consider

How can the study of psychology improve my life?

How can I learn more about the field of psychology?

In what ways can I apply what I learned to my everyday life?

Can what I believe really change my life?

Lesson Assignments

Before viewing the video program

Read the Questions to Consider, Lesson Preview, and Course Objectives included in this lesson. Use this information to guide your reading, viewing, and thinking.

View the video program, "Making Psychology Part of Your Life"

After viewing the video program

Review the vocabulary listed in the Key Terms and Concepts section in the previous twenty-five lessons. (Page references are keyed to the Hockenbury textbook, *Psychology*. Remember: there is a complete Glossary at the end of the textbook.)

Review the reading assignments for the previous twenty-five lessons.

Complete the exercises found in the Study Activities section and check your answers with the Answer Key at the end of this lesson.

Use the Study Matrix found at the end of this lesson to review and assess your knowledge of all Course Objectives.

Lesson Preview

Imagine that you could videotape your life, edit it, make changes, and replay it over again. Imagine what it would be like if you were some sort of magical person who could see inside and know each person's innermost fears and desires. What would life be like if we knew all that was or all that would ever be?

Of course, this is not possible. All of us are only human. We cannot relive life's events. We cannot know what goes on inside other people. And, it is very unlikely we will ever become an all-knowing mystical guru. This is life. We live it every day, imperfect in our knowledge, unsure of what other people will do. We make mistakes. We, being human, all have faults. We all commit follies.

In this video, the final program in this series, we will discuss how you can use psychology in your everyday life. You will discover that psychology is a practical science.

> Psychology is the most exciting science that exists. Throughout this telecourse, you've seen how psychologists apply the tools of science, sometimes very ingeniously, to understand why we humans do what we do. But equally important, psychology can affect our lives in ways that are real and beneficial. Whether it is dealing with the common experiences of everyday life or with more extreme events, psychology provides many insights into human behavior and mental processes. More so than other science, psychology provides us with the opportunity to enhance virtual every dimensions of the human experience.
>
> Don and Sandy Hockenbury, authors of *Psychology*

You will learn that the science of psychology can help in our everyday lives. By studying psychology, we can learn more about ourselves. We can also learn more about other people. We can use the science of psychology to help us live a more productive and personally satisfying life. This, above all else, is the real value of studying psychology.

As many different psychologists explain in this video, we all learn best when we can apply new concepts and new knowledge to the world we know. Psychology allows us to do just that. Psychology is not a cold science of numbers and ideas. Psychology is real—it can be applied each day.

What better way to learn material—to make it alive, interesting, practical and memorable—than to demonstrate to yourself the principles you have learned?

You do not simply need to learn about memory; you can improve your memory. You do not simply need to understand how motivation affects behavior; you can motivate yourself. You can use psychology. You can apply psychology in your work, in your relationships, at home—in virtually every aspect of your life. What you have learned in this course is only an introduction. There is much more you can study and much more you can learn, including how to:

- Fight prejudice on a personal level.

- Avoid making bad decisions.

- Study more effectively.

- Build long-lasting relationships.

- Control your anger by minimizing frustrations.

- Stop procrastinating.

… and on and on.

While you learned many things in this introductory course, the lessons available to you from psychology are endless. You now have a wonderful opportunity to apply the psychological principles you have learned in this course to your own life.

As Yale psychologist Peter Salovey explained in the video program for Lesson 1, advances in scientific knowledge occur at an ever-increasing pace. Neuroscience is changing our understanding of how our brains function. New brain-imaging techniques are providing researchers with more and better ways to help unravel the mystery of the human brain. New psychoactive medications are providing hope and relief to people who just a few years ago would have been doomed to a life of endless suffering. Psychology is learning more about how stress affects the body, how emotions affect intelligence, and so much more.

Consider these questions: Do you know what makes people happy? Do you know how treat an infant who constantly cries? Do you know what to say to an older person whose memory is failing? Do you know how to deal with a hostile employer? Do you know the best methods for treating depression or anxiety?

As you have seen in this video series, psychologists in colleges, clinics, research facilities, and universities around the world are working hard to find answers to these everyday questions. Psychologists are conducting research experiments and publishing their findings in an ongoing stream of knowledge. You are invited to join in and share in the wealth of all this new knowledge.

As Stanford University professor and noted psychologist Albert Bandura will explain in this video, what you say to yourself and how much you believe in yourself is a major factor in determining whether you will succeed or fail at any given task. If you will continue to learn, and if you will believe in yourself, you can and will increase your chances of success. This, in the end, might be the most valuable lesson of all.

We encourage you to continue your exploration into the world of psychology. We hope what you have learned, and will learn, will improve the quality of your life.

Course Objectives

When you have completed this telecourse, you should be able to:

1. Define psychology.

2. Explain the goals of psychology.

3. Discuss the type of work done by psychologists.

4. Discuss the role and importance of science and research to the field of psychology.

5. Identify basic psychological terminology.

6. Explain fundamental psychological concepts.

7. Identify the major contributors to the field of psychology.

8. Explain how biological and social factors interact with psychological factors to affect behavior.

9. Provide a general explanation of how psychologists define and treat mental disorders.

10. Discuss the ways in which psychology can affect people's lives.

11. Discuss the breadth of the field of psychology and the importance of continuing to stay current with new discoveries.

12. Recognize and appreciate the differences and similarities between people.

Study Activities

These self-test questions are designed as a study exercise to aid you in understanding the most important terms and concepts in this lesson. To ensure that you have an accurate understanding of the key terms and concepts in this lesson, please check your answers with the Answer Key provided at the end of this lesson.

Short-Answer Questions

1. Define psychology.

    _____

    _____

    _____

2. List the four basic goals of psychology.

_____

_____

_____

3. Identify the contributions to psychology made by Wilhelm Wundt, Sigmund Freud, B. F. Skinner, and Carl Rogers.

_____

_____

_____

4. Describe some of the various types of work done by psychologists.

_____

_____

_____

5. List the steps of the scientific method.

_____

_____

_____

6. Describe the different types of research methods used by psychologists.

_____

_____

_____

7. Briefly describe the nervous system and the function of neurons.

_____

_____

_____

8. Define biological psychology and explain why psychologists are concerned with human biology.

_____

_____

_____

9. Distinguish between sensation and perception, and explain how they interrelate.

_____

_____

_____

10. Define consciousness, and explain what William James meant when he described conscious "stream of thought."

_____

_____

_____

11. Describe Ivan Pavlov's famous experiment and explain the basic concepts of classical conditioning.

_____

_____

_____

12. Define cognition and thinking, and describe how mental images and concepts are involved.

_____

_____

_____

13. Define the term intelligence and explain what an Intelligence Quotient is.

_____

_____

_____

14. Define sensation and perception, and explain how they relate.

_____

_____

_____

15. Distinguish between motivation and emotion, and give an example of a motivation theory.

_____

_____

_____

16. Define stress, and describe the biopsychosocial model of health psychology.

_____

_____

_____

17. Compare and contrast psychoanalytic therapy, behavioral therapy, and cognitive therapy.

_____

_____

_____

18. Explain how psychologists define a mental or psychological disorder and discuss the prevalence of these types of illnesses.

_____

_____

_____

19. List some of the common misconceptions about what psychotherapy is and what it can accomplish.

_____

_____

_____

Answer Key

Short-Answer Questions

Your answers should include the following:

1. Psychology is defined as the science of behavior and mental processes. (page 3)

2. The four basic goals of psychology are to describe, explain, predict, and control or influence behavior. (page 16)

3. Wilhelm Wundt established the first research laboratory exclusively for psychology; he is credited as the founder of psychology as an experimental science. Sigmund Freud developed psychoanalysis, a personality theory, and the form of psychotherapy; he is recognized as one of the most influential thinkers of the twentieth century. B. F. Skinner popularized behaviorism by experimentally demonstrating various learning principles, and he coined the term "operant conditioning." Carl Rogers is credited as being the principal founder of the school of psychology called humanism. (pages 4–5 and 7–9)

4. Psychologists' work is very diverse. The most common type of work done by psychologists is in the study and treatment of psychological disorders. Studying the relationship between behavior and biological forces, conducting research experiments, and developing educational material and tests are also common of the work performed by psychologists. (pages 14–16)

5. Your answer should include these four steps: (1) formulate a question that can be tested (hypothesis), (2) design a study and collect data, (3) analyze the data and draw a conclusion, and (4) report the results. (pages 18–21)

6. There are five types of research methods: experimental method, correlational studies, and the three types of descriptive research studies—naturalistic observation, case study, and the survey method. (pages 22–28)

7. The human nervous system has two parts: the central nervous system and the peripheral nervous system. Communication throughout the nervous system takes place via neurons—cells that are highly specialized to receive and transmit information from one part of the body to another. (pages 47 and 56)

8. Biological psychology is the study of the relationship between biological activity and behavior and mental processes. Psychologists are concerned with human biology because ultimately all behavior and mental processes can be traced back to some biological event. (page 44)

9. Sensation refers to the detection and basic sensory experience of environmental stimuli, such as sounds, objects, and odors, and that perception occurs when we integrate, organize, and interpret sensory information in a way that is meaningful. (page 90)

10. Consciousness is defined as the personal awareness of mental activities, internal sensations, and the external environment. William James' "stream of thought" refers to the idea that consciousness is not chopped up in bits and pieces, but rather continuously flows and is unified and unbroken, much like a stream or river. (page 137)

11. Ivan Pavlov's experiment, for which he was awarded the Nobel Prize, demonstrated how a dog could be conditioned to salivate (conditioned response) at the sound of a ringing bell (conditioned stimulus) by pairing a natural stimulus with a natural reflex. This experiment led to the principles of classical conditioning. Essentially, classical conditioning involves learning an association between two stimuli. (pages 187–188)

12. Cognition is defined as the mental activities involved in acquiring, retaining, and using knowledge. Thinking is the manipulation of mental representation of information in order to draw inferences and conclusions. Mental images and concepts are what we think with. (pages 280–281)

13. According to the textbook, intelligence is defined as the global capacity to think rationally, act purposefully, and deal effectively with the environment. An IQ (intelligence quotient) is a global measure of intelligence derived by comparing an individual's score with the scores of others in the same group. (pages 296–297)

14. Motivation is defined as the biological, emotional, cognitive, or social forces that activate and direct behavior. There are several motivation theories: instinct theory; drive theory; incentive motivation; arousal theory; and the

humanistic theory that focuses on psychological needs as motivators. Emotion is defined as a complex psychological state that involves subjective experience, a physiological response, and a behavioral or expressive response. (pages 321–324 and 344)

15. Sensation is the process of detecting a physical stimulus, such as light, sound, heat, or pressure. Perception is the process by which a form of physical energy is converted into a coded neural signal that can be processed by the nervous system. Many psychologists do not differentiate between sensation and perception primarily because you cannot have one without the other. (page 90)

16. Stress is a negative emotional state that occurs when a person is confronted with a situation or event that he or she does not feel able to cope with effectively. The biopsychosocial model of health psychology is based on the belief that biological, psychological, and social factors interact and influence health and illness. (page 540)

17. Psychoanalysis, developed by Sigmund Freud, is a type of psychotherapy in which free association, dream interpretation, and analysis of resistance and transference are used to explore repressed or unconscious impulses, anxieties, and internal conflicts. Behavior therapy is a type of psychotherapy that focuses on directly changing maladaptive behavior patterns by using basic learning principles and techniques; it is also called behavior modification. Cognitive therapy refers to a group of therapies based on the assumption that psychological problems are the result of maladaptive patterns of thinking. (pages 622–623, 628–629, and 636)

18. Psychological disorder or mental disorder is a pattern of behavioral and psychological symptoms that causes significant personal distress, impairs the ability to function in one or more important areas of daily life. The prevalence of psychological disorders is much higher than most people think. Almost one in two adults—48 percent—have experienced the symptoms of a psychological or mental disorder at some point during their lives. (pages 575–576)

19. Common misconceptions arise when people expect certain things to occur in psychotherapy. In psychotherapy, the client is required to work at the process of change. Change does not occur simply because of an insight or catharsis. Change takes time and effort. The psychotherapist does not make decisions for clients, but rather helps them better understand their choices. Finally, a psychotherapist will often challenge a client's thinking and actions. Such challenges may be upsetting and unflattering. (pages 659–660)

Study Matrix

Lesson 26

Making Psychology Part of Your Life

Please Note: Use this matrix to guide your review and achieve the learning objectives of this course. Listed next to each objective are page°numbers in the textbook, the video lesson numbers, and the lesson numbers in this guide where you can find more information to help strengthen your knowledge of concepts you do not feel sure of.

Course Objective	Textbook	Telecourse Video Lesson and Student Guide
Define psychology.	p. 5	Lesson 1.
Explain the goals of psychology.	p. 18	Lesson 2.
Discuss the type of work done by psychologists.	pp. 1–15	Lesson 1.
Discuss how psychologists use science and research to evaluate why people behave as they do.	pp. 12–17	Lesson 2.
Identify basic psychological terminology.	Entire Text	All lessons.
Explain fundamental psychological concepts.	Entire Text	All lessons.
Identify the major contributors to the field of psychology.	Entire Text	Lessons 1, 5, 6, 7, 11, 12, 13, 14, 15, 17, 21, and 25.
Explain how biological and social factors interact with psychological factors to affect behavior.	pp. 43–85, 497–533	Lessons 3, 4, 19, 20, and 21.
Provide a general explanation of how psychologists define and treat mental disorders.	pp. 620–628, 636	Lessons 23, 24, and 25.
Discuss the ways in which psychology can affect people's lives.	Entire Text	All lessons.
Discuss the breadth of the field of psychology and the importance of continuing to stay current with new discoveries.	pp. 10–15	Lessons 1 and 26.
Recognize and appreciate the differences and similarities between people.	pp. 498–514	Lessons 17 and 18.